Palgrave Studies in Economic History

Series Editor
Kent Deng
London School of Economics
London, United Kingdom

Palgrave Studies in Economic History is designed to illuminate and enrich our understanding of economies and economic phenomena of the past. The series covers a vast range of topics including financial history, labour history, development economics, commercialisation, urbanisation, industrialisation, modernisation, globalisation, and changes in world economic orders.

More information about this series at
http://www.springer.com/series/14632

Gabriel Tortella

Catalonia in Spain

History and Myth

palgrave
macmillan

Gabriel Tortella
Universidad de Alcalá
Madrid, Spain

Palgrave Studies in Economic History
ISBN 978-3-319-85529-5 ISBN 978-3-319-54951-4 (eBook)
DOI 10.1007/978-3-319-54951-4

Sofcover reprint of the hardcover 1st edition 2017

Cover illustration: age fotostock / Alamy Stock Photo

Printed on acid-free paper

This Palgrave Macmillan imprint is published by Springer Nature
The registered company is Springer International Publishing AG
The registered company address is: Gewerbestrasse 11, 6330 Cham, Switzerland

To
José Luis García Ruiz,
Clara Eugenia Núñez,
Gloria Quiroga,
Who made this book possible

Contents

List of Figures

Map 1 Spain and its Regions (Autonomous Communities)

Introduction

Catalan separatism is the number one political problem that Spain faces today. The problem has become more serious after the 'Brexit.' The possibility of disintegration of the Union has markedly increased after a member as important as the United Kingdom has decided to quit. The history of Catalonia in its relation with the rest of Spain, therefore, should be of interest not only to Spaniards but also to non-Spaniards, especially to citizens of the EU.

Catalan separatism is the number one political problem that Spain faces today. It is far from a bilateral question, however. The problem affects the European Union (EU) as a whole and also some of its individual members, France especially. For the EU, the secession of a part of one member state is a problem in any case. The Union is the consequence of a long, difficult, and unfinished process of integration, and the disintegration of a part of one of its members would pose serious questions, for several reasons, among others because one of the Union's expressed premises is respect of the territorial integrity of its member states. The Treaty of the EU, however, foresees the eventuality of the separation of a region and its immediate consequence is that this region automatically ceases to be a part of the Union. It is obvious that the Union considers such eventuality with disquiet, chiefly because other regions might want to follow the example of the leaver.

The problem has become more serious after the 'Brexit.' The possibility of disintegration of the Union has markedly increased after a member as important as the United Kingdom has decided to quit. If after the United Kingdom leaves the Union, Catalonia should split from Spain, thereby leaving the Union too, the whole European edifice would be under threat of dissolution or at least of considerable shrinkage. Even though Catalonia is much smaller (its population is less than 1.7 percent of the EU population, excluding the United Kingdom), its leaving the EU after the United Kingdom would be extremely ominous.

The history of Catalonia in its relation with the rest of Spain, therefore, should be of interest not only to Spaniards, but also to non-Spaniards, especially to citizens of the EU. The most directly affected country should be France, because Catalan separatism has a strong imperialistic component. Catalan nationalists like to speak of the *països Catalans* (Catalan countries), referring to regions where Catalan is spoken and/or used to belong to the old kingdom of Aragon. This includes Valencia, the Balearic Islands, part of eastern Aragon, and the Roussillon, a region north of the Pyrenees which used to be part of Catalonia until the French conquered it during the War of the Reapers (see Ch. 2). Catalan nationalists think that these territories should have the right of self-determination, just as Catalonia has, according to their views. This right of self-determination means that these territories have the right to abandon their present status and elect to join a 'Grand Catalonia,' whose nucleus would be, of course, an independent Catalonia. The Catalan *Parlament* recently (October 2016) approved a declaration to this effect, something which immediately provoked a protest of the French government to the Spanish ambassador in Paris.

The basis of the present book is a Spanish version which was published in January 2016 by myself and three more coauthors, José Luis García Ruiz, Clara Eugenia Núñez, and Gloria Quiroga, to whom this English version is dedicated. The Spanish version was sponsored by the Foundation Alfonso Martín Escudero and by the Colegio Libre de Eméritos and published by Editorial Gadir. The former considerations about the international dimensions of the Catalan conflict made me seriously think about producing an English version of the book and even before it was finished, I contacted my friends at Palgrave Macmillan suggesting the possibility of carrying out my idea. The present book is a little more compact than the Spanish version; I have eliminated part of the scholarly apparatus and shortened the bibliographical appendix. Facts and reasoning presented, however, are exactly those of the Spanish version. And, of course, more recent events have been taken into account in the present version.

An additional reflection weighed in my mind. My conversations with English and American friends, plus my readings of books, journals, and magazines made me see that opinion in Anglo-Saxon countries was (and is) slanted in favor of Catalan independence. One reason for this, I am sure, is the memory of the Franco dictatorship with its ferocious centralism and ruthless suppression of dissenting opinion; as happened within Spain, the liberal and enlightened opinion sympathized with Catalans and Basques as oppressed peoples under the boot of the military dictator. By and large, I agree with this view; but things have changed, and the oppressed have become oppressors, not *manu military*, but through a 'white dictatorship,' as Josep Tarradellas, the first Catalan president in democratic, post-Franco Spain, predicted. One of the aims of this book is to show how this 'white dictatorship' works. Unfortunately, there are in the world today abundant examples of those mixtures of oligarchical government with elections, so the reader will not be surprised or consider the Catalan case a rarity.

Another, related, perception is that publications in English about Catalan modern history are slanted in the same way. This not only the case with Allison Peers, who wrote in the 1930s and whose sympathies for the Republicans extended to the 'Catalan nation.' Peers was too serious an academic not to also see the flaws, if not of Catalan nationalism, of some Catalan nationalists. But many of the more modern books that circulate in English about Catalonia are less scholarly and more slanted than Peers's *Catalonia Infelix* was. Here are two examples I recently came across: Simon Harris, *Catalonia is not Spain* and Liz Castro, *What's up with Catalonia. ¿Qué le pasa a Cataluña?* Harris's book title says it all; Castro's book is really a propaganda piece by the *generalitat* of Artur Mas. I have been unable to find equivalent books in English trying to present a non-nationalist-separatist standpoint. This is what *Catalonia in Spain* tries to do.

I have contracted many debts while writing this book. First of all, with those institutions I mentioned in the first paragraph and the persons heading them, Ramón Parada Vázquez and Elisa Polanco of the Foundation, Juan

Torres and Álvaro Delgado-Gal of the Colegio, and Javier Santillán of Gadir. Professor Parada and the Foundation he presides were kind enough to cede their publication rights in English. When carrying out our research for the Spanish book, we were aided by numerous persons and institutions which are mentioned in the Introduction to that book. While working on the English version, I was kindly aided by my coauthors in the Spanish version in many ways which it would be long to detail here. Javier Santillán also has made valuable contributions. Luis Múzquiz, of GeaCron, has made a map for me (no. 2) and generously ceded his copyright. I also want to thank Palgrave, and especially Aimee Dibbens and Thomas Coughlan, for their assistance with the production of the book.

Madrid, November 2016

1

Medieval Origins of the Spanish Nation

The Slow Birth of Spain: One Thousand Years of History (479–1479)

Modern Spain occupies about 84 percent of the Iberian Peninsula's surface (the rest is occupied by Portugal); it encompasses also the Balearic Islands, the Canary Islands, plus two nearby north-African cities, Ceuta and Melilla, plus a few minor islands and islets in the Mediterranean between Spain and Morocco. The Iberian Peninsula is very mountainous, and its rivers are scarcely navigable. Except for the northern coast, Spain is a sunny, dry country, with wide semi-desertic areas.

The Peninsula has been inhabited since pre-historic times by a variety of peoples (Iberians, Celts, and others). Greeks, Phoenicians, and Carthaginians established coastal colonies, but the Romans conquered it almost in its entirety, and divided it into five provinces. When the Roman Empire fell, the Peninsula became unified under the Visigothic kingdom, which adopted Roman Christianity. The Muslim invasion and conquest, starting in 711, put the Peninsula under the rule of the

G. Tortella, *Catalonia in Spain*, Palgrave Studies in Economic History, DOI 10.1007/978-3-319-54951-4_1

Emirate (later Caliphate) of Córdoba, which encompassed the whole of the Peninsula except for the northern mountainous areas: the Cantabrian Mountains and the Pyrenees, where small Christian counties and kingdoms survived. Around the year 1000 the tables turned: the Caliphate collapsed and was replaced by a number of smaller Muslim kingdoms (called *taifas* by the Christians, from the Arab word meaning 'band'), while the Christian kingdoms started expanding toward the south at the expense of the *taifas* in a centuries-long process commonly called the *Reconquista* (re-conquest). The *Reconquista* ended in the fifteenth century when the last Muslim kingdom in Spain, Granada, surrendered, and the whole of the Peninsula was left in Christian hands under two kingdoms, Spain (including Navarre) and Portugal.

Geographical factors explain the strength and variety of the Peninsula's regions, the multiplicity of its languages, customs, and identities. Transportation and communication have been difficult in the past due to high mountain chains and non-navigable rivers. However, there were also factors favoring unity: the Pyrenean Mountains, a barrier separating the Peninsula from the rest of Europe, turned it almost into an island. The massive, compact Peninsula has been designated with the name Hispania (also Iberia) since Roman times at least. Aside from relative geographical isolation, two historical factors fostered unity: Christianity and the memory of the Visigothic kingdom. The Latin language must also have contributed to give cohesion to Christian Spain. Although Latin gradually evolved into a series of dialects, in the late Middle Ages Castilian Spanish had become the most widely spoken language, and it acquired the character of *lingua franca*. The other two significant Latin dialects or languages were Galaico-Portuguese in the west and Catalan in the east. The Basque language, of uncertain origin, was spoken in the Basque country, straddling the Pyrenees.

Another unifying element was the *Reconquista* itself: taking the lands from the Muslims was justified in the name of religion and by the fact that these territories had belonged to the Visigothic kingdom. But in reality the *Reconquista* was part of a European-wide phenomenon. In the late Middle Ages Europe expanded in several directions: to the east at the expense of the Slavs and to the south and west at the expense of the Muslims. The most noted episode of this European expansion was, of course, the Crusades in the Middle East. Many Spaniards thought the *Reconquista* to be part of the crusading movement. This was a period when many peoples from northern Europe, especially Frenchmen, crossed the Pyrenees, some as pilgrims to visit the shrine of Saint James (Santiago) in Compostela, others to establish themselves in the lands taken from the Muslims. The participation of 'foreign peoples' in crucial battles of the *Reconquista* (Englishmen in the conquest of Lisbon, Frenchmen at the Navas de Tolosa – the decisive battle which opened the Andalusian plains to the Christian armies in 1212) was widely acknowledged. Alfonso VI, the conqueror of Toledo in 1085, had married his two daughters to Frenchmen. One of these, Henry of Burgundy, became count of Portugal, originally a dependency of the kingdom of Galicia. Henry's son, Afonso Henriques, became the founder of the Portuguese kingdom.

A clear manifestation of this unifying trend was the merging of Asturias, Galicia, León, and Castile into a single kingdom *de facto* under Alfonso VI. The youngest of these realms, Castile, became the most powerful and in the end gave its name to the whole unified kingdom. The three Basque counties south of the Pyrenes, Biscay, Guipúzcoa, and Álava, voluntarily joined Castile in the twelfth, thirteenth, and fourteenth centuries, respectively. A similar phenomenon was taking place in the east: several Pyrenean counties united to form the kingdom of Aragon in 1035 under king Ramiro I. To the west of Aragon, the kingdom of Navarre remained independent until the sixteenth century, while to the east a group of Pyrenean counties were loosely united under the count of Barcelona into what was to become Catalonia. The Pyrenean counties, western (Aragon) and eastern (Catalonia), originally belonged to the Carolingian empire and were collectively known as the *Marca Hispanica* (Hispanic March or Mark), a fortified territory guarding the imperial frontier from the Muslims to the south. The Carolingian empire had similar fortified territories in the North (Danemark) and the East (Ostmark). These Pyrenean counties gradually severed their ties with the French and coalesced into Aragon and Catalonia.

As a consequence of these unifying trends, the Peninsula was divided into five separate kingdoms at the end of the Middle Ages: Portugal to the west, Castile in the center, and Aragon to the east. Navarre was pressed between Castile and Aragon, and, to the south, Granada was the only remaining Muslim kingdom. Portugal had been a single unit from its origins, but Castile and Aragon were the results of the accretion of diverse political units: the crown of Castile comprised Asturias, León, Galicia, plus several former *taifa* kingdoms such as Toledo, Seville, Córdoba, and others, the Basque counties and of course Castile itself. The crown of Aragon comprised Catalonia, plus the former Muslim kingdoms of Mallorca and Valencia, plus the kingdom Aragon itself. Granada and Navarre were conquered and added to Castile in 1492 and 1512, respectively. A little earlier it was evident that Castile, being the largest and most powerful of the three major kingdoms, and centrally located, would absorb at least one of its neighbors, if not both; it eventually absorbed both. The earlier and more lasting union was that with Aragon, which took place largely through the decision of Isabel of Trastámara, soon to become queen of Castile, who in 1469 preferred marrying her cousin Fernando, son of the king of Aragon, rather than Afonso V, king of Portugal.

This is the period (late fifteenth century) when, after long and often bloody vicissitudes, the earliest large kingdoms of Western Europe (Portugal, Spain, France, England, and Scotland) were formed and initiated their long process toward becoming modern nations. Soon other kingdoms (Sweden, for instance) would follow the same path toward nationhood. After five centuries of rivalries and wars, the European nations undertook the road toward unity, a road they are still engaged on. The European Unión is a reality today, but its future is not as clear and assured as one would desire.

In a recent book on the history of Catalonia, the nationalist historian Josep Fontana (2014) states that 'identity' (he is referring to Catalan identity) is something born out of a long shared coexistence, but historically this coexistence is not limited to Catalonia. The truth is that Catalonia has been part and parcel of Spain (or Hispania) at least since Antiquity. The land which is Catalonia today was a part of a Roman province (*Tarraconensis*), one of the five which formed Roman

Hispania (the others were *Carthaginensis, Baetica, Lusitania*, and *Gallaecia*); it later became part of the Visigothic kingdom; after the demise of the Goths and the Muslim invasion, it was part of the Caliphate, except for the Pyrenean counties, which were part of the Carolingian empire (*Marca Hispanica*). First as Carolingian suzerainties, later on more or less on their own, these counties engaged in the *Reconquista* as other Christian Hispanic counties and kingdoms did; then the nascent Catalonia became part of the crown of Aragon, which in turn would merge with Castile to form Spain.

This gradual process of formation of the Spanish nation by gradual accretion of former smaller political units was not unique; it took place in a parallel way in other future nations, such as France and England (and then Britain). In Spain, however, it was a little different in that it proceeded *pari passu* with the *Reconquista* and the consequent process of repopulation. But during all this formative medieval period the history of Catalonia conforms in its broad contours to that of the kingdoms of the rest of Spain.

Medieval Catalonia

The history of Catalonia during the Middle Ages turns around five great topics: 1) The *Reconquista,* 2) The association, and then enmity, with France, 3) The relation of cooperation and rivalry with Castile, 4) The union with Aragon, and 5) Its seafaring activities and its interest in the Mediterranean where it created an empire which was the cause and the consequence of its commercial activity.

Catalan seafaring and commercial activities were already paramount in Antiquity, when Greek sailors founded the fabled port of Emporion (today's Ampurias, or Empuries in Catalan). Phoenicians and Carthaginians also founded colonies in the area. One tradition says that Barcelona was founded by Hamilcar Barca, father of Hannibal, and that its original name, Barcino, referred to this powerful Cartaginian family. It certainly was re-founded by the Romans, but the main 'Catalan' port at that time was *Tarraco* (today's Tarragona), capital of the *Tarraconensis* province. By the late Roman Empire Catalonia and the rest of Hispania's Mediterranean area was pre-dominantly Christian.

Even before the fall of the Empire in 479, Hispania was exposed to the invasions and incursions of the Barbarian peoples. From 411 on Vandals, Suevi, and Alans crossed the Pyrenees and established themselves. Vandals and Alans traversed the Peninsula, and many also crossed the Gibraltar strait and invaded northern Africa. The Suevi established themselves in Galicia and northern Portugal and created a kingdom there. But those who left a longer and deeper imprint were the Visigoths, Germanic as the most of the other barbarians, but semi-civilized after a long stay in the eastern part of the Empire. They entered Spain through Catalonia, occupied Barcino and Tarraco, and established their royal court in both cities successively and momentarily. After being defeated by the Franks at Vouillé in 507, the Visigoths vacated France, occupied most of Hispania, and made Toledo the capital of the Hispano-Visigothic kingdom. The Goths were a minority in the Peninsula, and practiced a version of Christianity called Arianism; the pre-dominant Hispano-Roman population was orthodox Roman. Later the Visigoths officially adopted the religion of the majority, but this caused a split among their governing elite and contributed to the downfall of their kingdom and the invasion of the Muslims from northern Africa in 711. Most of Hispania fell to the Muslims, who went on into France only to be defeated by the Franks at Poitiers (732). They then fell back into Hispania, which they called Al-Andalus. Initially, Muslim Spain was but a province of the gigantic Umayyad Caliphate of Damascus, ranging all the way from Syria to the Atlantic Ocean along the southern shore of the Mediterranean. However, the Umayyad dynasty was deposed, and its descendants moved to Spain, where they established an independent emirate in 750, with Córdoba as its capital. The Umayyads ruled Muslim Spain for two and a half centuries; in 929 the emir Abdel-Rahman III proclaimed himself Caliph; under him and his immediate successors, the Cordoba Caliphate became one of the richest and most cultivated of medieval kingdoms, but in 1002 it disintegrated into the *taifa* kingdoms. The last leader of the Caliphate was not a caliph, but a warlord commonly called Almanzor (from *Al-Mansur*, the Victorious in Arabic), who in 981 became an all-powerful *hajib* (sort of prime minister), a post he held until his death in 1002. For twenty years Almanzor fought and terrorized the Christian kingdoms, capturing and pillaging their cities, from Compostela to Barcelona. It can be fairly said that he was the last Muslim overlord in Spain. After his death the Caliphate broke down, the Christians took the initiative, and the *Reconquista* started in earnest.

The Muslims never occupied the Peninsula in its entirety. The northern mountain chains (the Pyrenees and the Cantabrian mountains) sheltered a host of Christian statelets or counties, later kingdoms, which the Muslim emirate never could dislodge. While the Pyrenean counties became attached to the Frankish empire, the western counties and kingdoms (of which Asturias was the most important) were independent and comprised a mixture of Goths and Hispano-Romans who had fled the Muslims, with peoples of local origins (Cantabrians, Asturians, Basques) who had largely escaped Roman influence and who now converted to Christianity and learned Latin from the southern newcomers. These new kingdoms started inching southward toward the plains which lay between the Duero river and the mountains. Thus in 856 the city of León, on the southern slopes of the Cantabrian mountains, became the capital of the new kingdom of León. This slow southward movement accelerated perceptibly after the fall of the Caliphate. Two symbolic events were the conquest of Toledo by Alfonso VI (1085) and of Valencia by the Cid (Rodrigo Díaz de Vivar, a Castilian warlord) in 1094, although this city fell to the Muslims again after the death of its Christian conqueror.

In eastern Spain the *Reconquest* proceed more slowly due in part to rivalries and dissensions among the Christian counties and between them and the Carolingians. The easternmost counties were quite numerous (around 12) although Barcelona soon became paramount and absorbed most of the others. Hence the term *Principado* (Principality; *Principat* in Catalan), which is often used to designate Catalonia: the count of Barcelona was considered as the principal (prince) of the Catalan counts. Perhaps for this reason Catalonia never acquired the rank of kingdom. The semi-legendary founder of this budding Catalonia *avant-la-lettre* was *Guifre el Pilós* (Wilfred the Hairy) who was count of Barcelona and made his son his heir, something which entailed some degree of independence, since up to then the counts had been appointed by the Frankish authorities. Legend has it that the French king Charles the Bald, who had made Guifre count, created the Catalan ensign (four red stripes over a yellow background) when, attending a wounded Guifre after a battle against the Muslims, he dipped his fingers in his count's blood and drew four red stripes over a golden shield. In reality the ensign was not used until several centuries later.

What is true, however, is that Guifre founded the Barcelona dynasty, and that he and his immediate descendants took advantage of the weakness of the Frankish kingdom. This relative independence was aided, paradoxically, by the destruction of Barcelona by Almanzor, which demonstrated the inability of the French overlords to defend it or at least help in its reconstruction. At this time (eleventh century) as in the rest of Christian Spain, population grew, to which immigration from France contributed, and the economy showed some vigor. Agriculture prospered and even some technical progress took place (water mills). Counties issued money and commerce developed.

This relative prosperity fostered rivalries and hostilities among the counties; the Church tried to foster peace and created assemblies of 'peace and truce' (*pau i treva* in Catalan), which met often to reduce violence and which, in the long run, became the embryo of the future *Corts* (Catalan Parliament), when the counts turned these assemblies into instruments for the collection of taxes. One of the early counts of Barcelona, Ramon Berenguer I, published the *Usatges de Barcelona* (Customs or Uses of Barcelona), the first legislative text written in Catalan.

Historians have written about the *fet diferencial* (Catalan for 'differential fact or trait'), meaning that Catalonia was and is different from the rest of Spain. The phrase was coined in the twentieth century, in the apogee of nationalism, and its validity is dubious. As we have seen, regional differences are strong in Spain for geographical and historical reasons, and some regions can claim differential factors as strong as Catalonia. Referring to medieval times, the main Catalan *fet diferencial* would be that, due to French influence, feudalism would have been much stronger there than in the rest of Spain, where *seignioralism*, a diluted form of feudalism, prevailed due to the fact that in frontier territories vassals enjoyed more independence, and social mobility was greater than in more self-contained societies. But Pierre Vilar (1962, I, pp. 377–392), a noted French hispanist and author of a monumental history of early modern Catalonia, points out that southern Catalonia was also a frontier territory, and that its social structures were, with very minor differences, more similar to those of Castile than to those of northern ('old') Catalonia, while the institutions of old Catalonia have more similarities with those of León, Asturias, and Old Castile.

The *Reconquista* brought about cooperation between different Christian kingdoms, buy also rivalry. We saw that the Cid conquered Valencia, up to then a Muslim kingdom which the counts of Barcelona considered within their area of influence. The Cid was Castilian, although he operated independently, having been ostracized by his king, Alfonso VI. The count of Barcelona tried to expel the Cid from what he considered Catalan territory, but was defeated by him. Later on they made peace and became allies. This state of changing and perilous relations lasted long, because the coastal *taifa* kingdoms (Valencia, Murcia, Huelva, etc.) were coveted by Aragonese, Catalans, and Castilians. As in the times of the Cid, this gave rise to alternations of tensions, skirmishes, and treaties, a situation which went on almost until the end of the *Reconquista*. This is probably why another count of Barcelona, Ramon Berenguer IV, seized an opportunity to unite Barcelona with the kingdom of Aragon by marrying Petronila, the heiress to the Aragon throne, in 1151. Petronila's father had been a monk who was forced to become Ramiro II and marry a French princess after his brother, Alfonso I the Battler, king of Aragon, died without issue. Ramiro preferred to leave politics in the hands of his son in law and go back to monastic life as soon as possible. Ramon Berenguer did not become king of Aragon officially (only prince) but his son did, becoming Alfonso II (the Chaste) of Aragon. It was not only fear of Castile's power which pushed Barcelona and Aragón to their union. The Muslim kingdoms had been strengthened by the fanatical Almoravid (eleventh century) and Almohad (twelfth century) invasions from Africa, which among other victories recovered Valencia from the Cid's heirs; France still claimed its feudal rights over the Pyrenean counties, and there were several maritime powers which challenged Barcelona's increasing Mediterranean influence: Genoa, even the faraway Germanic Empire, and top and foremost the Ottoman empire. Another factor favoring union was that the two economies were complementary: Aragon was agrarian and stockbreeding, while Catalonia was commercial and seafaring.

After the marriage of Ramon Berenguer and Petronila, Aragon was ruled by the Barcelona dynasty. Both territories were governed separately; they kept their separate administrations and even languages: Aragon spoke Castilian, whereas Catalonia used mostly Catalan (it is around this time that documents start giving Barcelona and its associated counties the name of Catalonia). Both territories together are known collectively as the Crown of Aragon.

It is obvious that (contrary to what some nationalist historians claim) Catalonia as such has never been a 'nation', at least in the political sense of being an independent territory ruled by a single government. Before uniting with Aragon, it was a conglomerate of counties led by Barcelona and dependent, at least formally, of the French kingdom, a link which was not dissolved until the treaty of Corbeil, more than a century after the union of Aragon and Barcelona. Furthermore, the modern concept of 'nation' is a product of the revolutions of the early Modern Era, the English revolution of 1688 in the first place (Pincus, 2009, p. 348), the French and American revolutions later on, which created states with all the attributes ascribed to national states today; late eighteenth-century France was the country where the word 'nation' was first used in a political revolutionary sense. To pretend that medieval Catalonia was a nation is, therefore, a serious anachronism.

Toward Union

Starting around the end of the twelfth century, especially after the battle of the Navas de Tolosa (1212), several pacts were reached between Aragon and Castile intended to allocate zones of influence and thus coordinate the reconquest of the southern half of the Peninsula still in Muslim hands. This comprehended the kingdoms of Seville, Cordoba,

Granada, Malaga, and Huelva, in the Guadalquivir valley, plus Valencia, Murcia, and Mallorca. Of course, things were far from simple, because these treaties and others dealt not only with the apportionment of future conquests but with several other questions pertaining to the always difficult relations among the Christian lords. For example, in 1137 Ramon Berenguer IV had declared himself a vassal of the king of Castile (Alfonso VII) in exchange for this king returning to Aragon a series of towns Castile had won in war, among them none other than Saragossa, the capital of Aragon. Later on, in 1179, the son of Ramon Berenguer, Alfonso II of Aragon, renounced his right to conquer Murcia in exchange for Alfonso VIII of Castile relinquishing his right to call the king of Aragon his vassal.

The consequence of all these complicated agreements was that Alfonso VIII and Fernando III of Castile, and Jaime I (Jaume in Catalan) of Aragon, known as the Conqueror, carried out the programmed conquests so that by the mid-thirteenth century only the kingdoms of Huelva and Granada remained in Muslim hands. Huelva was conquered soon after (1262) by Alfonso X the Wise of Castile. Granada gained a two-century reprieve because its rulers, the wily Nasrids, astutely allied themselves to the Christian kings in their struggle against the other Moorish kingdoms.

The Christian kingdoms, enriched with their newly acquired territories, enjoyed an economic boom, as did most of Western Europe at this time. Churches, palaces, and cathedrals were built in several architectural styles: Romanesque, Gothic, and, characteristic of Spain, *Mudéjar*, a mixed style with strong Moorish influence. Alfonso X, the Wise, of Castile, especially favored learning and the arts (he himself was a remarkable poet and historian). The first universities were established in Palencia (1208, later moved to Valladolid), Salamanca (1218), Murcia (1272), Coimbra (1290), and Lérida (1300). At this time the three main Latin languages of the Peninsula, Portuguese, Castilian, and Catalan, became fixated, and their earliest written texts were published. But only Castilian, perhaps just due to its central location, became the *lingua franca*.

The main protagonist of Aragonese expansion was Jaime I, the Conqueror. He was the organizer and leader of the campaigns to win

Mallorca (1229) and Valencia (1238–1245) which were added to the crown of Aragon as kingdoms, thus keeping, formally at least, a rank superior to Catalonia. Later on Jaime also re-conquered Murcia (ca. 1261; it had surrendered peacefully earlier, but there had been a Muslim rebellion), and he gave it to Castile in accordance with previous agreements. By means of the treaty of Corbeil (1258), he obtained from the French king (Louis IX, the Saint) the renunciation of his feudal rights, inherited from Charlemagne, over the Catalan counties, included those north of the Pyrenees (Roussillon, Cerdanya, Montpellier), which thereby became part of the crown of Aragon. In exchange, Aragon relinquished its rights over Languedoc and Toulouse. Nationalist Catalan historians have been critical of this treaty as too conservative.

The conquests of Jaime I had thus reached the limits of Aragonese expansion within Spain and across the Pyrenees. From then on Aragon started to expand in the Mediterranean, in the wake of the conquest of Mallorca. Menorca and Ibiza were taken soon afterwards; Sicily (1282) and Sardinia (1323) were added later. In 1319, an expedition to succor the Byzantine emperor against the Turks undertaken by a special section of Catalan troops, a sort of foreign legion called the *almogàvers*, led by the fierce Roger de Flor, ended in the creation of two Catalan duchies on Greek soil, Athens and Neopatria. This was due to the Catalans's intervention in internecine Byzantine struggles in addition to their victorious defense of Constantinople against the Turks.

The Mediterranean expansion was closely related to the economic prosperity which the kingdoms of Aragon experienced in the thirteenth and early fourteenth centuries; maritime trade flourished and the Catalan-Aragonese merchants organized a network of consulates coordinated by the *Consolat de Mar* (Consulate of the Sea) in Barcelona, which issued maritime legislation commonly known as the *usatges de la mar* (customs of the sea) which in the fifteenth century were collected in a code called *Llibre del Consolat de Mar* (Book of the Consulate of the Sea), widely used and translated into several languages. To facilitate the expansion of commerce new money was issued in 1285 in Barcelona, coins known as *croats* because they showed a cross on their reverse. Fontana claims that this was the 'first base of the Catalan monetary system' and 'a capital sign of sovereignty' of Catalonia, statements which would appear to be excessive, since the effigies on the obverse of the coins were those of the kings of Aragon; the coins were later issued in Saragossa, and many medieval feudal lords issued their own coins.

Jaime's successor, Pedro III the Great (1276–1285), finding himself in serious financial straits, was the first king to call the Aragonese *Cortes* (Parliament) in 1283. Jaime I had summoned the first Catalan *Corts* in 1213, but they did not meet in full until that later date. The Catalan *Corts*, therefore, were constituted remarkably early, but they certainly were not the first of their kind. The first Parliament in Europe (probably in the world) met in León in 1188 (Myers, 1975, pp. 59–65). Similar assemblies were gathered later on in Castile, Catalonia, Aragon, Valencia, and Navarre. They met more or less regularly until the *Nueva Planta* (New Start) decrees of Felipe V (early eighteenth century) abolished those of the Crown of Aragon. Parliaments also met early in other countries, such as England (whose Parliament started gathering in the early thirteenth century), Portugal (1254), or France (where the first *Estates General* met in 1302). As medieval assemblies that they were, the *Cortes* or Parliaments were divided into three or more levels (called *brazos* or arms, in Spanish) representing their respective estates (nobility, clergy, and townsfolk – in Aragon the nobility was subdivided into two distinct estates, high and low nobility), and they were separately summoned by the king.

At the first general Cortes of the crown of Aragon meeting in Monzón in 1289, it was decided that in addition to these *general Cortes* of the *Crown*, i.e., the whole realm, the Cortes of Aragon, Valencia, and Catalonia (Mallorca's deputies met jointly with the Catalan *Corts*) could meet separately to deal with matters privative of each kingdom. These first general Cortes also approved the so-called Privilege of the Union which granted a series of immunities to the nobility and required the intervention of the Cortes in international affairs. Of course the main function of these parliaments was not only to solve the financial needs of the crown, mostly for war expenses, but also to allay problems of conflicting legislation or relations between the estates, which expressed their grievances (*greuges* in Catalan) immediately after the king's opening address; they also had legislative power, although kings usually, except in Catalonia, could issue laws by themselves.

Pedro III's financial problems forced him to summon the *Cortes*; he needed money to be able to suppress Muslim revolts in Valencia, for instance. But the Aragonese *Cortes* were never easy to deal with. The nobility resisted new excises and rebelled against the king for having issued taxes before being sworn as count of Barcelona. Remarkably, Pedro was finally able to defeat the Valencia rebellion and also to quell the nobility's revolt. He also added Sicily to the crown of Aragon, after marrying a Sicilian princess and supporting the island's rebellion against a French invasion in the episode known as 'the Sicilian vespers'.

The Aragonese Cortes were more powerful than the Castilian ones. But to see them as a budding democratic parliament, as some nationalist historians, such as Fontana, have suggested, is both an exaggeration and an anachronism, since these Cortes were dominated by the nobility who had little else but their own interests in mind. The middle classes, let alone the poor, were weakly represented in the Cortes, if at all. The third estate had some powerful representation in Catalonia, although not in the *Corts*, but in some municipal bodies of Barcelona. In the late Middle Ages Barcelona became a commercial and crafts center; merchants and artisans constituted a robust middle class which struggled to share municipal power with the nobility. The class struggle was reflected in the ferocious urban wars of the fifteenth century, which we will examine later on. But already Jaime I had created the *Consell de Cent* (Council of the One Hundred) in Barcelona, a consultative body in principle chosen by lots where the *ciutadans honrats* (honorable citizens, i.e., non-noble worthy townsfolk) were eligible. Let me add here that the process of appointment to the *Consell* was much less random than it was supposed to be.

One problem for the Aragon dynasty was that their kings often followed the custom of dividing their kingdoms among their sons: typically, they left their continental possessions to their eldest sons and some islands and minor dependencies to their younger children. This created serious complications, because on several occasions the younger brothers, in their desire to expand their dominions, teamed up with foreign rulers against their own brother (or uncle or nephew, as the case might be). The last great king of the dynasty was Pedro IV, commonly called the Ceremonious or 'of the Small Dagger'. Nationalist Catalan historians call him Pere III. *Pere* is Pedro in Catalan. In fact, calling the

Aragonese kings by their Catalan names is legitimate since they very often spoke in Catalan and used that language in their chronicles. What is not legitimate, however, is to designate them as though they were not Aragonese kings but only Catalan counts. This is the case with the Pedros and the Alfonsos, because there were two kings with those names in Aragon before the Barcelona counts became kings of that kingdom. For nationalist historians these two Aragonese kings do not count, because they did not belong to the Barcelona dynasty. This is a typical example on nationalist historical distortion, and origin of considerable confusion. These were kings of Aragon, a title which took precedence over that of count of Barcelona, and all the kings of Aragon were numbered as such in the chronicles.

Pedro IV was the last great king of the Barcelona dynasty. His reign (1336–1387) straddled the watershed year of 1348, which marked the end of the secular boom of the late Middle Ages and the onset of the 'crisis of the fourteenth century', although popularly 1333 was known in Catalonia as *lo mal any primer* (the first bad year), because a poor harvest caused hunger and was like a harbinger of what was to come. Nevertheless, 1348 was the year when the bubonic plague epidemic broke upon Europe, Catalonia being one of the hardest hit areas.

Among Pedro's accomplishments was to put an end to the nobility's extraordinary privileges by abolishing the Privilege of the Union after defeating their army in the battle of Épila which took place in 1348, the year the plague started. It is said that after that battle, Pedro publicly tore the parchment containing the Privilege by means of a small dagger (*punyalet* in Catalan), hence his nickname: Pere *el del punyalet* or *el cerimoniós*. He was remarkable for his astuteness and his cruelty; he forced the defeated rebels to drink molten bronze, a horrendous death which he thought was 'just'. Pedro managed to unify the Aragonese possessions again: to do this he fought a long war against his distant cousin and brother in law Jaime III of Mallorca, who in the end was defeated and killed. He also fought to recover land lost by Athens and Neopatria and became duke of these Greek territories, which had been carved out by the *almogàvers* in the time of his grandfather, Jaime II. But it was an ephemeral re-conquest: they were definitively lost to Florence three years after Pedro's death. Even worse was the long, confusing and futile wars between Pedro IV of Aragón and Pedro I, the Cruel, of Castile (it is difficult to tell who of the two Pedros was the most cruel). Castile was stronger and richer, but it was torn by civil war between Pedro I and his half-brother Henry of Trastámara, who after seventeen years of on and off wars defeated and killed Pedro, and became Enrique II of Castile; he had been helped intermittently by Pedro of Aragon and by France, while England had supported his half-brother. In fact all these wars in Spain were just an extension of the Hundred Years war between France and England. The end result of all this conflict was that both kingdoms, Aragon and Castile, became exhausted and impoverished, but in the long run Aragon came out worst.

The Crown of Aragon was hit hardest by the plague in all of Spain, but especially Catalonia and especially Barcelona, which during the fifteenth century became second to Valencia as the most important port of Aragon. Catalonia was depopulated and ravaged by hunger, epidemics, and even an earthquake in 1373. The Aragonese Treasury was depleted, and the crown was forced to sell assets massively and to increase fiscal pressure by creating new taxes which fell hardest on foreign commerce (especially on imports), textile production, and consumer goods. In compensation Pedro established a new institution, the *Generalitat* (also called *Diputació*), a parliamentary committee which functioned while the Cortes were in recess and was charged with handling some taxes independently of royal officials. In the long run the *Generalitat* became a powerful body until it was disbanded in 1714. The name was resuscitated in the twentieth century, as we shall see. The *Generalitat* was not exclusively Catalan: similar bodies existed also in Aragon and Valencia. When the Catalan economy recovered later, the volume of the taxes handled by the Generalitat became very large, in fact much larger than those accruing directly to the royal Treasury.

All these are very interesting institutional developments, but they do not warrant statements such as: Catalonia 'had attained, by the mid-fourteenth century, the political and fiscal structure of a modern national state, such as was established in Holland and England three centuries later' (Fontana, 2014, pp. 73–4). To compare depressed and stagnant late fourteenth-century Catalonia with societies as prosperous and dynamic as seventeenth-century Holland or England borders on the ridiculous. The simplest proof is that Holland, and especially England, were at that time (the seventeenth century) on the verge of periods of momentous growth and international hegemony, while the early modern period for Catalonia was, as we shall see, one of stagnation and insignificance. It would be more accurate to say that in the late Middle Ages the different parts of the Crown of Aragon followed distinct paths of development and that, up to the late fourteenth century, Catalonia had outpaced the others and had attained not only greater degrees of prosperity and political and economic expansion, but also clear signs of institutional renewal and distinction. Unfortunately, all this came to an end with the late fourteenth-century crisis, and Catalonia never did really recover until the eighteenth century.

Pedro IV was succeeded by his son Juan I, who was a rather mediocre ruler and inherited a calamitous situation. In turn he was succeeded by his brother Martin I (the Humane), who was a better king but whose reign was marred by anti-semitic riots (a widespread phenomenon in all of Europe at the time) which the king made his utmost to quell. This was also the time of the Avignon schism, and Martin sided with Benedict XIII, the Avignon pope who was from Aragon, and with his ally, father (later saint) Vicente Ferrer, from Valencia. Both played a signal role in the appointment of his successor. Martin also sided with the common folk against the nobility in questions of jurisdiction. His only son, who was king of Sicily, died in combat there, so that when Martin the Humane died a few years later the Aragon throne remained vacant, and the problem of succession became paramount.

The Penultimate Step

The death of Martin in 1410 brought about the end of the dynasty of Barcelona. A procedure was set up to appoint a successor among the many available pretenders, all near relatives of the deceased. Naturally, each of them was supported by a fraction of the nobility. After pressures and deliberations it was decided that a small group of notables (nine, three from Aragon, three from Catalonia, and three from Valencia) would meet at Caspe, on the banks of the Ebro river, and nominate a successor. Among the Valencians was Vicente Ferrer, who had the support of Pope Benedict. Ferrer maneuvered adroitly and was able to muster six votes in support of his candidate, Fernando de Trastámara, who at the time was regent of Castile in the name of his nephew, the future Juan II. Fernando was an accomplished ruler and also famous for his military prowess in the conquest of the Moorish fortress of Antequera. He was grandson of Pedro IV of Aragon, and therefore cousin in the first degree of Martin I. The runner-up, Jaime de Urgel (Jaume de Urgell in Catalan), took up arms more than once against Fernando I, counting on the support of some Catalan nobles and troops of the duke of York (the Lancasters supported the Trastámaras; Catherine of Lancaster was the queen mother of Castile). In the end the count of Urgel was defeated and died in prison. He became a romantic hero for Catalan nationalists.

Fernando I of Aragon died young and reigned only four years. He had time to learn about the problems of dealing with the Aragonese *Cortes* while trying to gather funds to finance his war against Jaime de Urgel; he ended up making many concessions in exchange for the wherewithal. He left several sons who several times took advantage of the weakness of their nephew Enrique IV of Castile to try to wrest the crown from him; they were collectively known in Castile as 'the *infantes* of Aragon'. Although they did not achieve their aims in Castile, two of them became kings of Aragon: Alfonso V, the Magnanimous, and Juan II, the Great. Alfonso V spent most of his reign in Naples trying to consolidate and aggrandize Aragon's Mediterranean empire. He left the affairs of Aragon proper in the hands of his wife, María of Castile, of his right-hand man, Galcerán de Recasens, and of his brother Juan, who became king of Navarre after marrying Blanca, princess of that kingdom. It was at this time (first half of the fifteenth century) that a sort of urban civil war raged in Barcelona between the *Biga*, the armed party of the high nobility, and the *Busca*, the faction of the low nobility and the bourgeoisie. Aside from the plain power struggle between these two groups, a clear issue between the two was commercial policy: the Biga, predominantly a consumer group of luxury goods, favored free trade; the Busca craftsmen wanted protection from imports. It is interesting that

Catalan protectionism manifested itself so early in history. Generally speaking, this was clearly a class conflict typical of the transition from a feudal to a capitalistic society. But Catalonia was rent by conflict not only in Barcelona; in the countryside another chronic discord raged between the aristocratic landowners and their serfs and tenants. Many Catalan peasants were under the frequently tyrannical yoke of the nobility, who submitted them to humiliating vexations and abusive exactions, known as *malos usos* (bad customs); these peasants, however, could buy their liberty by paying a ransom (*remensa*) to the lord. They had trouble collecting the required ransom and wanted the *malos usos* abolished. These tensions had been intensified by the crisis, which decimated the countryside and pushed the lords to try to increase their control over their subjects. In consequence, there was a situation of chronic rebellion in the Catalan countryside between the *remensa* laborers and the landlords.

In 1443 the Busca obtained control of the Barcelona government, with the support of Recasens, who was in favor of widening the access to municipal posts so as to include the bourgeoisie, to devalue the *croat*, and to tax imports of woolens. In the *remensa* problem, although the king did not want to antagonize the nobility and the clergy, who controlled the *Corts* and thereby the purse, he also wanted to bring peace to the countryside, and therefore promoted a settlement, which worked for a few years.

When Juan II acceded to the throne in 1458 the situation was critical: the *remensa* conflict raged in the country and the *Biga-Busca* rivalry divided Barcelona. He managed to appease both temporarily. But these were not his only problems: in Navarre he refused to step down and let his son Carlos de Viana succeed to the throne when Blanca died. This caused a war between father and son; Carlos had the support of many Catalans so that the Navarrese conflict in the end caused a flare-up of another civil war in Catalonia. When Carlos died in strange circumstances, Juan (or his second wife, Juana Enríquez) was accused of parricide (without proof: he most likely died of tuberculosis), and the hostilities continued. It was a long and confusing war, in which some combatants changed sides, often more than once, and where the rebels offered the position of counts of Barcelona to four foreign magnates consecutively, the first of them Enrique IV of Castile who soon abandoned the enterprise. Other prospective rulers of rebel Catalonia were a Portuguese prince, a French duke, and his grandson. All came to naught when the rebels capitulated in Pedralbes in 1472. Although this war has been seen by nationalist historians as struggle for Catalan liberty, it really was a complex civil war where the *remensa* quarrel, the Biga-Busca rivalry, and the conflict between the nobility and the monarchy were the real issues, while the disputes between Juan II and Carlos de Viana were only the detonator. For Aragon, and for Catalonia in particular, the war was the last straw, a pretty heavy one at that, after the series of demographic, political, and economic disasters which had devastated it since the mid-fourteenth century.

Juana Enríquez, the second wife of Juan II of Aragon, was the daughter of Fadrique Enríquez, admiral of Castile, and the mother of a son who would reign in Aragon as Fernando II and in Castile as Fernando V. She was a strong woman who participated in the Catalan civil war as much or more as her husband, and who had previously pressured Juan to push aside Carlos de Viana to improve the chances of her son Fernando to reign in Aragon and eventually in Castile. The idea of marrying her son to Isabel of Castile, a distant cousin of hers, probably was her own in the first place. After exploring other possibilities, Juan came around: he needed the help of Castile against France and against his rebellious subjects; furthermore, he was a Trastámara, one of the *infantes* of Aragon who had coveted the Castilian throne: Isabel was the daughter of his cousin in the first degree, Juan II of Castile. Fernando and Isabel, therefore, were second degree cousins. The wedding of Isabel and Fernando was full of obstacles, however, because the king of Castile, Isabel's half-brother, Enrique IV, had a daughter and, in any case, he wanted Isabel to marry Afonso of Portugal, his brother in law.

Enrique's daughter, Juana, was probably not his. Although married twice, the second time to Afonso's sister, he showed little interest in women: the opinion that he was impotent, homosexual, or both, was widespread. Many believed that Juana had been engendered by one of Henry's generals, Beltrán de la Cueva; this is why she was nicknamed *la Beltraneja*. Enrique may have believed it too:

his Portuguese wife was unfaithful to him, and he finally had her expelled from the court. But, more important, he appointed Isabel his successor in 1468, implicitly recognizing his wife's infidelity. In exchange, Isabel promised not to marry without his brother's permission, a promise she broke the following year by wedding Fernando in semi-secrecy. Enrique did not react to Isabel's breach of promise and when he died in 1474 she was proclaimed queen of Castile, and Fernando became king consort although he always thought his rights to the throne of Castile as good as those of his wife. Afonso of Portugal then married Juana la Beltraneja and claimed the Castilian throne. A war ensued, but Isabel and Fernando won (battle of Toro, 1476) and this put an end to Portugal's bid for union with Castile.

Union

Juan II of Aragon died in 1479. At that moment Fernando became king of Aragon which from then on has been politically united to Castile. It is true that, as we will see later, both kingdoms were ruled separately and they kept their own institutions, *Cortes*, etc., for a long time. Nevertheless, there were a curious set of asymmetries which, to a certain extent, contributed to the gradual (very gradual) convergence of both kingdoms. If Castile was stronger and played the senior role in the new political body, Fernando was the more accomplished politician (although Isabel was certainly no pushover); furthermore, he considered himself monarch of both kingdoms on an equal footing with his wife; Isabel, however, disagreed: she saw herself as queen consort of Aragon, and her husband as king consort of Castile. They disagreed about this until the end, and this disagreement had troublesome consequences. In any case, foreign policy, especially in Europe, was left almost entirely in Fernando's hands, and in fact, in this field at least, he acted as ruler of a single kingdom. A clear example of this was the war to defend Naples from the French. Naples had been conquered by Alfonso V of Aragon, so it was an Aragonese dependency. Fernando and Isabel, however, appointed an Andalusian, Gonzalo de Cordoba, a former member of Isabel's guard, as captain general of the army, and his troops were mostly Castilian. There were other fields, such as religious policies, which were also carried out in a united way.

Fernando is not a popular figure with nationalist historians. He spent relatively little time in Aragon after his marriage and was somewhat impatient with the Catalan *Corts*'s fastidiousness and nitpicking. Also, he was a Trastámara, i.e., a descendent of a Castilian dynasty, no matter that he was born in Aragon; his mother was Castilian and during his childhood he was in her care. Most of his childhood and adolescence he spent in Catalonia, though, and in rather difficult circumstances, since Juana Enríquez was deeply involved in the Catalan civil war; he himself fought as a young captain in it (he was twenty when the Pedralbes capitulations were signed). This was good training; he was not only a consummate politician (Machiavelli took him as a model for his *Prince*) but also a very able military commander.

Be it as it may, Catalan nationalist historians abhor of Spanish unity and hold Fernando responsible for it. So they have accused him of several charges: betraying the *remensas* and the bourgeoisie in favor of the nobility; introducing the Inquisition in Catalonia; allowing corruption in Catalan or, more precisely, Barcelonese institutions by leaving control in the hands of a few families who took advantage of their position to enrich themselves, etc.

Of course, Fernando's record is not unblemished: undoubtedly he committed some serious mistakes; but all in all his achievements clearly outweigh his errors. First of all, he pacified Catalonia after almost a century of internecine strife; he did not sell out to the nobility, as some say, on the contrary: in the final entente he reached with the diverse groups the Busca obtained far more than the Biga (chiefly, albeit not only, protectionism), but he was no revolutionary and was not out to destroy the nobility in spite of their antagonism against him. In addition, he also put an end to the *remensa* contest, after the peasants rebelled again in 1484. He issued the Sentence of Guadalupe in 1486 which abolished the *malos usos* and introduced *emphyteusis*, a type of long-term or indefinite lease, which granted peasant families stability of tenure conditional to payment of rent to the landlord. Serfdom and feudalism were not abolished, but the conditions of laborers were improved and the countryside pacified. There were no more agrarian conflicts in Catalonia for a long time. Fernando also increased, as far as he could, the power of the crown in Catalan institutions, introducing reforms according to the absolutist model which was being imposed by European monarchs at the time. To say that this brought about 'a considerable setback for democracy' (Fontana, 2014, p. 122) makes little sense, since Catalan institutions at the time were not democratic but oligarchic, i.e., they were controlled by the nobility and the wealthy commoners. Fernando wrested power from the nobility in favor of the monarchy; this is why he was unpopular with the upper classes, although many were happy to see the king assume the responsibility of imposing order after so many years of war and chaos. Democracy was out of the question in Renaissance Catalonia, as in the rest of Europe at the time. Fernando also managed to put some order in the finances of the Barcelona municipality, as we have seen.

It is true that Fernando and Isabel introduced the Inquisition in Spain and therefore in Catalonia, where it was unpopular. Their intention was to make Spain religiously homogeneous, and they were not the only Renaissance rulers striving for this kind of homogeneity. Due to geographical and historical factors, Spain was a mosaic of religions and cultures, and they saw this as a source of potential weakness. Their motives, however, differed somewhat: she was more religious, he more political. She saw the Inquisition as an agency for saving souls, whereas for him it was a political instrument for increasing royal power and attaining social discipline and strength. This striving for religious unity moved them to commit a terrible blunder, which was the expulsion of the Jews in 1492. It must be admitted, however, that there was considerable support for the expulsion of Jews in Catalonia and in Spain at large. In any case, their critics usually omit to say that the papal Inquisition had been functioning in Aragon since 1242. The Inquisition now established by Ferdinand and Isabel, although authorized by the Pope, was placed under the jurisdiction of the Spanish state, so it did not depend directly on Rome, as was the case with the papal Inquisition.

Another success of Fernando was the recovery for Aragon of the counties of Roussillon and Cerdanya, which had been ceded to France by his father (Juan II) in exchange for military support during the Catalan civil war. Astute diplomatic maneuvers brought about the treaty of Barcelona (1493) whereby Charles VIII of France returned these counties. All these successes, plus the conquest of Granada (1492) and Naples (1504), plus, of course, the discovery and colonization of America, moved the admiration of writers, among them most notably Niccolò Machiavelli, who in *The Prince* (1994, p. 176) said about him that he was 'by fame and glory the leader among Christian kings; and when his exploits are considered, they are all very great and some extraordinary'.

His most remarkable success, however, was possibly his marriage to Isabel (Valladolid, 1469), which, added to the conquest of Granada, marked the beginning of the Spanish nation state under a single monarchy. It is true that both kingdoms (Aragon and Castile) were quite dissimilar, being in turn the product of earlier agglomerations of separate kingdoms in differing degrees of convergence. It is true also that Navarre and Portugal were still separate political units in the Peninsula at the end of the fifteenth century. But Navarre was added to Castile in 1512 (after Isabel's death), and Portugal was united with Spain in 1580, although it separated again in 1640. Together, Fernando and Isabel (they are known as the Catholic Monarchs, a title bestowed upon them in 1494 by pope Alexander VI Borgia, of Spanish origin and a frequent ally) formed a remarkable and unusual team. They not only jointly obtained signal successes on the international scene (to the conquests and victories just mentioned, one must add their diplomatic successes and alliances, especially their marriage policies, only marred by the deaths of some of their children), but their ability to pacify and reorganize their realms after all the turmoils of the mid-fifteenth century is also admirable. Regarding their matrimonial diplomacy, of their five children only two daughters survived and, married according to their carefully devised policies, they lived difficult and tormented lives. The youngest, Catherine of Aragon, was the estranged but strong-willed wife of Henry VIII of England, and the mother of Mary Tudor. The other, Juana the Mad, was married to Philip the Handsome, duke of Burgundy and heir to the Holy Roman Empire. She was mistreated by her husband (whom she loved to madness), her father (who confined her to a castle), and her son, Charles V (who kept her there to the end of her life). Nevertheless, Carlos (I of Spain, V as Holy Emperor) became the most powerful ruler of the world and the first officially acknowledged king of Spain.

In spite of all their triumphs, the Catholic Monarchs also committed serious blunders: the main ones were establishing the Inquisition, expelling the Jews, treating the kingdoms of Castile and Aragón in an asymmetrical manner, and giving Castile the monopoly of the Indies (America). As we saw before, the first two decisions were determined by the monarchs' wish to unify and homogenize their kingdoms to foster internal peace and external security. They committed a grievous miscalculation (ethical considerations aside): the Inquisition exercised a secular ideological oppression which gravely affected and damaged the intellectual resources of Spanish society; the expulsion of the Jews, one of the most dynamic groups in this society, only aggravated the deleterious effects of the Inquisition.

As to the asymmetric treatment of Castile and Aragon, it is, of course the consequence of the pre-existing asymmetry of the two kingdoms, but the policies of the Catholic Monarchs contributed to augment and perpetuate it, with grievous political consequences in the long run. As we have seen, Castile was more powerful and easier to run, chiefly because their *Cortes* were more compliant. Therefore, Castile was the center of the attention of Fernando and his main foreign policy instrument. The asymmetry was carried to the extreme in relation to the Americas, and this was due to Isabel's preference for her own subjects over those of her husband. This was already expressed in the Treaty of Tordesillas (1494) which divided the western hemisphere between Portugal and Castile, and even more in her testament, where she stated that the discovery and colonization of the Indies had been carried out by Castile only (which was not totally true, since Aragon also played a considerable supporting role in both tasks) and therefore 'the deals and profits with them [the Indies] are to be made and transacted from my kingdoms of Castile and Leon, and all that may be brought from them be carried to said kingdoms'. It seems, however, that Isabel's mandate was not followed literally; Fernando would not be inclined to exclude his own Aragonese countrymen from the Americas, and Carlos V would not either (Martínez Shaw, 1980, p. 233). The fact remained, nevertheless, that the relations between Aragon and the Indies were rather tenuous until the eighteenth century, and that nationalist historians, citing Isabel's testament have attributed this to unfair discrimination, instead of to Aragón's stagnation during these centuries, as was the case according to Martínez Shaw.

Another asymmetry, this one of an opposite sign, pertained to fiscal matters. Since Castile was wealthier and more powerful, she was subject to higher fiscal pressure not only in money and commodities but also in men for the armies. We saw before that Castilian soldiers fought to defend Naples, Aragon's most valued overseas possession, possibly because Castilian troops were more disciplined and easier to recruit. In the medium run this posed no problem, but in the seventeenth century Castile's strength diminished, its economy stalled, and its capacity to contribute money and men diminished, while the burdens of Aragon and Portugal were light indeed. Attempts to redress this asymmetry caused bloody conflict at that time.

Conclusions

Spain can be proud to be the remotest cradle of European democracy, as Leon, Castile, Aragon, and Navarre produced the earliest rudimentary parliaments in the Continent and very probably in the world. It can be proud too that Aragon exported the parliamentary tradition to its dependencies in southern Italy. An embryo, however, is not a mature human being. One cannot (or should not) speak about democracy in medieval or early modern Europe. Furthermore, it was very often that these representative medieval institutions, in Spain and in other neighboring countries, were really in the hands of oligarchies who were opposed to the changes and social reforms that modernization required. In addition, in most European countries (save England and the Low Countries) representative institutions receded during the Renaissance and Early Modern period, when absolute monarchy was the rule. Absolute monarchy had less and less recourse to parliaments and used its renewed power to streamline and make more efficient the administration of the state. England, however, followed a different course: its Parliament, instead of withering, was reinforced to prop up the absolute monarchy in its sweeping sixteenth-century reforms, although in the seventeenth it revolted against absolutism and monarchy. In France the old parliament was the focus of revolution against absolutism in the eighteenth century, and several countries tried to follow the same path with varying success. Although Europe was the cradle of modern democracy, therefore, its history followed diverging and tortuous paths before reaching maturity in the twentieth century. In general, the democratic movement was carried out by the bourgeois and urban classes of flourishing commercial cities. This may explain why, in spite of their early start, Spanish parliaments suffered secular stagnation until the nineteenth century: Spain's economy experienced a long interlude of decline and depression between the late sixteenth century and the mid-nineteenth century – with the exception of eighteenth-century Catalonia. A strong urban bourgeoisie was missing in early modern Spain.

Another European creation is the nation-state; by the end of the fifteenth century there were four (or five) buddying nation states in Europe: Spain, Portugal, France, England, and Scotland. In Scandinavia three kingdoms hesitated between becoming three separate nations or a single one. The cases of Spain, France, and England show considerable similarities in that they emerged as single nations after a turbulent medieval period of gradual and discontinuous process of integration of smaller units. Due to geographical and historical reasons, Spain is the extreme case for the large number of kingdoms and principalities which were agglomerated through complex processes of re-conquest and absorption. Catalonia, however original, was far from a unique case; it was the product of the gradual aggregation of frontier counties which converged toward unity and were merged with a larger kingdom, Aragon, before total unity was completed. Aragon in turn was the resultant of a similar unification of several Pyrenean counties. It is, therefore, inappropriate to speak a 'medieval nation' when referring to Catalonia. First, it was never a real, consolidated, political unit; second, modern nations, in the sense we commonly use this word today, did not exist until the eighteenth century; applying this term to a medieval county, even to a kingdom, is a flagrant anachronism.

References

FONTANA, Josep (2014), *La formació d'una identitat, una historia de Catalunya*. Vic: Eumo Editoral.

MACHIAVELLI, Niccolò (1994 [1515]), *Il Principe*. Milano: Rizzoli Libbri.

MARTÍNEZ SHAW, Carlos (1980), 'Cataluña y el comercio con América, el fin de un debate', *Boletín Americanista*, 30, pp. 223–236.

Myers, A. R. (1975), *Parliaments and Estates in Europe to 1789*. London: Thames and Hudson.

PINCUS, S. (2009), *1688. The First Modern Revolution*. New Haven, Conn: Yale University Press.

VILAR, Pierre (1962), *La Catalogne dans l'Espagne moderne. Recherches sur les fondements économiques des structures nationales*. 3 vols. Paris: SEVPEN.

2

Catalonia in Early Modern Spain

The Difficult Welding of Two Crowns

The asymmetry of Aragon and Castile at the time of their union was one the most serious problems faced by Spain in the Early Modern Era. This lack of symmetry was the consequence of the diverging evolution of both kingdoms in the late Middle Ages, their different sizes, and their diverse institutional structures.

Elliott (1984, pp. 3–6) describes the problem thus:

> The late fifteenth century [. . .] found Castile ready for a fresh challenge and new opportunities. The prosperity of the wool trade had brought it vast new riches. The ending of the *Reconquista* had freed it from internal wars. The discovery of the New World, and the European wars undertaken by Ferdinand in defense of Aragonese interests, would provide an ideal opportunity for canalizing the immense energies of a proud and triumphant nation, which found itself for the first time with the occasion, the resources and the incentive to turn outwards, towards Europe and a wider world. [. . .] Where Castile was entering a period of economic and military expansion, the Crown of Aragon, after centuries of expansion

G. Tortella, *Catalonia in Spain*, Palgrave Studies in Economic History, DOI 10.1007/978-3-319-54951-4_2

> followed by a period of decay, was entering on a new age which, at the best, was likely to be no more than one of consolidation and slow recovery.
>
> Unfortunately, this great upsurge of national vitality in late fifteenth-century Castile was matched by no comparable upsurge in the Crown of Aragon to which it now found itself united. The Crown of Aragon's medieval history was quite the reverse of that of Castile [. . .] While the Castilians were still engaged in dynastic struggles, and their crusade against the Moors was far from complete, the inhabitants of the eastern regions had already expelled the Arabs and were laying the foundations for one of the most imposing States in medieval Europe [. . .] The thirteenth and fourteenth centuries were the great age of the Catalan-Aragonese empire. [But t]he fifteenth century was for Catalonia, the predominant partner in the federation, a century of commercial, social, and political crisis [. . . which . . .] plunged into civil war a country which had already been weakened by economic crisis [. . .] The Catalonia that emerged from these struggles was a battered and exhausted country, with its spiritual and economic impetus lost.

The union of the two kingdoms was purely personal. 'Other than the marriage contract of Ferdinand and Isabella, there was no formal document of union' (Elliott, 1984, p. 7). Both monarchs made a point of ruling two different states; when Fernando acceded to the throne of Aragon at the death of his father, some members of the Royal Council proposed that they should adopt the title of kings of Spain, but they rejected the suggestion (this did not prevent their contemporaries calling them so). Isabel's testament was written as queen of Castile, and she named her daughter Juana (the Mad) her successor who only in case of incapacitation would be replaced by Fernando as governor or regent. She thus showed her disagreement with her husband, who considered himself king of Castile on his own right. The same applied to the exclusive adscription of the Indies to Castile.

The consequences of this asymmetry were harmful, but it is difficult to see how they could have been avoided. To start with, as Nadal (2011, p. 20) pointed out, 'the empire was Castilian [. . .] There is no gainsaying that the Castilian kingdoms responded better to the requirements of Carlos's policies'. This, however, was not necessarily advantageous for

Castile, whose Cortes lost a large share of their liberties and prerogatives. In addition, or maybe as a consequence, Castile bore most of the burden and the cost of Habsburg and Aragonese imperialism: we already saw this in regard to the conquest of Naples under Fernando. More attention and effort was devoted to the European scene than to the colonization of the Americas (Sánchez-Albornoz, 1956, II, p. 499). Although American silver permitted the pursuance of quixotic European enterprises by the Spanish crown for a while, in the seventeenth century these enterprises failed in all fronts: not only in Europe, but also in the Americas and even inside Spain itself. Aragon also suffered. Its political situation 'could not be more distressing', says Nadal: 'its constitutional autonomy [was respected, but this brought about] the paralysis or sclerosis of its administrative apparatus'. Furthermore, Aragon was kept out of the great decisions, subordinated to 'Castilian extraversion'.

It is also true that the definitive union of the kingdoms after the demise of the Catholic Monarchs appears to have been largely the product of chance. If Felipe I (the Handsome) of Burgundy, Juana's husband, had not died prematurely, he would have consolidated his rule in Castile and excluded from it Fernando, his father in law, as he did during his short reign (1505–1507), when Fernando was relegated to king of Aragon only. But Felipe's death and Juana's disability made Fernando regent of Castile and king of Aragon for the remaining ten years of his life (numerous contemporaries, Machiavelli among them, still called him king of Spain, and so did Fernando himself on occasion). He married again, to Germaine de Foix, a niece of Louis XII of France. She gave him a son who, had he survived, would have been king of Aragon, and this kingdom would have become formally independent of Castile. The child, however, died early, and so both crowns were inherited by Charles of Gaunt, eldest son of Juana and Felipe, hence grandson of Fernando and Isabel. He became Carlos I of Castile and Aragon and Charles V of the Holy Roman Empire, and, thereby, the first undisputed king of Spain. Although there is an undeniable random factor in Carlos's becoming the sole heir of the kingdoms of Castile and Aragon, it seems very improbable that both kingdoms might not have been united again in the medium term in one way or another.

Interestingly, Carlos, who was so different from his grandfather Fernando, whom he never met, behaved in a similar way once he assumed the crown: he made Castile his abode and visited Aragon seldom, although initially he seemed to prefer Barcelona to Valladolid, then the capital of Castile. In the long run, however, his reasons for residing in Castile appear the same as those of his grandfather: this kingdom was richer and more powerful, and its *Cortes* were more pliable than those of Aragon, thus making it easier to obtain from them the means Carlos's expensive imperial policies required. According to Lynch (1964, p. 10), Carlos and his successors respected the privileges of Aragon because

> these kingdoms had little to offer so they had little to protect and the crown had few reasons for breaking the protective barriers. Had the eastern kingdoms been richer in resources, then it is difficult to avoid the conclusion that their institutions would have suffered the same fate as those of Castile [. . .] Aragon and Catalonia were saved from the more extreme forms of absolute government by their poverty, and their immunity survived with the permission of the crown. The proof of this lies in the fact that when it was necessary the crown had no hesitation in imposing its will, even in the face of resistance. In the Catalan cortes of 1510 the representatives of Barcelona opposed the grant of subsidy on constitutional grounds, because the king had not given satisfaction to their demands; Ferdinand promptly ordered the recall of the Barcelona representatives and this was enough to bring them to heel [. . .] And it was not until the seventeenth century, precisely when Castile had reached the end of its resources, that the central government attempted to break the immunities of the eastern kingdoms in order to tap their manpower and money.

And, we might add, it was in the eighteenth century, when Catalonia committed the egregious error of joining England in alliance against Felipe V, its lawful monarch, and to resist heroically but futilely the king's armies, that Felipe took advantage of his victory to put a definitive end to all those old privileges and immunities.

These often praised privileges and immunities (the laws and customs which sustained its political system, also called liberties, constitutions, or *fueros*) were certainly not democratic at all, although they enjoyed a certain popular support. According to Elliott (1984, p. 16), in Aragon

> the Crown was not the only potential oppressor [. . .] with the king far away, it was not difficult for the nobles of the States of the Crown of Aragon to turn the *fueros* to their own advantage and to harass their vassals at will [. . .] The true contrast is not between a 'free' Crown of Aragon and an 'enslaved' Castile; it is a more subtle contrast between a Castile which enjoyed justice and good government, but had little defense against the arbitrary and fiscal demands of the Crown, and a Crown of Aragon well protected against arbitrary taxation and royal absolutism, but possessed of a constitution easily abused by an irresponsible aristocracy.

Lynch (1964, pp. 33) makes a comparable description: 'The "liberties" of Aragon [. . .] were not popular or democratic ones [. . .] Above all, they shielded an archaic social structure. Behind these legal barriers lurked a feudalism more primitive than anywhere else in western Europe [. . .] The *fueros*, then, worked to the advantage of the ruling class, not of the mass of the people'.

These assessments by two respected British scholars are frequently overlooked by nationalist historians. Regarding Catalonia, Elliott (1984, pp. 101–102) shows that, pretending to resist the pressures of kings and viceroys, the Catalan 'constitutions were being exploited in the interests of the select few [. . .] The *Diputació* [also called *Generalitat*, a permanent committee of the Corts in charge of tax collection], once the bastion of Catalan liberties, had fallen victim of sectional interests, and now appeared little more than a bastion of aristocratic privilege'. These aristocratic elites controlled the *Corts*, where the peasantry – the majority of the population – was not represented (this was also true of all medieval parliaments), and used this control to negotiate with the monarchs, thereby obtaining favorable legislation in exchange for the coveted subsidies, whose burden fell almost exclusively upon the voiceless peasants. The nobility also shared the control of the municipal government (the *Concell de Cent*, the council of the One Hundred, the city assembly) with the *ciutadans honrats*, the wealthy commoners, and used this power as an additional lever in its relations with viceroys.

Thus 'the Crown's power in the Principality was gradually whittled away over the course of the sixteenth century [until] the constitutions tied the hands of the viceroy and his officials. It was this that made them sacrosanct to the Catalan governing class'.

***

After the death of Fernando the Catholic, two monarchs reigned in Spain for the rest of the sixteenth century (until 1598 precisely), Carlos I and Felipe II, his son. They ruled over an 'empire where the sun never set'. Felipe was not really emperor (his uncle Fernando succeeded Carlos on the see of the Holy Roman Empire) but even shorn of the Austrian territories Spanish holdings in Europe (from Italy to the Low Countries) were quite impressive, to which must be added the American possessions, the Philippine Islands (named after Felipe), plus several footholds in Africa and islands in the Pacific and Indian oceans, plus, of course, Portugal and its colonies in the Americas, Africa, and Asia after 1580, when Felipe II became king of Portugal after his nephew, king Sebastian, died without issue. Felipe was even king consort of England during his brief marriage to Mary Tudor (1544–1548).

Homogenization between Castile and Aragon proceeded through the 'council system' of government: there were Councils of Castile, of Aragon, of the Indies, of the Inquisition, of Finance (*Hacienda*), and several others (Portugal, Flanders, etc.). The role of these Councils was advisory in theory, but in fact they often had semi-executive powers. This system brought about some administrative convergence, although, for instance, the Council of Aragon had more trouble dealing with the Aragonese Cortes than the Council of Castile had with those of Castile. The council system was combined with that of viceroys, a post which had been created in the Aragonese Mediterranean empire. There were viceroys in Aragon and Naples, and also in the Indies, but there was no viceroy in Castile, something which underlined its centrality. While it is true that the Aragonese were not excluded from trading with the Indies on an equal footing as the Castilians, it is also true that the transatlantic commerce was controlled and supervised in Seville through the *Casa de Contratación* (Commerce House), a typically mercantilist institution located on the largest (fluvial) port city on the Atlantic.

During the sixteenth century Catalonia partook of the general prosperity although its role was relatively minor in the great empire. There were several reasons for this. First, Catalonia was still recovering from the catastrophes of the previous centuries. Probably the most important factor, however, was the one underscored by John Lynch. Catalan authorities and institutions did their best to remain aloof and to avoid paying taxes. The Catalan *Corts* were extremely fastidious and mistrustful of royal power: they required that the king pledge respect to the constitutions of the principality before starting any discussion of subsidies or contributions. Then they also required that the king should solve problems and grievances (*dissentiments* and *greuges*) which the deputies might submit at any time in the session, something which would interrupt and postpone the main discussion. All this involved long and tedious sessions, which were clearly out of place in such a complex political machine as the Spanish crown was, and which were deliberately used by the deputies to obtain new concessions from the crown. The king of Spain had many matters to attend to and was more pressed than the local deputies were during these long and convoluted procedures. Since Catalonia was not very rich but very argumentative and tight-fisted, the kings preferred to leave it alone and look for subsidies elsewhere. This explains the progressive '*effacement*' of Catalonia from imperial enterprises, as Vilar (1962, I, p. 529) pointed out.

Nevertheless, the Catalan economy became more dependent on its western neighbors as the Mediterranean empire stagnated due to the development of the Atlantic spice trade, which rivaled the Mediterranean route after the Portuguese reached the Indian Ocean navigating around Africa; and, later on, due to the Turkish maritime expansion. To compensate this, Catalonia sold an increasing share of its industrial and craft production (textiles, leather goods, soap, glass, weapons) in Castile, which re-exported part of it to the Americas. Barcelona also became an important port of transit for American silver which the Spanish crown remitted to Italy and finally to Flanders to pay for the *tercios* that fought the rebellion in the Low Countries after 1566.

Catalonia's relative prosperity and its depopulation after the wars and plagues of former centuries attracted migrants, especially from France. The pacification of the countryside after the sentence of Guadalupe must have been an added attraction. Most of these French migrants settled in the country and took up agriculture and husbandry; by century's end they were about 20 percent of the Catalan population.

The Seventeenth-Century Crisis

A Time of Depression

After the defeat of the Armada in 1588 Spain experienced a long (125 years) century of depression, misfortunes, and catastrophes unparalleled in its history. Military disasters, disunion, dismemberment (Francisco de Quevedo, poet and satirist, compared Philip IV to a well, grander the more soil he lost), and economic decline succeeded one another. The causes of 'the decline of Spain' are clear: intellectual sclerosis, the consequence of religious intolerance, the Counter Reformation and the Inquisition; the political asymmetry between Castile and Aragon we already referred to; the persistence of feudal values; absolute disregard of economic realities; and a growing disproportion between the real possibilities of the country and the aims pursued by the political elite, a disproportion which could endure for a long time thanks to the inflow of precious metals from the Americas and the crippling taxes paid by Castile.

All the foregoing are causes specifically referring to Spain. Other wider causes must be taken into account; the central decades of the seventeenth century witnessed depression on a world scale, due to a factor independent of human action: a cooling of the weather caused by a diminution of solar activity. This caused the phenomenon known as the *little ice age*, a fall of the mean temperature of the globe which affected agricultural production, something which, in a society with limited technical capabilities, could only cause famine, plague, and war. Parker's monumental book (2013) offers in its opening pages an impressive accumulation of evidence about the interrelation between climate change, dearth, and violence all over the world; the revolts that erupted in the Iberian Peninsula were only a fraction, albeit substantial, of a disturbing panorama of conflict on a planetary scale.

Within the great world crisis of the seventeenth century Spain is probably the country which came out worse off, whose status went from that of hegemonic power to third-rate player. This may be due to an extra factor which should be added to the foregoing: the physical endowments of Spain were not well adapted to the military and economic conditions of the seventeenth century, where cereal cultivation and large armies were the sources of economic welfare and military might. Spain's dry, rocky land yields poor wheat crops and therefore allows only low population densities. The economy of Medieval Spain was based upon transhumant sheep rearing which was well adapted to the characteristics of the land and to sparse population (Alvarez Nogal and Prados de la Escosura, 2013), but military power in the Early Modern era required numerous armies. Spain could compensate its shortage of military manpower by hiring mercenaries with American silver, and she did, but in the long run this became too costly and silver output also fell. The defeat of the Armada required new taxes, which impoverished Castile and even so were insufficient. So from the early seventeenth century Felipe III started to issue debased *vellón* coin (*vellón* being an alloy of silver and copper, which in the end was almost pure copper), which caused inflation and ruined Castile.

The seventeenth century witnessed a global crisis, but this crisis did not hit all regions equally. In Europe the south was the most battered while northern Europe forged ahead and gained an economic and political advantage it never lost since then (Cipolla, 1976, Ch. 10). Within southern Europe Spain possibly was the hardest hit.

Spanish historians have debated the magnitude of the crisis in their country. A few of them have denied the seriousness of the slump. Given what we know today about the decline in population, the cessation of French immigration, the fall in tax income, the effects of galloping inflation alternating with ruinous deflation, and the political and military disasters (defeat in the Low Countries, recurring defeats in the wars with France, rebellions of Catalonia and Portugal with the consequence of definitive independence of Portugal, and dismemberment of Catalonia) it would be foolish to deny the evidence of a grave crisis. Literary testimonies (picaresque literature), essayists, and pamphleteers (*arbitristas*) all coincide in showing an impoverished society trying to keep appearances and in need of desperate measures to fend off disaster.

More than fifty years ago Vilar (1962, I, p. 588) wrote: 'Between 1598 and 1640 Catalonia shows signs of crisis which are common to the whole Spanish economy'. There are signs, for instance, that Barcelona's commerce declined in the first decades of the seventeenth century. The same seems to be true of industry: the indications, although not conclusive in themselves, are too numerous to be dismissed. There are proofs of efforts on the part of entrepreneurs to lower salaries, or use peasant manpower to sidestep guilds, of unemployment, hunger, street protests, and other traces of malaise. Catalan agriculture seems to have withstood better than Castilian agriculture, but it also underwent subsistence crises in 1604–1606, 1627–1631, and 1640; the last one no doubt was among the immediate causes of the Catalan rebellion which we will presently examine.

An endemic sign of distress in Catalonia was banditry, a scourge which blighted Catalonia from the fourteenth to the seventeenth century, with especial rigor in the last period. Early bandits tended to be noblemen who incurred in rivalries and vendettas. Somehow linked to the *busca* and the *biga*, there appeared in the late Middle Ages in Catalonia the rival bands called *nyerros* and *cadells* (these words referring to the names of two noblemen who were the original leaders of the two factions). Their frequently violent confrontations were also related to political rivalries, the *nyerros* being more reactionary. Seventeenth-century banditry, however, was more popular and driven by the search for booty. Silver convoys crossing Catalonia on their way to Flanders were frequently assaulted by these bandits.

The seventeenth-century Spanish Habsburgs (Felipe III (1598–1621), Felipe IV (1621–1665), and Carlos II (1665–1700), commonly called the 'minor' Habsburgs, by contrast with Carlos I and Felipe II, the 'major' Habsburgs) tried to repress banditry, not only for reasons of law and order but also for political and religious reasons: they suspected that foreign bandits crossed the Pyrenees bringing with them Protestantism and subversion. Furthermore, banditry was a sign of the division of Catalan society: a part of the nobility and the church sympathized with the bandits, and so did other groups. There were even problems for the viceroys to get the *Corts* to pass legislation prohibiting the making and owning of *pedrenyals*, long barreled guns widely employed by bandits. Finally, however, the Spanish crown prevailed and the last famous bandit, Joan de Serrallonga, was hanged in Barcelona in 1634. But this was by no means the end of troubles.

The War of the Reapers, the First Catalan Rebellion

The Low Countries were added to the Spanish crown as the estate of Felipe I, the first Habsburg king of Castile; they have been called 'the fatal inheritance', for they were the first cause of the decline of the Spanish empire. Due to religious dissent (Protestantism had gained many adepts there) and Felipe II's intransigence, they rebelled in 1566 and thus started the Eighty Years War which ended with the division of the provinces and the independence of the northern region, Protestant Holland. This war sapped the strength of Spain, consumed rivers of silver coming from the Indies, and irremediably crippled the Spanish economy. It also embroiled Spain in the Thirty Years War (1618–1648), an international conflict which started in central Europe, within the Holy Roman Empire, pitching a Roman Catholic Emperor against his Protestant subjects in Bohemia. This war drew in most of the European great powers who took sides according to their religion, except Catholic France, which supported the Protestants.

Spain was also embroiled in this war. It helped the Catholic side, but its foremost interest was to keep open and safe the road from Barcelona and Genoa to the Low Countries, which was vital to convey supplies of money and soldiers for the fight against the Dutch rebels. France felt menaced by Spain's struggles along the Rhine and declared war in 1635, threatening Catalonia, which Cardinal Richelieu, France's strong man, shrewdly thought to be a weak point.

The wily Cardinal was right. Catalonia was already in turmoil against the Spanish crown over the Union of Arms, a plan devised by the Count-Duke of Olivares, the Spanish counterpart of Richelieu. Olivares was an Andalusian nobleman who had gained the trust of Felipe IV, a king bored by the daily chores of politics. Olivares had plans for the gradual unification and homogenization of Spain's diverse components and also for the immediate pooling of resources from the undertaxed portions of the kingdom: the Aragonese crown (Catalonia included) and Portugal. This was called the Union of Arms because the basic idea was that all dependencies should contribute equally to the war effort, a burden which up to then had fallen mainly upon Castile. Olivares's plan involved pooling money and, especially, manpower. Catalonia resisted on several grounds: as usual, she appealed to her *fueros*, which prohibited her soldiers to fight outside her territory unless the *Corts* gave specific permission; she also claimed that she was being asked to contribute an excessive number of men. This last claim was true, but at the time it was moot, because there were no accurate censuses taking into account the recent demographic decline. When Felipe IV visited Barcelona in 1626 and assembled the *Corts* to get the approval of the Union of Arms, he found hostility and passive resistance, endless procedures and interruptions, *greuges* and *dissentiments*, and, after months of endless wrangles, he finally left angry and empty-handed because his main point had not even been considered. In the end he proclaimed the Union by decree.

Problems became keener with the French invasion, which took the Catalan counties north of the Pyrenees and prepared for an assault across the mountains. In order to organize the defense, Spanish troops had to be brought to Catalonia and billeted there. Billeting was extremely unpopular with the local inhabitants and caused endless conflicts. This gave rise to an impossible situation: the Catalans had to be defended from the French, but they did not want to supply native troops or billet Castilian soldiers. The tensions between royal officials and Catalan authorities mounted by the day, especially with Pau Claris, a passionate priest who was the president of the *Diputació*, and Francesc de Tamarit, a nobleman who was the military member in the same body. Both Claris and Tamarit carried out an obstructionist policy regarding the billeting of troops and military operations in general, although Tamarit distinguished himself in the siege of the fortress of Salses, in northern Catalonia, which was taken from the French in January 1640. Due to his obstructionist attitude, Tamarit was imprisoned by the viceroy, Dalmau de Queralt, count of Santa Coloma, who thought that stern measures would make the hinderers toe the line; he paid his mistake with his life. The detention of Tamarit brought matters to a pitch. The

Catalan countryside was in a state of rebellion, with insurgent bands roaming in the territory. In May 1640, two months after Tamarit's detention, one of these bands entered Barcelona, assaulted the jail, and freed not only Tamarit and a few other rebellious notables, but also all the common criminals who were locked in there. Incidents continued while Santa Coloma and the Madrid authorities hesitated between using force and showing leniency. In the end they decided for leniency, but it was of no use.

It was traditional in Barcelona that early in June reapers or harvesters (*segadors*) from the countryside would flock to the city to look for employment from landowners, as the harvesting season approached. This entry usually coincided with the *Corpus Christi* festivity; these *segadors* being tough, uncouth, boisterous men, ready to enjoy the pleasures of the city for a few days, the visit was ordinarily not without its perils, but in the summer of 1640 it was an almost infallible occasion for disaster; and so it was, giving occasion to a journey which is known since then as the *Bloody Corpus* (*Corpus de sang*). Mixed with the *segadors* many rebels and bandits entered Barcelona intent on mayhem and pillage. After a number of incidents and street fights, the *segadors* attacked the viceroy's palace. Santa Coloma, betrayed by some of his councilors, had left and tried to board a galley in the port, but the galley, harassed by a mob at the dock, left without him. He returned and was sighted by his pursuers, who knifed him to death. Several days of rampage followed.

All of Catalonia was prey to chaos and anarchy, as the mobs and bands started attacking the nobility and the well-to-do, turning a rebellion against the king into a mutiny against the wealthy. While the king abandoned leniency and started organizing an army to pacify Catalonia by arms, the *Diputació* under Claris opened negotiations with the French and proclaimed a Catalan Republic, which lasted no more than a week. Under pressure to defend Barcelona against the royal army which was fast approaching, Claris and the French envoy, Bernard Duplessis-Besançon, agreed that French troops would defend Barcelona in exchange for Catalonia becoming a French suzerainty under the authority of Louis XIII, who was acknowledged as the new count of Barcelona. 'Catalonia had exchanged one master for another'

(Elliott, 1984, p. 522). It is interesting that these Catalan-French conversations were carried out in Castilian Spanish, which was the only language both parties knew.

Thanks to French help the royal army was stopped at the gates of Barcelona (battle of Montjuic, 26 January 1641). Claris could not see the consequences of his policies, as he died just a month afterwards. Meanwhile, Portugal had seceded from Spain in December 1640 with English support. Thus, while trying to reorganize in order to win the war in the Low Countries, Spain found itself forced to fight two more wars, one in Catalonia and one in Portugal. This was the lowest point in a dismal century. As Olivares put it: 'This year can undoubtedly be considered the most unfortunate that this Monarchy has ever experienced' (cited in Elliott, 1984, p. 523). In the end Spain only recovered Catalonia, and not all of it, for France kept the northern counties, Roussillon, Conflent, Vallespir, and the northern half of Cerdanya.

The Thirty Years War ended with the Peace of Westphalia (1648), where Spain accepted the loss of most of its northern European territories, notably the Dutch Low Countries. The Peace of Westphalia signaled the end of Spain's hegemony in continental Europe and the transfer of this hegemony to France. This country, however, suffered a period of turmoil after the deaths of Richelieu (1642) and Louis XIII (1643). The heir to the crown, the future Louis XIV, was born in 1638, so during his childhood his mother, the Spanish Anne of Austria, and Cardinal Mazarin, governed France. Both were unpopular and had to fight the rebellion of the nobility called *la Fronde* which ravaged France until Louis became of age in 1653. Northern Catalonia suffered from these internecine struggles and in the end became much more subject to the centralized power of Louis XIV than southern Catalonia ever was to Spanish centralism. The Catalan language gradually died down there, and in the end it just became one more French *département*.

Southern Catalonia, what today is called just Catalonia, in the end returned to the fold, largely of its own accord, although the military and diplomatic abilities of Juan José de Austria, Felipe IV's illegitimate son, played a decisive role. During the intervening years the royal armies slowly reconquered about half of Catalonia. Two important towns, such as Tarragona and Lérida (Lleida in Catalan), were in Felipe IV's hands since 1644, and from there the royal army proceeded very slowly to converge upon Barcelona. It still took eight long years, because Spain was exhausted and bankrupt. Meanwhile the Catalans subjected to French rule had time to lament Claris's submission to the new masters. To fight the Spaniards, the French employed the same tactics as Spaniards had used to fight them. Their troops had to be billeted, local men had to be recruited, and taxes had to be raised. To their surprise French soldiers found that the Catalans were as averse to fighting Castilians as they had earlier been to fight Frenchmen, so they had to be forced or imprisoned to make them toe the line. In fact, Catalonia was treated as a colony. It became more dependent upon French imports, and French merchants made fortunes dealing in war supplies. Catalan businessmen felt displaced, and their interests subordinated to those of the newcomers. In contrast, Felipe IV repeatedly made it known that he would always respect the Catalan *fueros*. Furthermore, the French became less interested in their Spanish war as their nobility became involved in the Fronde and other fronts; in Barcelona the population became increasingly demoralized and divided. Don Juan José de Austria, instead of attacking the city frontally, wisely preferred to avoid excessive bloodshed and lay siege to it while blockading it by sea. An epidemic was added to the hardships and hunger so that in October 1652 the city capitulated peacefully. In January 1653 Felipe IV published a pardon of the Catalans and confirmed the *fueros*. Only a few rebels were persecuted for notorious misdeeds. What Don Juan José did, as the new viceroy, was to appoint his own men to key posts and remove those he considered as hostile.

The war with the French, however, continued until the Peace of the Pyrenees in 1659, when Spain definitively ceded northern Catalonia to France. Felipe IV's goodwill was shown in the inclusion in the treaty of a general pardon and the restitution of their belongings to all those who had been dispossessed during the Catalan war. There also was a clause aiming at preserving Catalan institutions in French Catalonia, something which was not respected under Louis XIV. All in all, the War of the Reapers was an unmitigated disaster for Spain in general and for Catalonia in particular. Both came out definitively ruined, dismembered, and diminished. There is no doubt that the independence of Portugal was a consequence of the Catalan rebellion. Pau Claris carries the main burden of responsibility for all this; no single individual could be blamed to a greater extent for the unfortunate episode. Nevertheless he is still considered a hero in modern Catalonia.

As to the wider historical meaning of the war, Elliott's (1984, pp. 548–549) words are clear and accurate:

> In retrospect [. . .] the Catalan Revolution of 1640 had only succeeded in buying the Principality a little more time. It perpetuated for a further fifty years a form of government which had already begun to appear anachronistic by the third decade of the seventeenth century, and which, in the light of contemporary developments elsewhere in Europe, seemed destined to eventual extinction. Like other insurrections of the sixteenth and seventeenth centuries, it would thus appear a typical revolt of the old order – a 'medieval' revolt against the new-style monarchy.

Recovery

All available signs suggest that Catalonia recovered during the second half of the seventeenth century. In general, the entire Spanish economy improved somewhat after the catastrophes of the previous half century. The alternations of galloping inflation and severe deflation which ravaged the economy under Felipe III and Felipe IV were stopped by means of a protracted monetary reform (1680–1686) which devalued the *real* and put an end to the issues of *vellón* money. The Peace of the Pyrenees, humiliating though it was, restored peace for a while and permitted a substantial reduction of military expenditure, which was the root cause of inflation and bankruptcy. The treaty also established free trade between the former contenders (France and Spain), which also facilitated economic recovery although it alienated Catalan businessmen. In Spain, and in Catalonia in particular, population also recovered from the decline of the earlier period.

But not everything was normalcy and redress. Louis XIV was not satisfied with the Peace of the Pyrenees. Once Spain weakness was clearly established, he unleashed a series of limited wars to attain new objectives. The theaters of the new wars were not exactly new: the Spanish Low Countries (today's Belgium) and Spanish Catalonia, which France invaded in 1667, 1683, and 1689. The repeated French invasions exasperated the Catalans who simultaneously complained about the inadequacy of the troops sent to defend their land and about the cost and inconvenience of having to billet them. Protests and complaints led to peasant revolts in the years 1688–1689; the French took advantage of these revolts to invade once more and lay siege to Barcelona in order to obtain more concessions from a country whose weakness was aggravated by the physical and mental feebleness of the king (Carlos II). The occupation of Barcelona lasted no more than a few months; the war ended in 1697 with the Peace of Ryswick and more French acquisitions at the expense of Spain in the Antilles. In view of all this it is not surprising that France was the object of hatred in Catalonia, something which in a few years would be an obstacle to the plans which Louis XIV was drawing for Spain. In the long run, therefore, his aggressive policies turned counterproductive.

The nature and extent of Catalan recovery in the second half of the seventeenth century has been a topic subject to differing interpretations. On one side, there are those scholars who aggrandize the import of the recovery in order to fulfil 'an old longing of the Catalanist historiography: to discover that the economic renaissance of Catalonia had its origin in the seventeenth century, that is to say, that it was not due to the hated Bourbon regime' (Arranz and Grau, 1991, p. 131). On the opposite side, there are those who want to rehabilitate the Bourbon regime. In the middle there are those who, like Leopold von Ranke, just want to know 'what really happened'.

Standing out in the first group of scholars there is Josep Fontana, who in a recent book (2014, p. 198) states that by the end of the seventeenth century Catalonia was on its way to become a democratic nation, in the wake of England and Holland and that, consequently, Felipe V (grandson of Louis XIV and successor of Carlos II, see next chapter) committed a heinous crime when he aborted such noble project and imposed absolutism and tyranny by abolishing the Catalan (and Aragonese in general) *fueros*. This theory had been expounded by Fontana in other works, but mere repetition does not make it more convincing. Fontana's mentor, Jaume Vicens Vives (the outstanding Catalan historian of the twentieth century), for instance, would not have agreed with his student on this point. According to Vicens (1970, p. 115), 'the elimination of privileges and fueros produced unexpected benefits'. Exactly the opposite of what Fontana sustains.

There are various reasons to doubt Fontana's theses. Comparing Catalonia with England and Holland in the seventeenth century is not very appropriate. England and Holland were the two largest commercial powers at the time, something Catalonia, unfortunately, was not. As Arranz and Grau (1991, pp. 122, 125) say, 'at the start of the eighteenth century, on an international plane, Barcelona was no more than a second rate port in the western Mediterranean [...] Amsterdam and London were very far away'. In 1700 Barcelona's population was a mere 43,000, while Amsterdam had 200,000 inhabitants and London almost 600,000 (Maddison, 2001, p. 54); in comparison with the northern metropolises, Barcelona was a dwarf. Furthermore, both Amsterdam and London had grown spectacularly between 1500 and 1700 (their populations multiplied by a factor of 14), while Barcelona's population only grew by a factor of 1,5. We are referring to Amsterdam and London because they were the cradles of the Dutch and English revolutions. Their astounding growth and the dynamism of their economies provided the medium and the spark of the political and religious revolutions which took place in their respective countries. Something similar, although on a minor scale, happened in their respective countries: Holland and England doubled their respective populations between those same dates, while Catalonia's population remained static. The whole Spanish population grew very little, but that of Catalonia stagnated. It was the economic and demographic dynamism of Holland and England which brought about the institutional developments in these two countries; nothing comparable occurred in Catalonia (or Spain, for that matter). The role of religion in the Dutch and English revolutions was crucial: they were to a large extent protestant revolutions. Protestantism was a social ferment in many areas; even Catholic France had a Huguenot party. No such thing ever existed in Spain, the fortress of the Counter-Reformation, let alone in Catalonia. The fact is that Catalonia, with all its *fueros*, constitutions, etc., remained in a state of secular stagnation and that, after these *fueros* were abolished by Felipe V, it started an unprecedented process of demographic and economic growth which put it at the head of Spain socially and economically. This is what stands out in the history of this period, and something which Fontana and his school have not adequately explained so far.

All this does not mean that Catalonia stagnated in the late seventeenth century. On the contrary, there is evidence of a vigorous recovery from the ravages of the preceding decades. But, as Arranz and Grau (1991, p. 124) say, 'the low starting point of Barcelona's redress in the second half of the seventeenth century and also [. . .] the modesty of the results obtained before 1714' are evident. It is true, though, that, as Vilar (1962, I, p. 650) points out, economic recovery took place in the countryside to a larger extent than in Barcelona. Agriculture expanded, and so did the activity of a series of smaller northern ports, probably because they exported agricultural products harvested nearby. Even industry migrated to the countryside, probably to avoid the high taxes and wages of Barcelona. Rural repopulation kept local industries well supplied with cheap manpower. Arranz and Grau think the main cause of this displacement was the strength of urban guilds, which made Barcelona uncompetitive 'not only relative to foreign production centers, but also relative to the small towns, villages and rural districts of Catalonia'.

The trends seem clear, but there are few reliable figures to add precision. Only several series collected by Vilar, Fontana (1955), and Arranz and Grau give us a fairly accurate idea of the evolution of maritime traffic in the port of Barcelona. What they show is a rapid pace of growth in the very final years of the century. These figures have fed excessive optimism; they did so at the time, so that royal officials in the early decades of the eighteenth century thought the Catalan economy was richer than it really was; and they have done so more recently, among some scholars who have seen in these figures a harbinger of a take-off into self-sustained growth, or little less. In fact, what these figures seem to indicate is a renewed demand of military supplies due to the French invasion in 1689.

Summing up, the economic improvement of the late seventeenth century in Catalonia and in all Spain was little more than the recovery after the terrible events of the first half of the century. As Arranz and Grau (1991, p. 125) said about mercantile activities in Barcelona, they were 'hindered by the ideological dead weight, which was inseparable from antiquated social outlooks. Only the distinctive growth model of the eighteenth century could start to erode those ideological relics'.

References

ÁLVAREZ NOGAL, Carlos y Leandro PRADOS DE LA ESCOSURA (2013), 'The rise and fall of Spain (1270–1850)', *Economic Histoy Review*, 65, pp. 1–37.

ARRANZ, Manuel y Ramón GRAU (1991), 'L'economia urbana de Barcelona i la Guerra de Seccessió', *Recerques*, 24, pp. 115–142.

CIPOLLA, C.M. (1976), *Before the Industrial Revolution. European Society and Economy, 1000–1700*. London: Methuen.

ELLIOTT, John H. (1984), *The Revolt of the Catalans. A Study in the Decline of Spain (1598–1640)*. Cambridge, UK: Cambridge University Press.

FONTANA, Josep (1955), 'Sobre el comercio exterior de Barcelona en la segunda mitad del siglo XVII. Notas para una interpretación de la coyuntura catalana,' *Estudios de Historia*, V, pp. 197–218.

FONTANA, Josep (2014), *La formació d'una identitat, una historia de Catalunya*. Vic: Eumo Editoral.

LYNCH, John (1964), *Spain under the Habsburgs. Volume One. Empire and Absolutism, 1516–1598*. Oxford: Basil Blackwell.

MADDISON, Angus (2001), *The World Economy. A Millennial Perspective*. Paris: OECD.

NADAL, Jordi (2011), *España en su cenit (1516–1598). Un ensayo de interpretación*. Barcelona: Critica.

PARKER, Geoffrey (2013), *Global crisis, war, climate change and catastrophe in the seventeenth century*. New Haven and London: Yale University Press.

Sánchez-Albornoz, Claudio (1956), *España, un enigma histórico, II*. Buenos Aires: Editorial Sudamericana.

VICENS VIVES, J. (1970), *Approaches to the History of Spain*. Translated and edited by Joan Connelly Ullman, Berkelely & LA: University of California Press.

VILAR, Pierre (1962), *La Catalogne dans l'Espagne moderne. Recherches sur les fondements économiques des structures nationales*. 3 vols. Paris: SEVPEN.

3

Reform and Progress in the Eighteenth Century

The War of Succession, Catalonia's Second Rebellion

The consequences of the War of Succession (1703–1714) were even more disastrous for Catalonia and for Spain as a whole than those of the War of the Reapers, or of Secession, had been. In the War of Succession there was no question of Catalonia's independence. This was a dynastic civil war, and Catalonia (indeed, the whole old kingdom of Aragón) took the side of the Austrian pretender in the belief that Felipe V, the new Bourbon king, was intent on abolishing the *fueros*. As Vicens wrote (1970, p. 111),

> This time the Catalans were fighting stubbornly to defend their pluralistic concept of the ordering of the Spanish monarchy. They did not realize that this was precisely the system that had led to the agony of the last Hapsburg kings and that without a broad margin of reforms (both of the laws and of the traditional regional fueros) it would be impossible to put

G. Tortella, *Catalonia in Spain*, Palgrave Studies in Economic History, DOI 10.1007/978-3-319-54951-4_3

the country back on its feet. The Catalans were fighting against the current of history and the price for this is usually very high.

Carlos II, the Bewitched, died in November 1700 nearing on his 39th birthday. He had been a cripple since birth, mentally and bodily feeble, impotent, and deformed. He had been married twice but he had no children. In his testament he appointed as his heir Philip of Anjou, grandson of Louis XIV and of his Spanish wife, María Teresa of Austria, daughter of Felipe IV. Philip was therefore nephew of Carlos II and ascended to the Spanish throne as Felipe V. There were other contestants to the post, however, notably Charles, archduke of Austria, a Habsburg, second son of Emperor Leopold I, and a close relative of Charles II of Spain, although not as close as Felipe. The Spanish succession had been exercising all the diplomatic minds in Europe for several reasons. First and foremost, it was well known that Carlos would leave no direct heir. Second, having a Bourbon as king of Spain worried many, especially in England and the Low Countries, who dreaded the power this could put in the hands of Louis XIV. Of course, having a Habsburg on the Spanish throne and another, his father (later his brother), as Holy Roman Emperor was not very reassuring either. Third, the enormous Spanish Empire, weakened after the catastrophes of the seventeenth century, had many elements that were coveted by other European powers. A plan had been drawn up to dismember it and apportion parts to the various pretenders. The plan finally could not be carried out, but several nations, England and the Low Countries in particular, hoped to gain if a Habsburg ruled in Spain, the more so if his ascent to the throne were due to the intervention of these powers.

Strict legitimacy favored Felipe, who was named in the royal testament and was the closest male relative of the deceased Carlos. He was crowned and sworn by the Cortes of Castile, Aragon, and Catalonia. He visited Barcelona in 1701–1702 and made several economic and legal concessions to the *Corts* which were very well received in the Principality. He never said anything about abolishing the *fueros*, but some misgivings subsisted in anti-French circles, which were approached by English and Austrian agents. As the hostilities between France and the Low Countries intensified, and Britain and Austria joined the

Dutch, the pro-Austrian party grew in Aragon and most notably in Catalonia, where the bitter memories of French incursions at the end of the seventeenth century still rankled. This party claimed that the successful *Corts* of 1701–1702 had been carried out under the pressure of Felipe's army, a very dubious statement.

The hostilities in Spain started in 1703 (England had declared war on France in 1702), but for two years they were chiefly maritime; France and Spain fought virtually alone against a British, Dutch, and Austrian coalition. Spain was not the only theater of war: parallel to operations in Spain, the hostilities were carried out mostly in the Rhineland. British naval superiority was shown by the conquest of Gibraltar in 1704 and Menorca in 1708, and by British virtual domination of the Mediterranean. In 1705 plans started for the assault of Barcelona. A British agent, Mitford Crowe, who had been a businessman in Barcelona, organized the pro-Austrian party in Catalonia and convinced a group of rebels to sign a pact in Genoa whereby the English would provide ships and troops for the invasion of Barcelona with the help of the pro-Austrian party. Barcelona was bombarded and then assaulted in October by an English army; once the city was secured, the archduke Charles of Austria disembarked, and held *Corts* there, where he was sworn king as Carlos III. In the following months the whole kingdom of Aragon joined the rebellion. In reality it was the 1705 *Corts* in Barcelona that were held while the English army was still in the city, after taking it by assault, whereas the 1701–1702 *Corts* had taken place in wholly peaceful circumstances.

By 1706 the archduke seemed on the verge of winning the war; his troops entered Madrid in the summer, and Felipe V seemed in complete retreat. However, the Madrid populace received the archduke coldly. Castile as a whole remained hostile, so that two months later the archduke's army left the capital. Then the winds of war changed again: in April 1707 a Spanish-French army commanded by the duke of Berwick routed and English-Dutch-Portuguese army, commanded by the marquis of Ruvigny, at Almansa, near the border of Valencia and Castile. This was an almost decisive battle: the archduke's army was destroyed, and Valencia and Aragon definitively passed into the hands of Felipe V: only Catalonia (not all of it) and

Mallorca remained faithful to the Habsburg pretender. Curiously enough, the victorious Bourbon army was headed by an Englishman, and the army of the archduke was led by a Frenchman. This is a remarkable case of crossed destinies: James Fitz-James, duke of Berwick, was the illegitimate son of James II Stuart and Arabella Churchill, sister of John Churchill, first duke of Marlborough, who headed the English armies and diplomacy in the northern European theater. Berwick was born in France during the first exile of his father and received a Catholic education. He fought for the English army while his father was king, but fled to France after 1688, and became a French citizen and soldier. Ruvigny was a Huguenot who abandoned France on account of his religion and became an English soldier.

The war went on, chiefly because the English coalition was more successful in the Rhineland. In 1709 Louis XIV was almost defeated, and counseled Felipe V to abandon Spain and look for a position elsewhere. Felipe refused and went on in spite of the archduke's string of victories which permitted him to enter Madrid again, with the same result as before: he left the capital a second time under the threat of Felipe's army. Finally, in 1711 something unexpected happened: emperor Joseph I died without male issue and was succeeded by his brother, the archduke. He departed for Vienna leaving his partisans in Barcelona somewhat in the lurch. Meanwhile the English were getting tired of war, and this was reflected in the election of 1710, which was a victory for the tories, who favored peace. Negotiations were being conducted with France, and they were aided by the elevation of Charles of Austria to the imperial throne. Having the emperor as also king of Spain was as bad if not worse as having a Bourbon scion on the Spanish throne. Negotiations continued and the English (now British) obtained what they wanted. Felipe renounced his rights to the French crown, Britain kept Gibraltar and Menorca, plus a series of advantages in the Spanish-American trade (which we will see later in some more detail), and the Spanish Netherlands were acquired by the Empire. The old Aragonese Mediterranean Empire was partitioned: in addition to the southern Netherlands, Austria kept Naples and Sardinia; Savoy kept Sicily. All this was finally established in the treaties of Utrecht and Rastatt (April 1713 and March 1714). It was the end of the international war, but the civil war in Spain was fought to the bitter end. Emperor Charles VI (the former pretender) refused to recognize Felipe as king of Spain for eleven more years until the Treaty of Vienna, in 1725.

Barcelona resisted, heroically but futilely, for a few more months, refusing Berwick's entreaties until Felipe's troops were already inside the city, in the second week of September 1714. Not until then did the rebel leaders propose to discuss the conditions of surrender, to which Berwick answered that the time to negotiate was long past and that now they were at the mercy of the king. When the news of Barcelona's surrender arrived, Mallorca capitulated in 1715.

Barcelona's resistance had been heroic, but also obtuse and counter-productive. If its leaders had taken a more rational and serene approach, they might have been able to bargain about the reforms that Felipe wanted to make in Catalonia and which they so much dreaded. By refusing to negotiate, the Barcelona rebels in the end placed themselves at the mercy of the king they hated so much. With a little foresight, the pro-Austria party should have realized that their side was bound to lose. Those who did realize had little influence, were accused of treason, and forced to remain silent or leave to the other side. From Almansa on, the pro-Austria party was cornered in the eastern half of Catalonia plus Mallorca. They were poorer, smaller, and lacked the trade with the Americas. Furthermore, the Catalans (the whole kingdom of Aragon) were used to paying very light taxes, and the efforts of the archduke to make them pay for the war made him unpopular. Short of revenues, he resorted to debasing the coinage, which caused inflation and did not endear him with the people either. Unlike Felipe, who renounced his rights in France, Charles abandoned Spain with relief when he became emperor. If the Catalans could go on with their resistance it was because the war was going badly for the French in the northern theater, and because their allies supported them as they could. Their cause was lost since 1707, and even more so since 1711. They fought on obstinately, and this was disastrous for Spain and for Catalonia. Both lost bargaining power by the day during the war. Spain's weakness was made evident at the negotiations of Utrecht, and Catalonia placed herself at the mercy of a resentful Felipe, who saw the Catalans as the cause of his kingdom's vulnerability and as a bunch of renegades and traitors who had broken their oath of fidelity sworn in the *Corts* of 1701–1702.

Repression followed after the end of the war, something lamentable but not outrageous, especially when compared to other similar episodes of the period. In Scotland, for instance, after the Jacobite rebellion of 1745, '[o]ne hundred and twenty men were executed after some form of trial; more were shot out of hand' (Ross, 2014, p. 236). The duke of Cumberland, head of the English army, ordered 'to harry, burn and kill men, women and children' in reprisal (Lynch, 1991, p. 338). Nothing so brutal happened in 1714 Catalonia, where the death sentences were few. Rafael Casanova, the maximum civilian and military leader of the Barcelona resistance, was not persecuted, although his goods were confiscated. He took refuge in his parents' house and was left alone. He spent the rest of his days working as a lawyer and a loyal subject of Felipe V. His second in command, Salvador Feliu de la Peña, also went on with his profession as a merchant. Not only lives, but also properties were respected according to the generous terms offered by Berwick; only a few blocks of modest houses to the north of the city were expropriated and leveled to build a citadel, much resented by the local populace afterwards.

A cursory examination of the records of the two pretenders to the Spanish throne could be interesting. Felipe V has been criticized for being a puppet in the hands of his grandfather, Louis XIV, but this is at best an exaggeration. It is only natural that Felipe, as the offspring and pupil of the great monarch, and greatly depending on French military support, should have listened to his grandfather especially when choosing his advisers. Nevertheless, he frequently differed from his ancestor's counsel and showed character and a will of his own. Three telling examples come to mind. First, during the dismal year of 1709 Louis, foreseeing defeat, was ready to abandon his plans and asked his grandson to accept the dismemberment of Spain and its empire, and even to quit Spain and accept a minor kingdom in Italy as a consolation prize. Felipe refused squarely, and vowed to struggle on; in the end he proved right. Second, he did not acquiesce when Louis advised him to promise that he would respect the Catalan *fueros*, as a measure to mollify the rebels.

On this point he remained adamant. Finally, when, during the negotiations which led to the Treaty of Utrecht, Felipe's father died, leaving him in a very favorable situation to aspire to the French throne, he renounced his right in order to facilitate the bargaining, since Britain would never have accepted him as monarch of both kingdoms. In this Felipe clearly differed from his rival the archduke who, among loud protestations of fidelity to his Catalan subjects, abandoned them as soon as he had his opportunity to become emperor in Vienna. Although in old age Felipe had symptoms of mental degeneration, in his youth he showed remarkable qualities of military and political leadership.

The reign of emperor Charles VI, the old Spanish pretender, was characterized by two traits: constant warring, not only against the Ottoman Empire but also against his Christian neighbors, and by the issuing of the Pragmatic Sanction, a law regulating the order of succession to the imperial throne. It is well known that thanks to this law, which established the ability of women to be crowned as empresses on their own right, his daughter Maria Theresa succeeded him on the throne (not without another long war). But this was not the main aim of the Pragmatic Sanction, which was issued in 1713, much before Maria Theresa's birth; its main aim was to put some order and uniformity in the tangled norms of succession of the multifarious dependencies of the Empire, where the estates of the Habsburg family were mixed pell-mell with imperial territories; the norms of succession in this territorial crazy-quilt were a source of discord and even war (Kann, 1980, pp. 59-61; Jaszy, 1961, pp. 57-60). In conclusion, the emperor carried out a uniformity policy in his domains which was exactly the opposite of what his Spanish supporters championed when he was pretender to the Spanish throne.

Spanish historians of the pro-Austrian school have been very critical of the measures taken by Felipe V in Aragon, and especially in Catalonia (see later), after the war, rarely mentioning that the pro-Austrian faction was guilty of felony, disloyalty, and perjury, as they had rebelled against their king after having solemnly paid homage and sworn fidelity to him, something he repeatedly mentioned during the war. He no doubt also remembered that his great-grandfather, Felipe IV, had pardoned his Catalan subjects for similar crimes and respected their *fueros* half a century earlier, and they had corresponded by rebelling again. Furthermore, as we have seen, the Catalan rebels had many offers to negotiate during the war and they rejected all of them. It must also be added that the rebels stated in justification that Felipe was planning to abolish the *fueros*, something which is negated by the fact that he respected those of the Basque country and Navarre, which did not rebel, and also by Felipe's respecting and even expanding the Catalan *fueros* in the *Corts* of 1701–1702, to the point of eliciting protests in Castile. Nationalist historians have also complained that Felipe not only abolished old privileges and institutions, but also appointed non-Catalans to political posts. This is true, but this policy is natural: after the conflict Felipe wanted to have persons he trusted in the delicate posts of postwar Catalonia: he appointed Catalans and non-Catalans to those posts and established the principle that capacity rather than geographical considerations should prevail in his choice of officials. As we shall presently see, this was not the only case where outsiders were appointed to key posts in a post-war situation.

After the American Civil War, for instance, in spite of the US being a basically democratic country and the times very different, the behavior of the victors had very much in common with that of the Bourbon side after the War of Spanish Succession. In both cases the victors abolished many institutions of the losing side. In the US it was in large part a Federal Congress, with the full support of president Ulysses S. Grant, that, when in the midterm elections of 1866 the old confederate politicians won in most Southern circumscriptions, annulled the proceedings outright, militarized ten old confederate states, disenfranchised about 15,000 residents in these states, removed the elected from their posts and appointed provisional officers in those states, commonly outsiders (who received the derogatory appellation of *carpetbaggers*), incarcerated confederate president Jefferson Davis and his vice president Alexander Stephens (let us recall that neither Casanova nor Feliu de la Peña were detained), condemned to death a prison officer, and established the *ironclad oath* whereby all Southerners wanting to run for office had to swear under oath that they had never supported the confederate government or fought in the confederate army. Congress also enacted a sharp increase in taxes in Southern states, with two objectives: burdening the losers with the cost of the war and punishing southern planters (Foner, 1989, pp. 261–80, 365, 383; Morison, 1972, II, pp. 498–522, 518). Many similar things happened in vanquished Aragon after the War of Succession which have elicited wrath and invective from nationalist historians.

There were differences between the two cases also. In the US the *Reconstruction* period ended around 1877, when Southern racist politicians returned to power under the passive gaze of Northern voters. In Catalonia, however, the *Nueva Planta* policies were applied without remission for several decades. Although there are some indications that the Southern economy benefited in the long run from Reconstruction policies, it took many decades for it to shake off its initial inertia. In Catalonia, as we will see presently, economic recovery came in a couple of decades and then unprecedented growth took place.

The experiences of Germany, Italy, and Japan after World War Two inspired Professor Mancur Olson (1982) to develop his theory about the advantages for some societies of losing wars and submitting to profound reforms that would remove old and decadent institutions which constitute an obstacle to economic growth and social progress, and often are sources of conflicts. Olson (1982, p. 101) showed that the Southern US benefited from Reconstruction policies (excoriated by some Southern historians), although in the very long run. The available evidence suggests that in the Catalan eighteenth century case growth was more vigorous because the Nueva Planta policies were applied with more intensity and perseverance.

The *Nueva Planta*: Political, Economic, and Fiscal Innovations

The Political *Nueva Planta*

Nueva Planta (New Plant or Plan) was the name given by Felipe V's officials to the new set of measures applied in the kingdom of Aragon to replace the old *fueros*. Contrary to what some historians have stated, the New Plant did not sweep away all the old legislation, either in Catalonia or in the whole kingdom of Aragon. In Catalonia, however, institutions as old as the *Corts* and the *Generalitat* were abolished; the post of viceroy was abolished too, and in its stead that of captain general was substituted. In both cases the office was that of chief executive power in Catalonia, dependent upon the king's government. The change in denomination was intended to underline the military, rather than civilian, character of the post. The captain general was assisted by a *Real Audiencia*, a body with governmental and judicial capacities. Another venerable institution abolished was the municipal assembly, the *Concell de Cent.* From then on all municipal posts were appointed by the Spanish government.

Other old Catalan institutions were respected, however, such as the traditional civil and criminal law, the *Consolat de Mar*, most guilds and professional associations, etc. Castilian Spanish was made the language of the government, but Catalan was not prohibited.

A bitterly criticized measure was the abolition of the *prohibición de extranjería*, which involved prohibiting the appointment of non-Catalans to official posts in Catalonia. However unpopular, the abolition was natural for a king who wanted to govern the whole of Spain as a single territory; so the abolition decree proclaimed that 'in my kingdoms honors and dignities should be given to my vassals according to merit and not to having been born in one province or the other'.

Finally, the New Plant abolished the University of Barcelona and created that of Cervera, a city that had remained always faithful to Felipe. This measure has also been criticized, for obvious reasons. Barcelona was much larger and cosmopolitan than sleepy Cervera. It should be recognized, however, that the University of Cervera, which for about one hundred years (it was moved back to Barcelona in 1842) was the only such institution in Catalonia, played a far from negligible scientific and educational role.

The Fiscal Nueva Planta: The Catastro

It is common knowledge that from the time of the union of kingdoms in 1479 the contribution of the kingdom of Aragon to the common Treasury was very small. Old Regime figures present many problems, but one can say with confidence that around 1610 the kingdom of Aragon contributed about 4 percent of total Spanish government revenues (Sureda, 1949, p. 114). According to Nadal (1988, p. 40) the population of Aragon in 1591 was some 16 percent of the Spanish total. We know from Uztáriz (1968 [1742], p. 35) that around 1717 this proportion had mounted to 23 percent. A simple linear interpolation tells us that in 1610 the Aragonese population was 17 percent of the Spanish total. The disproportion between population and fiscal burden was, therefore, glaring. Furthermore, this paltry contribution was irregular, it being concentrated in wartime. Catalan tax payments in peacetime were practically nil (Albareda, 2012, p. 82). Catalonia's refusal to pay a higher proportional amount in time of war was the cause of the rebellion of 1640, and Felipe IV's appeasement policy sustained the rebels' fiscal privilege. This contributed to the continued deterioration of Spain's fiscal situation in the second half of the seventeenth century. Domínguez Ortiz (1990, p. 23) marveled that Spain should have been able to fight a second, long and hard civil war with her Treasury so depleted, and still manage to reorganize its still vast empire and recover from the war losses.

In view of all this it is not surprising that Felipe V, fulfilling vows repeatedly expressed during the war, should have carried out a fiscal reform intended to balance the tax burden between victorious Castile and conquered Aragon. Aside from its avowed punitive intention, the reform was logical and just; it had been previously established in Valencia (1707) and Aragon (1711). Although the principles were the same, the actual application varied somewhat from one kingdom to the other, so the reforms were even given different names: *Equivalente* in Valencia, *Única Contribución* in Aragon. In Mallorca it was called *Talla* and in Catalonia, *Catastro*. The basic idea in all cases, however, was the same: the resulting fiscal burden should be roughly equal to that of Castile (hence its name in Valencia), but the system should be simpler and fairer. These aims were best attained in Catalonia.

It is obvious that the Catalan legislators were careful and deliberate in the preparation of the decrees establishing the new tax system.

After the conquest of Barcelona the authorities issued provisional administrative and fiscal measures while they spent one year and a half preparing the definitive ones. The political and administrative reorganization contained in the first New Plan decree was issued on 16 January 1716, and the new decree revamping the tax system was not issued until 15 October of that same year. While in Valencia, Aragon, and Mallorca the new tax was collected on the basis of existing registers, and the apportioning of the tax burden was rather crude, quite close to a poll tax model, in Catalonia the taxable wealth was estimated by means of an accurately compiled cadaster (hence its name) whereby landholdings, industrial and craft tools, even wages and salaries, were noted down and used to estimate the individual payable tax. The nobility was exempt from paying 'personal' taxes (i.e., those levied upon profits, salaries, and wages), but not from 'real' taxes (i.e., those levied upon agriculture and real estate). Nationalist historians (Balcells, 2009, p. 517; Sobrequés, 2011, p. 44) consider this new tax as exploitative and oppressive. There certainly were many complaints of local taxpayers who were not used to the impost hike, which fell all the more harshly on the shoulders of a people who were impoverished by the war. These historians hotly deny that in the long run the new system may have contributed to the growth that the Catalan economy experienced since the 1730s, claiming that the *Catastro* was similar to the other systems established in the rest of Aragon. We know, however, that this is not true: the *Catastro* was more carefully devised and much fairer than the other imposts collected in the rest of Aragon. This was already well known by contemporary specialists, such as Zavala y Auñón (1732, pp. 38-40) and Uztáriz (1968 [1742], pp. 353-5), and recognized by modern ones (Nadal Farreras, 1971, p. 62; Vicens Vives, 1959, p. 533; Martínez Shaw, 1985, p. 97).

It is not surprising that, because the economy was devastated and the estimates of Catalan riches were considerably exaggerated, there should have been numerous and, by and large, justified complaints. Furthermore, Catalans were not used to paying taxes, and the whole system was brand new, so that the officials had to familiarize themselves with it and were liable to making more errors than normal. All this explains the tensions and complaints of the first years, whose testimonies have provided nationalist historians with ammunition to issue fulminations against the New Plan which they describe as 'despotic and arbitrary', 'exorbitant', etc. (for instance, Torras Ribé, 2013, pp. 300-1).

In spite of the novelty of the *Catastro*, it retained a very traditional trait, and this was the so-called *repartimiento* (apportioning, distributing). This means that the total amount to be collected was estimated beforehand, and then the individual quotas were calculated according to the *Catastro* rules. No matter how fair the apportioning might be, if the total figure was calculated in excess, the tax burden became oppressive. This is what happened in the first few years. The cause of the excessive burden was that, as we saw before, the partial recovery of the last decades of the seventeenth century made officials believe that Catalonia was richer than it really was.

Due to all these difficulties, somebody proposed to adopt the simpler systems applied in Aragon and Valencia; but the king rejected this possibility arguing that the *Catastro* was much fairer than the other systems and left less room for error or arbitrariness. The *Catastro* stayed and in the long run the initial difficulties were surmounted. Taxpayers and officials got used to the new system, improvements in the *Catastro* were introduced, and the total quota was considerably lowered after two or three years. Furthermore, the lower quota was left unchanged for the rest of the century so that as the economy grew and prices went up, the tax burden became progressively lighter.

Many historians attest to the increasing lightness of the Catalan tax burden as time advanced. Thus Mercader (1985, p. 183): 'the *Catastro* soon stopped being the calamity it had been for the Catalan populace and gradually became a normal and tolerable tribute'; or Artola (1982, pp. 229-31): 'the fiscal treatment applied to the Crown of Aragon [...produced...] a more modern and fairer fiscal system than that subsisting in Castile.' Or Vilar (1962, II, p. 192): 'the tax which seemed so burdensome in 1716 became very light seventy five years later'. Surviving accounts of merchants and industrialists also show that the *Catastro* tax was a very small part of total cost, and also that there

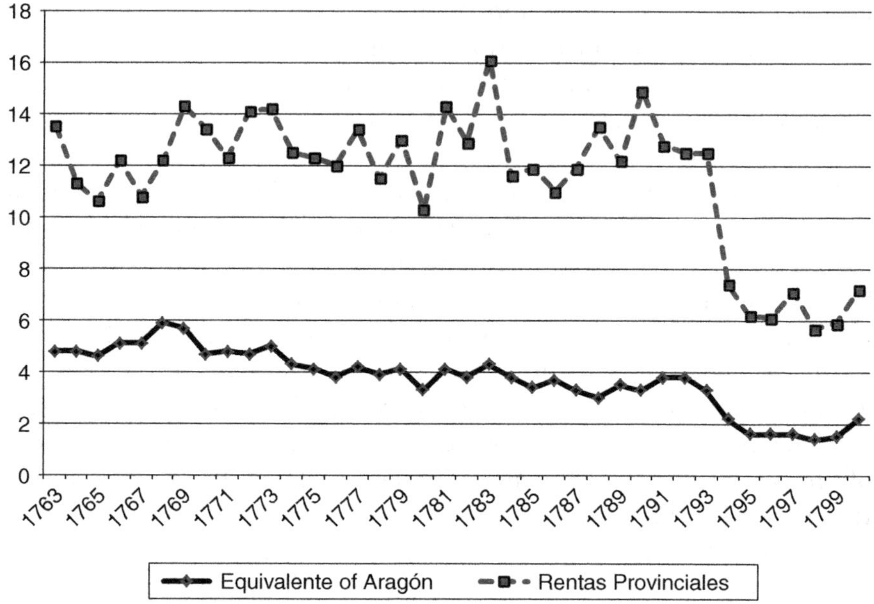

Fig. 3.1 *Equivalente* of Aragon and *Rentas Provinciales* (of Castile) as a Percentage of Total Revenue
Source: Merino (1987)

was a considerable amount of tax evasion, which of course made the burden even lighter.

Figure 3.1 shows how the relative tax burden of the Crown of Aragon, of which Catalonia was a substantial part, went down during the 1763–1800 period, while the relative tax burden of Castile did not fall at all (rather experienced a slight increase) in the 1763–1793 period. Let me explain a little. Both tax burdens (of Aragon and of Castile) reflected in the Graph are relative to the total tax revenue of the Spanish Crown, according to Merino (1987), who has collected and published the fiscal data of the Crown in the eighteenth and early nineteenth centuries. In the case of Aragon, the series reflects the revenues from *equivalente* taxes; in the case of Castile, the revenues from the indirect taxes (*alcabala* and others) collectively called *Rentas provinciales* (Provincial revenues) and whose fiscal pressure the *equivalente* was supposed to equal. 1763–1793 was a 'normal' period; the French wars unleashed in 1793 forced the

Spanish state to introduce new taxes and thus the relative weight of both the *Equivalente* and the *Rentas Provinciales* fell precipitously. The total tax burden, of course, went up.

From all this we can conclude that the *Catastro*, far from being an obstacle to the economic growth of Catalonia, probably contributed to it for being fair and predictable, unlike the previous taxes which, although lighter, were arbitrary and unfair. Under the Catastro, for instance, the nobility were exempt when they acted as merchants or industrialists, but not when they played the role of landlords. The new tax system, therefore, stimulated investment in industry and commerce, something which helps to explain the favorable evolution of the Catalan economy in the following decades.

The *Catastro* system was thought to be so superior that the enlightened ministers of Felipe V's successors (Fernando VI and Carlos III) repeatedly tried to adapt and introduce it in Castile. Unfortunately, these attempts ended in failure. According to Olson's theory, Catalonia turned out to have benefited from losing the War of Succession, for defeat permitted the modernization and streamlining of its institutions against the opposition the traditional forces (i.e., the nobility and the church). Exactly the opposite happened in Castile, where the traditional forces were reinforced by victory. The success of the Catalan *Catastro* moved Pedro R. Campomanes, the marquis of Ensenada and other royal officials, who had the support of Fernando VI and of Carlos III, to order the compilation of a *Catastro de la Riqueza Rústica* (Cadaster of Agrarian Real Estate) of Castile with the intention of using it as the basis of a land tax along the same lines as the Catalan system and which would be called *Única contribución* (Single tax). The *Catastro de Ensenada*, as it is commonly called, was formed, and it remains one of the jewels of archival sources for the study of the rural conditions and social structure of eighteenth-century Castile. But the opposition and passive resistance of the nobility and the church were able to stop its practical application: the *Única contribución* remained a utopian project of enlightened politicians and intellectuals while Castile remained subjected to an archaic, inefficient, and unfair tax system for almost one more century.

The Onset of Catalonia's Development

In the words of Martínez Shaw (1985, p. 55), 'for Catalonia the eighteenth century evolved under the sign of expansion'. For Vilar (1974, p. 11), 'development [was] evident and powerful.' After the catastrophe of the War of the Reapers and the recovery from it in the late seventeenth century, the War of Succession again devastated Barcelona, Catalonia, and the southeastern half of Spain. Afterwards, however, development in Catalonia proceeded apace and over a wide spectrum. It touched most areas and sectors in a characteristic process of *balanced growth*. Growth was based upon solid agrarian expansion which, in turn, demanded capital products and consumer goods, and supplied savings which permitted investment in industry and commerce. In spite of new wars and devastation in the transition from the eighteenth to the nineteenth century, it seems evident that the roots of the development of modern Catalonia are in the eighty years after the War of Succession.

Population

The testimonies about this economic growth are very numerous. Father Jaume Caresmar wrote in 1780: 'The industry of Catalans has extended throughout all the Continent [i.e., Spain], with an abundant traffic of carts and mules, with commercial shops over all the coast and in the main cities of the Kingdom [. . .] promoting the quality of its produce and distilling its surplus wine into brandy, which they sell across the Ebro river, together with olive oil, wool, silk and other staples' (cited by Carrera Pujal, 1947, IV, p. 429). Caresmar also referred to capital exports of Catalans, who lent to bishoprics, communities, and private individuals in the same regions where they sold their wares. He even makes one of the earliest references to the proverbial Catalan traveling salesman, who found his way even to popular and not so popular literature in modern times.

Many more witnesses could be cited; but quantitative evidence would be even more convincing. The only solid data of this kind we have, however, is that referring to population. According to Nadal (1992, pp. 58, 73), 'Globally, from 1300 to 1717, for more than 400 years, the Catalan population stagnated, unable to exceed the mark [of 500,000 inhabitants. By contrast from] 1717 to 1787, and from 1787 to 1857 population growth reached every single one of the 38 cantons of Catalonia'. In the same article Nadal supplies the following figures: Catalan population was 508,000 in 1717, and 899,531 in 1787. In those seventy years it went from 7.25 percent of total Spanish population to 9.5 percent. The eighteenth century was a period of general population growth in Europe, but Catalonia experienced this expansion to a much greater degree that the rest of Spain. Maluquer (1998, p. 54) draws an accurate and concise description:

> From the beginning of the eighteenth century, and for the first time, the Catalan economy produced enough to assure the survival of a rapidly growing population. It still was basically an agrarian economy. But a consistent agrarian recovery, with a decided market orientation, the increase of provincial incomes and the growth of internal demand, plus external competitiveness, provided the bases for a process of expansion and transformation of manufacture which was to lead directly to industrialization.

Agriculture

Unfortunately almost all documents of the *Catastro* have disappeared, so it is impossible to carry out a systematic reconstruction of agricultural production figures, but Vilar (1962, II, pp. 190-202), in his monumental work on eighteenth century Catalonia, has accumulated an amazing amount of disperse information, which, though fragmentary, because of the almost unanimous coincidence, allows a high degree of confidence as to the sign of the changes uncovered. 'With the possible exception of Cerdanya [a Pyrenean county], all districts or cantons of the Principality are named in one eighteenth-century document or another remarking a greater or smaller increase of the cultivated surface [. . .] no region of some importance in the Catalan economy missed this eighteenth-century agrarian renovation'. There are also studies of agrarian rents showing regular increases, and of agrarian wages, showing these to grow in parallel with wages in Barcelona. We also know that agrarian recovery and growth started almost as soon as the war was over, and there are even suggestions that the inherent disruptions in a way helped, because they stimulated the introduction of radical improvements, which otherwise might not have taken place or been postponed, and there are also indications that the *Catastro* might have favored the cultivation of marginal land, because it carefully classified lands according to quality and taxed them accordingly (i.e., applied lower rates to lower qualities.

The most important and fastest-growing crop was the vine, well adapted to Mediterranean conditions and also the raw material for the products which soon became the most important trade and export goods of Catalonia: wine and brandy. These exports helped finance increasing imports of grain, because, although the cultivation of cereals also expanded, population growth was faster. Thus Catalonia purchased in other Spanish regions not only wheat and other grains but also meat and salted fish. Local food output increased, but was not enough to feed a population which was growing at a yearly rate near 1 percent. Other crops which grew fast as well were olives and olive oil, rice, flax, hemp, almonds, and the products of animal husbandry.

The signs are not only of an expansion of cultivation but also of technical progress, especially of more intensive irrigation, through the building of small canals (*acequias*). The area where more irrigation permits were granted was that around Barcelona, and then, a distant second, the Gerona hinterland. There was an increase in the number of mills built, not only flour mills but also paper mills and fulling mills. Another sign of improved techniques was the reduction of fallow, something which was made possible through improved crop rotations and the more intensive use of natural fertilizers, some of them imported. There is also evidence of increased commercialization of crops and regional specialization.

Catalonia in the Spanish Empire: Commerce and Industry

Commerce

From the sixteenth century on the Spanish Empire has been subjected to rather stringent commercial laws, whereby the metropolis monopolized all trade with the Americas. The center of this monopoly was located in Seville during the sixteenth and seventeenth centuries and was moved to Cadiz in 1717. The *Casa de Contratación* was the institution in charge of controlling all trade with the Americas. Every ship coming or going to the Americas had to make stop at Seville and be registered, its cargo inspected and eventually permitted to sail or disembark. The crossing was also carefully regulated. Ships had to sail in convoys (*flotas*) escorted by warships. The so-called *Flotas de Nueva España* sailed to Mexico, while the *Galeones de Tierra Firme* were due for the Isthmus (Portobelo) or Cartagena de Indias (Cartagena in present day Colombia); the cargo of the ships arriving at Portobelo was unloaded, moved across the Isthmus, and loaded on the *Armada del Sur* which carried it to Lima on the Peruvian coast. Both *Flotas* and *Galeones* (gallions) usually stopped at Havana before sailing for the eastward crossing to Seville.

This cumbersome system was intended to provide safety, but posed some problems, because it prevented an effective coordination between supply and demand, which often hindered the rapid selling of goods; for the Crown, however, it had the advantage that it could keep a tight control over transactions which made easier the collection of taxes. The War of Succession played havoc with this tight scheme; English and Dutch ships interfered and menaced the security of the fleets and smuggled at leisure. When the war was over it was difficult for the Crown to return to the *status quo ante*. Among other things it had to move the *Casa de Contratación* to Cadiz, an excellent seaport, because Seville, a river port, posed serious problems with larger ships. Furthermore, the Treaty of Utrecht stipulated large concessions to the British, such as the *asiento de negros* (the monopoly of supplying African slaves to Spanish America) and the *navío de permiso* (the licensing of a

British ship yearly to participate in Spanish America trade). Both concessions permitted substantial smuggling in addition to the regular activities. On top of this, commercial links had been created between Spanish American importers and non-Spanish suppliers, who were often able to smuggle their goods one way or another. So the system was less airtight than had been prior to the war, and was subject to frequent adjustments in the following decades. By and large, the Cadiz monopoly was gradually relaxed, and this facilitated trade from other Spanish ports, notably Barcelona.

The War of Jenkins's Ear (1739–1748) again disorganized the Spanish trans-Atlantic trade, and contributed to generalize what were called *navíos de registro*, ships which traveled by themselves after having obtained a license from the *Casa de Contratación*. After 1765 a series of Spanish ports, Barcelona among them, were authorized to trade directly with a number of ports in the Americas. Finally, in 1778, the number of ports that could trade directly was further increased and freedom of trade was enlarged. These measures produced the expected results: trans-Atlantic trade vastly expanded, and so did the corresponding tax revenues.

As can be imagined all these reforms in the commercial regime benefited Catalonia considerably. As Vilar (1962, III, p. 341) said, 'transatlantic navigation passed into Catalan hands in a large measure'. In the early part of the century links between Catalonia and Cadiz expanded vastly, and Catalan merchandise had a growing share of Spanish exports to America. Among these brandy and wine were the leading items, with other vegetal products such as nuts and raisins. Brandy was really the star product: not only was demand strong (Northern Europe was a large importer as well), its high alcohol content prevented fermentation and made it stable and storage easy.

Industrial and craft products were exported also, but their peak arrived later in the century: silk handicrafts (stockings, handkerchiefs, lace), firearms, ironware, and even strings for musical instruments. In the second half of the century, cotton textiles, especially hand-painted cloths (*indianas*), were exported to America in increasing amounts, together with felt hats, leather goods, paper, books, iron ware (weapons, tools, knives), and soap. The Crown discouraged local industry in the Americas, since traded goods were easier to tax.

Two final remarks: first, the obvious: the increasing participation of Catalonia in the transatlantic trade stimulated the Catalan economy, as the abolition of the internal tolls, which had traditionally separated the kingdoms of Aragon and Castile, had done earlier in the century. Second: the Spanish Crown, possibly to compensate for the abolition of the *fueros* and the bitterness of defeat for the Catalans, made a definite effort to stimulate the commerce of Catalonia with the Indies; thus, for example, Catalan brandy was *de facto* exempted from the tight regulation which was applied to the rest of Spanish brandies in 1714; the facilities extended for the registration of Catalan merchants in Cadiz; the authorization of direct trade with the Americas to Catalan ships; and the authorization of the Royal Company of Barcelona in 1755, which actively promoted the exportation of *indianas* to America (Martínez Shaw, 1981, esp. ch. 2).

Industry

The removal of interior tolls between Aragon and Castile was crucial for the reason adduced in Adam Smith's famous dictum (*The Wealth of Nations*, Ch. III): 'The division of labour is limited by the extent of the market'. For Aragon as a whole, the customs union with Castile meant gaining access to a market four times larger than Aragon's own; for Catalonia it meant acceding to a market almost 14 times larger than Catalonia's own. Scale of output and specialization no doubt contributed mightily to economies of scale and capitalization. We have just seen a number of industries which found new markets in Spanish America. These were those that expanded faster, of course, but to these must be added shipbuilding, stimulated by the growth of commerce but also by the Crown's demand for warships. Construction and house building also developed as a consequence of population growth, improved standards of living, and also by royal demand for public works and military buildings. Vilar (1964, pp. 282-4) points out that bricklayers' wages in Barcelona grew much faster than in Madrid, and this he considers to prove that 'Catalonia had suddenly acquired the leading economic situation it had lost since the fifteenth century'.

There can be no doubt that Catalan textile industry benefited from the deliberate purpose of the Crown to favor the Principality, probably to compensate it for its war losses. Soon after the end of the War of Succession (1717 and 1718) Felipe V issued a series of decrees forbidding the importation of cotton textiles, abolishing internal tolls between Aragon and Castile, and according preference to domestic wares for the acquisition of military equipment. According to Thomson (1992, p. 71), 'this direct encouragement [. . .] probably made the nascent Spanish industry the most politically favoured of its time'.

However successful this policy in stimulating the growth of a domestic industry, it still necessitated state protection for a very long stretch of time, as we shall see, because neither its quality nor its prices were internationally competitive. One of the causes of this inferiority was the strength of guilds, the 'existence of a virtually complete guild system in Barcelona [as a consequence of which, t]here was no free labour market [. . .] These rigidities would have made the organization of the industry on a putting-out basis virtually impossible'. This contributes to explain why salaries were relatively high and productivity low. However, by import substitution and expansion in the domestic market, the Catalan textile industry kept growing. There was import substitution in spinning also at the very end of the century, all of which stimulated the importation of mostly second hand English machinery (*jennies* and *mules*) and coal in the already turbulent years of the late eighteenth and early nineteenth centuries (Delgado Ribas, 1990). At that time Barcelona was becoming a little London, polluted by the smoke of coal and the exhalations of tanneries and dye factories (Martí Escayol, 2002).

This industry, whose markets were located in Spain and the Indies, was badly hurt when war broke in 1793. Spain first fought France, which invaded Catalonia once more. Later on Spain changed sides and allied itself with France against England only to be badly defeated at the naval battle of Trafalgar. Then in 1808 there was a spontaneous popular rebellion against the occupying French troops. Thus started what is called the War of Independence in Spain and the Peninsular War in England, which we will examine in the next chapter. Suffice it to say here that these wars, which interrupted the normal transatlantic trade and made of Spain the theater of a bloody six-year war, gravely affected all the economy, but especially trade and industry. Most of the brilliant gains of the eighteenth century in these matters went up in fire and smoke during these approximately twenty years of war in which Spain changed sides and alliances. The metropolis emerged from the war independent from France, but continental Spanish America emerged independent from Spain. These momentous changes required deep internal reforms: these came, but at a frustratingly slow pace.

Conclusions

There is a debate going on in Spanish historiography about what effects the reforms introduced by Felipe V and his successors had in the Spanish economy. Nationalists historians, such as Fontana, Sobrequés, Balcells, or Torras Ribé, maintain that these effects were nil or worse. The non-nationalists, such as Vicens Vives, Domínguez Ortiz, Martínez Shaw, or even Vilar, tend to affirm that their effect was positive. I myself decidedly side with this opinion. I wonder what other explanation is there for the fact that Catalonia's economy and society hardly evolved at all during the three centuries from 1400 to 1700; while wars raged there abundantly during the period (only the sixteenth century was free of them) the economy and society remained remarkably static. Then, after the War of Succession, things changed rapidly, and both population and the economy grew in Catalonia much faster that in the rest of Spain. This mutation is difficult to explain if we overlook the Bourbon reforms; linking them with the Olson theory, we have a coherent explanation not only of the Catalan success but also of the stagnation of Castile. Because it lost the war, Catalonia was able to free itself of the feudal fetters which tied it up for so long. According to Vicens (1970, p. 115), after the New Plan reforms, the

> transformation was so violent that Catalonia hovered on the verge of ruin for fifteen years. But with time the elimination of privileges and fueros produced unexpected benefits: Catalans not only were forced to look toward the future but, under the auspices of a common monarchic regime, were offered the same opportunities open to Castilians. [. . .] This process of the social integration of the various peoples in Spain was far more substantive than any legislative measure devised since the time

> of Philip II: Catalonia played a decisive role because of her triple expansion –in population, commerce and the textile industry.

Nationalist historians who think that the Bourbon reforms were vengeful and destructive must have recourse to the recuperation on the late seventeenth century to postulate a continuity with the eighteenth-century expansion. But we already saw that the late seventeenth-century episode was little more than a recovery, with no structural change at all. In spite of the recovery of trade, Barcelona, according to Nadal and Giralt (1963, pp. 279 and 203), remained

> a model of pre-industrial society [which needed to change] a set of obsolete political and administrative institutions which were a major obstacle to expansion. Paradoxically, their removal was effected by means of a very cruel war [, but] defeat opened the gates of splendor for the city. [Barcelona went from being] an undeveloped society [to enjoying] the wonderful take-off of the eighteenth century. [. . .] Be it as it may, falling into the orbit of the Bourbons marked a watershed in the history of Barcelona.

Summarizing, it is difficult to understand how it would have been possible for Catalonia to develop its agriculture, its commerce, and its industry as it did after 1716, without a privileged access to Spanish and Spanish American markets, and without a fair and efficient tax system. Until this explanation is forthcoming, we will have to agree with Joan Batlle, a Catalan deputy who said in the Cortes in the early 1820s: 'If Catalonia had not broken the chains of the second Iron Age, abolishing the abuses of the feudal regime, it would not be reputed industrious as it is today, and it could not pride in this distinction which has made it celebrated the world over' (Cited by Vilar, 1974, p. 22).

References

ALBAREDA, Joaquín (2012), *La Guerra de Sucesión de España (1700–1714)*. Madrid: Crítica.

Álvarez de Cienfuegos Campos, Isabel and others (1963), *Homenaje a Don Ramón Carande*. Madrid: Sociedad de Estudios y Publicaciones.

ARTOLA, Miguel (1982), *La hacienda del Antiguo Régimen.* Madrid: Alianza Editorial.

Balcells, Albert, ed. (2009), *Història de Catalunya.* Madrid: La Esfera de los Libros.

CARRERA PUJAL, Jaime (1947), *Historia política y económica de Cataluña, siglos XVI al XVIII.* Tomo IV. Barcelona: Bosch.

DELGADO RIBAS, Josep M. (1990), 'De la filatura manual a la mecànica. Un capitol del desenvolupamente de l'industria cotonera a Catalunya (1749–1814)', *Recerques*, 23, pp. 161–178.

DOMÍNGUEZ ORTIZ, Antonio (1990), *Sociedad y Estado en el siglo XVIII español.* Barcelona: Ariel.

Fernández, Roberto, ed. (1985), *España en el siglo XVIII. Homenaje a Piere Vilar.* Barcelona: Editorial Crítica.

Foner, Eric (1989), *Reconstruction. America's Unfinished Revolution, 1863–1877.* NewYork: Harper & Row.

JASZI, Oscar (1961), *The Dissolution of the Habsburg Monarchy.* Chicago: The University of Chicago Press.

KANN, Robert A. (1980), *A History of the Habsburg Empire, 1526–1918.* Berkeley: University of California Press.

LYNCH, M. (1991), *Scotland. A New History.* London: Century.

MALUQUER DE MOTES, Jordi (1998), *Història econòmica de Catalunya, segles XIX i XX.* Barcelona: Universitat Oberta de Catalunya.

MARTÍ ESCAYOL, Maria Antònia (2002), 'Industria, medicina i química a la Barcelona del fins del segle XVIII. El tintatge i la introducció del carbó mineral des d'una perspectiva ambiental', *Recerques*, 44, pp. 5–20.

MARTÍNEZ SHAW, Carlos (1981), *Cataluña en la carrera de Indias, 1680–1756.* Barcelona: Crítica.

MARTÍNEZ SHAW, Carlos (1985), 'La Cataluña del siglo XVIII bajo el signo de la expansión' in Fernández, pp. 55–131.

MERCADER I RIBA, Juan (1985), *Felip V i Catalunya.* Barcelona: Edicions 62.

MERINO, José Patricio (1987), *Las cuentas de la Administración central española, 1750–1820.* Madrid: Instituto de Estudios Fiscales.

Morison, Samuel Eliot (1972), *The Oxford History of the American People, II, 1789–1877.* New York: Mentor.

NADAL FARRERAS, Joaquín (1971), *La introducción del Catastro en Gerona, contribución al estudio del régimen fiscal de Cataluña en tiempos de Felipe V.* Barcelona: Cátedra de Historia General de España.

NADAL, Jordi (1988), 'La población española durante los siglos XVI, XVII y XVIII. Un balance a escala regional' in Pérez Moreda and Reher, pp. 38–51.

NADAL, Jordi (1992), *Bautismos, desposorios y entierros. Estudios de historia demográfica*. Barcelona: Ariel.

NADAL, Jordi and Emilio GIRALT (1963), 'Barcelona en 1717–1718. Un modelo de sociedad pre-industrial', en Álvarez de Cienfuegos, pp. 277–305.

OLSON, Mancur (1982), *The Rise and Decline of Nations. Economic Growth, Stagflation, and Social Rigidities*. New Haven, Conn.: Yale University Press.

Pérez Moreda, Vicente and David Sven Reher, eds. (1988), *Demografía histórica en España*. Madrid: El Arquero.

Ross, David (2014), *Scotland, History of a Nation*. Broxburn: Lomond.

Sobrequés i Callicó, Jaume (2011), *L'Onze de Setembre i Catalunya*. Guerra, resistència i represió, Barcelona: Editorial Base

SUREDA, José Luis (1949), *La Hacienda castellana y los economistas del siglo XVII*. Madrid: Consejo Superior de Investigaciones Científicas.

THOMSON, J. K. J (1992), *A Distinctive Industrialization. Cotton in Barcelona, 1728–1832*. Cambridge: Cambridge University Press.

TORRAS i RIBÉ, J.M. (2013), *Felip V contra Catalunya. Testimonis d'una represió sistematica (1713–1715)*. 5th. ed., Barcelona: Rafael Dalmau.

UZTÁRIZ, Jerónimo (1968 [1742]), *Theórica y práctica de Comercio y de Marina*. Madrid: Editorial Aguilar.

VICENS VIVES, J. (1970), *Approaches to the History of Spain*. Translated and edited by Joan Connelly Ullman, Berkelely & LA: University of California Press.

VICENS VIVES, Jaime (1959), *Manual de Historia Económica de España*. Barcelona: Teide.

VILAR, Pierre (1962), *La Catalogne dans l'Espagne moderne. Recherches sur les fondements économiques des structures nationales*. 3 vols. Paris: SEVPEN.

VILAR, Pierre (1964), 'Transformaciones económicas, impulso urbano y movimiento de los salarios, la Barcelona del siglo XVIII', in Pierre Vilar, *Crecimiento y desarrollo. Economía e Historia. Reflexiones sobre el caso español*. Barcelona: Ariel, pp. 194–233.

VILAR, Pierre (1974), 'La Catalunya industrial, reflexions sobre una arrencada y sobre un destí,' *Recerques*, 3, pp. 7–22.

ZAVALA Y AUÑÓN, M (1732), *Representación al Rey N. Señor D. Phelipe V. (que Dios guarde) dirigida al mas seguro aumento del real erario y conseguir la felicidad, mayor alivio, riqueza, y abundancia de su Monarquia*, ... Madrid: Miguel. (available through Google).

4

The Peninsular War: Birth of a Nation

Introduction

The Peninsular War (*War of Independence* for Spaniards) is a key episode to understand modern Spain. It involves a remarkable paradox: the war started with a more or less spontaneous uprising of the Spanish people against the invading French troops (the spark flared in Madrid on 2 May 1808). The uprising hastened the crumbling down of the traditional Spanish state which had become just a vestige of the *Ancien regime*. In its stead there appeared, in an equally spontaneous manner, a series of local or provincial *Juntas* which immediately took in hand the tasks of daily government in a simultaneous but uncoordinated manner.

For many this was a return to the *taifa* kingdoms, and to the cluster of Christian statelets which formed after the Moorish conquest of Spain in the eighth century. However, out this fragmentation in 1808 a movement toward union developed, a surge of popular support for a vision of old Spain as a modern nation, which materialized in the meeting of national *Cortes* in Cádiz and the promulgation of the Constitution of 1812. As Domínguez Ortiz (2001, p. 254) wrote, 'The War of Independence gave

G. Tortella, *Catalonia in Spain*, Palgrave Studies in Economic History, DOI 10.1007/978-3-319-54951-4_4

Spain [. . .] the occasion to show that national unity, forged gradually for centuries, had penetrated every conscience and that it was possible to combine that will to unite with respect for regional diversity'.

Of course nationalism was a product of that era. The word *nation* was used by the French revolutionaries in a different sense from what is given it today; for them *nation* meant the set of free and equal *citizens* as distinct from the Old Regime monarchies, whose populations were not free but *subject* to the will of a monarch. The term *nation* of the French revolutionaries was closer to today's *democracy* or *citizenship*, or to the *people* as it is conceived in the United States Constitution (*We, the people*...), than to the local or tribal, when not racist, connotation it acquired later and which is most common today.

What was original about the movement started on 2 May 1808, and the armed rebellion that ensued was that the fight against the French invaders was carried out while appealing to concepts and rhetoric which had originated with the French Revolution. It is true that the people participating in the revolt harbored different ideas, and that in some what predominated was xenophobia and devotion to traditional monarchy and religion while for others the Spanish nation signified a modern and constitutional country of equal and free citizens. But these contradictions were not exclusive of Spain: the French army which invaded Spain included subjects of the empire and Jacobin republicans, and many of those who at that time hailed the emperor were willing a few years later to become subjects of a restored monarchy. Something similar occurred across Europe: the sympathy for equality and liberty proclaimed by the French Revolution coexisted with hatred against the hero turned despot: a case in point is Beethoven who changed his mind about dedicating his third symphony to Bonaparte.

The nation-state was the product of the great modern revolution which commenced in Holland and England in the eighteenth century and which became widespread with the independence of the United States and the French revolution which, in reality, was a European revolution that started in France. All this was established about fifty years ago by Louis Gottschalk and Jacques Godechot, among others. What is interesting about the Spanish case is not its long and frustrating struggle to become a modern nation during the nineteenth century. This happened to all of them, starting with France and continuing with the

Anglo-Saxon set, all of whom underwent a protracted transition to become a modern nation.

Spain's originality lays in that, being backward economically and intellectually in the early nineteenth century, it fought with extraordinary gallantry to preserve its identity while at the same time it endeavored to adopt and adapt the best parts of the revolutionary program: the parliamentary system, a constitution, popular sovereignty, the basic freedoms. In the absence of its king, Fernando VII, the 'felon king', as was called by the liberals after he showed his true despotic colors, Spain attained something which would seem way beyond its meager resources, i.e., to defy France, the hegemonic power, using its rival's political and intellectual weapons. That Spain bit off more than it could chew is shown by its long effort and strife along the nineteenth century to materialize the political ideals of the Cortes of Cádiz, by the long process of constitutional doing and undoing, and by the propensity to the *coup d'Etat*, the *pronunciamiento*, which hung over the political scene as a Damocles's sword. The reason for this frustration is simple: economic retardation brought about social and political stagnation.

Today's absurd paradox is that now, having reached social and economic maturity, Spaniards are now watching the strivings of nationalists to tear down, stone by stone, the edifice which it cost two long centuries to build. When Spain was weak and backward, and attacked by an enemy vastly more powerful, it moved almost miraculously from fragmentation to unity. Today, by contrast, in peace and prosperity, it seems to be ready to run the same way backwards, from unity to disintegration.

Spain's War of Independence

The immediate origins of the war go back to 1806, when the French emperor, Napoleon Bonaparte, tried to strangle Great Britain economically by means of the *continental blockade*, in other words, the interdiction of importing British goods to the Continent. Portugal refused to go along with the blockade and Napoleon, with the acquiescence of the Spanish government, introduced a French army in Spain with the intention of invading Portugal. On 18 October 1807, the army of general Jean A. Junot crossed the Bidasoa river into Spain, traversed the country, reached Portugal, and took Lisbon on 30th November. The Portuguese royal family had just left for Brazil. Manuel Godoy, a sort of prime minister *cum* favorite under Carlos IV of Spain, promoted the Treaty of Fontainebleau (October 1807) whereby, Portugal would be dismembered and apportioned to Godoy himself, the Spanish royal family, and the remaining third to be offered to the British in exchange for Gibraltar.

Napoleon had no intention of fulfilling the treaty. French troops occupied key cities near the Franco-Spanish border, such as San Sebastian, Pamplona, and Barcelona, and, finally, in March, marshal Joachim Murat entered Madrid peacefully but at the head of an armed column. Taking advantage of the rivalry and hatred which existed between king Carlos and his elder son and presumptive heir, Fernando, and the cowardice of both, Napoleon made them come to Bayonne, in France, near the border, with the pretext of trying to arbitrate their differences. In fact, by means of threats, cajolery, and offers of compensation, he forced them to renounce the Spanish throne in favor of his own elder brother, Joseph Bonaparte. To his surprise, however, the Madrid populace, on 2nd May, mutinied and was fired upon by Murat's troops. While the Spanish civil and military authorities took a passive attitude, a substantial part of the garrison of Madrid under the command of captains and lieutenants joined the rebels, and two days of urban war ensued. In the end the French troops dominated the situation and executed many of the prisoners taken. These scenes were immortalized in two large paintings by Francisco de Goya and can be seen in the *Museo del Prado* in Madrid.

The news from Madrid spread throughout Spain, and in many cities popular sovereignty was proclaimed and Juntas were organized to replace old regime institutions and to prepare for resisting the invaders. 'The breakup of power among the provincial Juntas saved Spain from the immediate shock of the French invasion under Napoleon, not only because it multiplied the country's resources, but due to the fact that it posed the problem for the invader that there was no clear center which could be decisively conquered' (Marx and Engels, 1960, p. 95). To this was added that the peasantry collaborated in the uprising and the guerrilla war that ensued (*guerrilla* in Spanish means 'little war' and the term was generalized at that time), which made effective control of the territory by the French army even more difficult (Fraser, 2006, p. 176).

The first Junta was organized in Asturias (25 May), and it immediately declared war on France; some days later it sent two representatives to England (one of them was José María Queipo de Llano, viscount of Matarrosa, later count of Toreno) to ask for help. Collaboration between the British government and the Spanish Juntas never ceased until the end of the war. The first victory of Spanish arms took place in Catalonia, in el Bruch, at the foot of Montserrat (the serrated mountain not far from Barcelona which harbors one of the most venerated shrines in Catalonia), where guerrillas and *somatents* (civilian militias) routed a French column under general Schwartz, coming from Barcelona toward the interior (7 June). According to legend, a drummer boy terrorized the French soldiers as the drum roll reverberated in the mountains making them believe that a big army advanced against them. Be it as it may, Schwartz was forced to return to Barcelona. Renewed French attempts to advance from that city toward Gerona and Valencia were also beaten back.

Juntas were also formed in Cartagena, the most important Spanish military port on the Mediterranean, and other large cities such as Valencia, Granada, and Zaragoza. Zaragoza, on the Ebro river, is quite close to France, to which it declared war. It was soon submitted to a long siege, which it resisted for two months under the leadership of the captain general of Aragon, José Palafox. This first siege ended in late July, when news arrived of the defeat of a large French army in Bailén, near Cordoba by a Spanish army commanded by general Francisco Javier Castaños (19 July). This was the only Spanish victory in conventional war, and it caused the intervention of the *Grande Armée* under the personal command of Bonaparte himself. Under Bonaparte the French repeatedly defeated the Spanish armies. Zaragoza was besieged a second time, and it finally capitulated after being almost totally destroyed and suffering tremendous losses. After the defeat of Ocaña in 1809, almost the whole Peninsula fell into French hands, save for Cadiz (where the Cortes met while the French besieged the city), Valencia, and most of the region of Galicia, in the northwest. The guerrilla resistance, however, continued.

It was from Galicia that British general Arthur Wellesley (later duke of Wellington) moved south at the head of an army which reached and conquered Lisbon in September 1808. He fortified the city and resisted repeated French attacks. The overextension of the Napoleonic empire and the preparations of the French campaign in Russia took away French troops from the Peninsula. From the mid-1811 Wellesley's army took the initiative and started pushing back the French from Portugal and penetrating into western Spain with the help of the guerrillas. Probably his most decisive victory came near Salamanca, at the battle of the Arapiles (the name of twin peaks near that city, 22 July 1812). After that battle Wellesley threatened Madrid, which Joseph Bonaparte (José I) abandoned precipitately. This was his second time: he also had run from Madrid after the Bailén defeat. But Wellesley, after entering Madrid in triumph, finding himself short of funds and his lines overextended, was unable to take Burgos, and withdrew to Portugal. José returned to Madrid. At that juncture the British Rothschilds, headed by Nathan Meyer, lent to the British Treasury the capital necessary for the final effort to defeat Napoleon (López Morell, 2013, pp. 7-18). José I left Madrid for a third and definitive time in March 1813. Pursued by Wellesley's renovated army, the French withdrew until they were defeated in Vitoria (21 June 1813) and were forced to retreat toward the Pyrenees. In December 1813 they signed the treaty of Valençay, recognizing Fernando, who had been prisoner in Valençay during the war, as king of Spain and granting his return. The Spain which Napoleon had characterized earlier as a bunch of ignoramuses and priests had turned out to be the 'fatal knot [. . .], the main cause of all the French *malheurs*', as he himself wrote in exile. Marx explained Bonaparte's error in that he ignored Spain's treasures of local energy, and 'it thus could happen that Napoleon who – as all his contemporaries – thought that Spain was an inanimate body, suffered the fatal surprise of discovering that, although the Spanish state was dead, Spanish society was teeming with life and each of its parts overflowed with power to resist' (Marx and Engels, 1960, p. 85).

The modern Spanish nation was formed and steeled during those years of fight against Napoleon. On 8 July 1808 José I swore the Statute of Bayonne (a pseudo-constitution granted by Bonaparte), which used the word *nation* several times in its text. It recognized the existence of a 'Spanish Nation' and started (Art. 1) by declaring that Roman Catholicism was the religion of King and Nation, and 'none other shall be permitted'. The Cádiz Constitution of 1812, by contrast, was truly democratic in origin and intent. The Cortes of Cádiz were composed of elected deputies (as legitimate as the circumstances of war permitted), and the successive Cortes were to be elected by universal suffrage by an indirect system (not unlike the system still used in the United States, where electors elect representatives who in turn elect the federal president). According to the Cádiz Constitution, the primary voters appointed representatives who in turn elected the deputies. The first Chapter of the Cádiz Constitution was entitled: 'About the Spanish Nation and the Spaniards', and placed sovereignty 'essentially in the Nation' (not the king). Article 2 memorably stated: 'The Spanish Nation is free and independent and is not, and cannot be, the patrimony of any family or person'. Spain included Spanish America and the Philippines, so that Spanish citizens were those 'having origin in the Spanish dominions of both hemispheres' (Art. 18). Fernando VII abolished the Cádiz Constitution in 1814, as soon as he returned from Valençay.

The 'War of the French' in Catalonia

The English call it 'The Peninsular War'; the Spanish call it 'The War of Independence', but Catalan historians call it 'The War of the French' (*La Guerra del Francès*). Catalonia was the Spanish region where the French presence was more deeply and longer felt. It was even incorporated to the French empire in January 1812, and divided into four *départements*. This lasted only a little more than two years; however, in March 1814 Catalonia reverted to its original status as a Spanish region, although it was not until May of that same year that the last French garrison abandoned Barcelona, which thus became the last Spanish town flying the flag of the French revolution.

The inclusion of Catalonia in the French empire found little support in the local population. General Mariano Álvarez de Castro, a native of Granada, headed the stubborn – or heroic – resistance to the French. First it was in Barcelona, where he defended the fortress of Montjuic, but was ordered to capitulate by an order of the weak-kneed captain general of Catalonia. In Gerona, however, he commanded the city during a very hard and courageous seven-month siege by the French general Gouvion-de-Saint-Cyr. Later another Spanish general, the liberal Luis de Lacy (a native of Cadiz and a descendant of an illustrious Irish military family), carried out even greater exploits. His life was that of a romantic, swashbuckling hero. In his early youth he was expelled from the Spanish army for wounding his superior in a duel over the love of a woman. He then enlisted in the French army, married a French lady, and fought under Napoleon in Germany. Sent to Spain with the invading French army and unwilling to fight against his country he tried to resign, then deserted and surrendered himself to the Junta in Madrid. He was reinstated in the Spanish army and due to his military prowess became captain general of Catalonia and led the resistance against the French; as he had no real regular army, Lacy resorted to guerrilla warfare, with very audacious operations, including raids across the Pyrenees to carry war to the enemy. Later on, Lacy admitted guerrilla fighters into the regular army. In his desperate fight Lacy employed what today would be called terrorist tactics, such as massive poisoning and blowing up a powder depot. Such savage tactics made him a hero to many, but not to the conservative Catalan upper classes who controlled the local Junta, who lobbied against him, and finally pressured him to accept the post of captain general of Galicia. After the war, as a radical liberal that he was, he conspired against Fernando VII, gathering the support of some Catalan military circles and staging a *pronunciamiento* in April of 1817. The coup failed and he was taken prisoner and shot in Mallorca. He was moved there because the authorities feared his popularity in Catalonia might incite riots. Sadly, general Castaños, the hero of Bailén, was instrumental in the death sentence of Lacy.

It may be surprising that an Andalusian general of foreign origins should have had such a following in Catalonia, usually so suspicious of outsiders. Lacy's popularity there, and that of Alvarez de Castro, seem proof of the widespread feeling of support for the Spanish cause against

Napoleon, in spite of the astute efforts of the French commanders to gather popular support there by making the Catalan language co-official with the French and giving the region some government autonomy.

The Catalan Junta, although quite conservative, duly sent its representatives to the Cortes de Cádiz. They were almost all of them rather reactionary except for their most distinguished individual, Antoni de Capmany, a moderate liberal and brilliant essayist and historian who, among his arguments (which he gathered in his booklet *Centinela contra franceses*, 'Sentry against the French') to oppose Napoleon, was the emperor's intention to replicate French uniformity in Spain, i.e., to smother the 'little nations' (that is to say, the regions, such as Catalonia, Castile, Andalusia, etc.) which made up Spain. Capmany was no Catalan nationalist but rather a warm supporter of the unity of Spain and of the use of the Spanish language, which was the only one he employed in writing, but he wanted to preserve the variety of regional institutions, of which he was a distinguished student. In the Cortes he was in favor of abolishing the guilds and the Inquisition; both proposals were enacted.

Catalonia, the region which suffered the longest and most rigorous French occupation, was among those that fought with more tenacity against the invasion, as the cases of the Bruch, Gerona, and the leaderships of Alvarez de Castro and Lacy would suggest. One can mention in this context that the great heroin of the Zaragoza siege, *Agustina de Aragón*, whose real name was, coincidentally, Agustina Zaragoza, was a native of Barcelona.

Fraser (2006, pp. 159, 171-2) poses the question of why Catalans defended so enthusiastically the Bourbon monarchy whose ancestors had abolished their cherished *fueros*. Their fight against the French, he adds, was longer, bloodier, and with a higher price in terms of lives and property than possibly that of any other Spanish region. Let me add that most authors, such as Mercader (1947, pp. 125, 141) and Lovett (1965, pp. 163, 178), have remarked the selflessness and patriotism of the Catalans. Fraser's answer to his question emphasizes economics: Catalonia, as we saw in the preceding chapter, enjoyed unprecedented prosperity under Felipe V and his successors during the eighteenth century. The working classes and the guilds were very active in organizing the resistance; this, plus the activity of the *somatents*, made the Catalan revolt more genuinely popular than in the rest of the country, he adds. Furthermore, the cotton industrialists were very aware that any foreign intrusion jeopardized their monopoly of national and colonial trade. To add insult to injury, Napoleon ordered that Spanish markets should be open to French textiles. Furthermore, according to Aymes (2008, pp. 88-9), Catalonia was more subject to French military than to civilian authorities, and the officers were ready to tolerate any sort of contraband from France, or even from England, in order to keep their men adequately provided.

The religious factor must also be taken into account. The church had a very strong influence in Catalonia, possibly even more than in some other regions. Catalan priests viewed the French invaders as an army of heretics and atheists. To this must be added the conservatism of the Catalan upper classes, who controlled the local Junta which, according to Fraser, was much more conservative than the other Juntas. These dyed-in-the-wool reactionaries abhorred of revolution, and though France was at the time an empire, they considered Napoleon a parvenu of revolutionary origins.

Conclusions

The Spanish modern nation was born in the fight against Napoleon, who tried to take advantage of what he thought was the political weakness and social inertness of Spain to annex it to his empire. In the short term, political weakness derived from the bitter rivalry between the crown prince, Fernando, and his parents, and from the corruption and mediocrity of the government and the political elite. There was also the structural weakness of all contemporary absolute monarchies in Europe. Compounding political feebleness there were economic archaism and stagnation. The immediate causes of economic problems were the recurring wars which had started in Europe in 1793 and were a consequence of the French revolution and the international reaction against it. For Spain they involved alternating confrontations with France and Britain which entailed invasions and naval defeats which interrupted Spain's relations with its American colonies, undermined the foundations of its empire, and bankrupted its Treasury. A profounder cause of Spain's economic malaise was the failure of its enlightened politicians to introduce the necessary fiscal and agrarian reforms (see Chapter 3 and Tortella, 2014). This failure was not due to lack of will or of vision, but to the stubborn and effective resistance of the nobility and church, who in the end turned out to be more powerful than the monarchy. Felipe V's successors, his sons Fernando VI (1746–1759) and Carlos III (1759–1788), supported (perhaps not with all the necessary determination) the reformist policies of their enlightened ministers, but in the end the passive resistance of the privileged prevailed (Herr, 1958; Tortella, 2014), and Spain, with the exception of Catalonia, the only region where reforms could be carried out, remained economically backward and stagnant.

To his surprise (and of many others), Napoleon found strong resistance south of the Pyrenees, especially in Catalonia, which spurned the special deal Napoleon granted it in the form of unusual political autonomy and recognition of Catalan as co-official language. Under the generalship of an Andalusian, Luis Lacy, Catalonia fought tooth and nail against the invaders, and sent 51 deputies to the Cortes at Cádiz, among whom Antoni Capmany shone for his intelligence and farsightedness.

The idea of a 'Spanish nation' which was enshrined in the Constitution of 1812 was modern and wide-encompassing, as it included as Spaniards those of 'both hemispheres' (i.e., it considered Spaniards the inhabitants of the American and Asian colonies as well). Furthermore, Capmany also thought (although this was not translated into the Constitution) that within the large Spanish nation there was room for the historical 'little nations' of Castilians, Catalans, etc. Spain might thus have become a sort of 'nation of nations' *avant-la-lettre* (we will discuss this concept later). At any rate, there is no doubt that in the Peninsular War a majority of peninsular Spaniards joined forces to remain independent and defend their common identity against a vastly superior enemy. This will to unite and resist, added of course to the power of the British army under Arthur Wellesley, made the weak strong and able to defeat Napoleon's soldiers.

References

AYMES, Jean René (2008), *La Guerra de la Independencia de España (1808–1814)*. [Trad. Pierre Conard]. 6ª ed. Madrid: Siglo XXI.

DOMÍNGUEZ ORTIZ, Antonio (2001), *España, tres milenios de Historia*. Madrid: Marcial Pons.

FRASER, Ronald (2006), *La maldita guerra de España. Historia social de la guerra de la Independencia, 1808–1814*. Barcelona, Crítica.

HERR, Richard (1958), *The Eighteenth-Century Revolution in Spain*. Princeton, NJ.: Princeton University Press.

LÓPEZ-MORELL, Miguel A. (2013), *The House of Rothschild in Spain, 1812–1941*. Farnham: Ashgate.

LOVETT, Gabriel H. (1965), *Napoleon and the birth of the modern Spain*. Vol. I. *The Challenge to the Old Order*. New York: New York University Press.

MARX, Karl y Friedrich ENGELS (1960), *Revolución en España*. Barcelona: Ariel.

MERCADER RIBA, Juan (1947), 'La anexión de Cataluña al Imperio francés (1812–1814),' *Hispania*, vol. 26, pp. 125–141.

Morales Moya, Antonio, ed. (2014), 1714. Cataluña en la España del siglo XVIII, Madrid: Ediciones Cátedra

TORTELLA, G. (2014), 'La renovación económica y social de los Borbones, la política económica de España en el siglo XVIII', in Morales, pp. 263–291.

5

Liberalism and Reaction

Economic Stagnation and Political Paralysis

A Growing Gap

From a comprehensive Spanish standpoint, the nineteenth century is characterized by the aggravation of a phenomenon which was already present in the eighteenth: economic development was very slow, close to stagnation for the country as a whole, while in Catalonia there took place what some have called, with some exaggeration no doubt, an 'industrial revolution'. However exaggerated the expression, there can be no doubt that dualism was marked and increasing. Catalonia was growing while the rest of the country nearly stagnated. The only other region where one could identify a process of industrialization was the Basque Country, but this process, which was centered upon metallurgical and mechanical industries, did not start in earnest until the final decades of the nineteenth century.

Economic stagnation was correlated with social stagnation. The Spanish population grew slowly by comparison with its neighbors of

G. Tortella, *Catalonia in Spain*, Palgrave Studies in Economic History, DOI 10.1007/978-3-319-54951-4_5

northern Europe, and the share of agricultural workers in total population hardly changed during the whole period, hovering around two thirds (Pérez Moreda, 1987, pp. 30-1, 35). The overall rate of urbanization also evolved tardily; in the words of Pérez Moreda, 'between the mid-eighteenth and mid-nineteenth centuries the urban population grew at a pace only slightly greater than that of the population as a whole.' In the second half of the nineteenth century the rate of urbanization accelerated a bit, but remained way below that of more advanced European countries. In this, as in many other aspects, Catalonia showed a different picture. Its population grew much faster between the mid-eighteenth and the mid-nineteenth centuries, moving from being 7 percent of total Spanish population in 1717 to about 11 percent in 1857. In the second half of the nineteenth century Spanish population grew a little faster, and the Catalan rate slowed down, so that Catalonia's demographic share hardly changed between 1850 and 1950. In the second half of the twentieth century the population of Catalonia again grew faster, as we shall see in Chapter 7.

The share of agricultural population in Catalonia went down appreciably faster than in Spain as a whole. By 1900 the Catalan proportion was 48 percent while in all of Spain it was 66 percent. Correspondingly, the share of those active in commerce and industry in Catalonia was higher than in Spain as a whole. Naturally, urbanization rates also differed: by 1900, only 9 percent of Spaniards lived in cities of more than 100,000 inhabitants, while for Catalonia alone the rate was 27 percent. The weight of Barcelona was great. Excluding Barcelona, Catalonia was slightly more rural than Spain as a whole.

There is little doubt that these differences in social, economic, and demographic structures were reflected in the political makeups. For most of the century Barcelona was the only city where the working class, plus the commercial and industrial bourgeoisie, had considerable importance; this favored the Progressive party there to a greater extent than in other cities, even though this party, almost exclusively urban, had a solid implantation throughout Spain. Two more remarks are in order: one, while Progressivism was strong in Barcelona, there were a considerable number of parties and groups to its left, such as democrats, republicans, anarchists, etc.; and two, the Catalan branch of the Progressives, unlike those of the rest of the country, was in favor of tariff protection. The Moderate or Conservative party, on the other hand, was not usually dogmatic in questions of commercial policy, which allowed its leaders to be opportunist and caused little dissension in its ranks. The Moderates veered toward protectionism, but there was neither unanimity nor serious contention in its bosom. Within the Progressives, by contrast, the tariff question caused a real fracture between the Catalans and the rest.

In summary, nineteenth-century Catalonia experienced a remarkable degree of economic development, through a process of industrialization which was especially centered upon the textile industry. As a consequence, there appeared a numerous urban working class and a solid entrepreneurial nucleus; although differing on many issues, both groups shared a strong protectionist sentiment. Outside the cities, however, there was a much more backward rural world where reactionary movements often found favor. This clear dichotomy of Catalan society has not always been recognized by historians. The differences in social makeup between Catalonia and the rest of Spain were sharply reflected in the political history of the nineteenth century, as we shall presently see.

Reactionary Catalonia: The *Carlist* Wars

In March 1814 Fernando VII returned to Spain from Valençay, in southern France. The liberal deputies in the *Cortes*, now assembled in Madrid, expected him to swear the Constitution as soon as he arrived. These were new Cortes, after elections in 1813, and they were deeply divided, as the country was. The conservatives had regrouped and they clamored for the return of absolutism and the abolition of the Constitution. This was exactly what Fernando had in mind. In the words of Stanley Payne (1973, p. 428),

> He proved in many ways the basest king in Spanish history. Cowardly, selfish, grasping, suspicious, and vengeful, D. Fernando seemed almost incapable of any perception of the commonweal. He thought only in

> terms of his power and security and was unmoved by the enormous sacrifices of Spanish people to retain their independence and preserve his throne.

Reluctant to swear the Constitution, instead of going to Madrid straightaway, Fernando followed a zigzag way through Catalonia, then to Zaragoza, and ended up in Valencia. It is apparent that he expected a better and more congenial reception in the lands of the old kingdom of Aragon than in Castile. He was right: in Valencia he was handed a message from reactionary deputies asking for the restoration of absolute monarchy. He also received the homage of anti-liberal generals guaranteeing their support for the restoration of absolutism and the disbanding of the Cortes. This is exactly what he did with a decree he issued in May, just before entering Madrid to the delirious reception of the rabble which shouted '*Vivan las caenas*' (Long live chains – misspelled). Payne calls this 'the first direct military intervention in modern Spanish government, the overthrow of the constitutional system by the army'. Fernando immediately proceeded to persecute and imprison liberals and constitutionalists throughout the country. Three years later, Lacy, the hero of independence in Catalonia, rebelled and was shot by Fernando's generals.

But the winds of history blew, although intermittently, in favor of the liberals: on 1 January 1820 an army was quartered in Andalucia waiting to be shipped across the Atlantic to fight against the independence movement in South America. Some battalions headed by coronel Rafael del Riego rebelled and asked the king to restore and swear de Constitution. The movement was slow to develop, but it was supported in other regions and finally Fernando was forced to take 'the constitutional path', as he himself put it. Thus started the period known to historians as the 'Liberal Triennium', when 'moderate' and 'exalted' liberals fought incessantly in the Cortes and in the streets, while the economy deteriorated. The politicians should not be totally blamed for the economic morass: after the Napoleonic wars there was a prolonged depression, and no Spanish politician of the time was intellectually equipped to find a short-term remedy to it. At any rate, the constant squabbling between both wings of liberalism was no help at all and prevented the possibility of enacting reforms which might have helped improve the situation. Peasant discontent spread and fostered the apparition of banditry and guerrillas. Early in 1823 the reactionary monarchies in Europe (practically all save Britain) decided to put an end to the liberal regime in Spain to prevent contagion. France was commissioned to carry out the assignment, something it did very willingly. A French army known as 'The One Hundred Thousand Sons of Saint Louis', headed by the duke of Angouleme (nephew of Louis XVIII), crossed the Pyrenees and found, unlike Napoleon fifteen years before, little effective popular resistance. Angouleme crossed the Peninsula to Cadiz, where the liberal government had taken refuge with the king. This time the French army entered Cadiz, disbanded the government, and restored Ferdinand as absolute monarch, to his entire satisfaction. He abolished all the 'Triennium' legislation, declared the three years as non-existent ('the three wrongly called years' was his expression), persecuted liberals fiercely, and hanged Riego. 'They won't be able to say "long live Riego" any more', he declared in a typical show of coarse and grisly humor. The reactionary Angouleme was horrified at Fernando's savagery, all the more so since he had made him promise leniency with the vanquished.

This was the liberals' second failure in less than ten years. Absolutism in its most despotic version was restored in 1814 amid popular enthusiasm, with much more ardor in the streets than when the Constitution was restored in 1820, and when a French army invaded Spain for a second time, it was received with indifference, even with sympathy, contrasting with the ferocity which the Napoleonic army encountered in 1808. The lack of popular support for liberalism can be explained in part by the errors of the Triennium politicians; but at bottom the problem was one of pure and simple backwardness. For a famished and illiterate populace the virtues of an advanced liberal Constitution were just incomprehensible, unlike the sermons of the parish curates, whom the vast majority of the people listened to each Sunday, condemning liberalism, equating it with atheism and impiety, and praising the conjunction of the altar and the throne. Paraphrasing Marx, one can say that for them the Cadiz Constitution was a just a wet rag compared to an actual flesh and blood king. The constitutionalist liberals were truly admirable in leading the resistance of the new nation against the immensely more powerful Napoleon and in undertaking the ambitious reform program embodied in the Constitution of 1812 and all the accompanying legislation, but the truth is that all these feats, plus their moral and intellectual superiority, were little appreciated by an ignorant and backward people whose shallowness and idiocy were epitomized in the wretched motto they proffered in 1814: 'long live chains'. The exasperating slowness at which Spanish liberalism progressed in the nineteenth century was due to the tardy pace at which the economy and the intellect progressed during that period.

The ten-year absolutist period which followed the second French invasion (called by the liberals the 'Ominous decade') ended with the death of Ferdinand and was characterized by the tug-of-war between moderate reformers and extreme absolutists. Incredible though it may seem, Ferdinand was blasted from the right. His brother Carlos headed this faction and, as Ferdinand had no children until very late in life, Carlos was expected by the 'apostólicos' (the name those of the extreme right gave themselves) to succeed him on the throne. The *apostólicos* (later *carlistas*) made an early show of strength with the so-called *War of the Aggrieved* whose main theater was Catalonia. This was a rebellion led by disgruntled priests and reactionaries who were aggrieved because Fernando had not fully restored the Inquisition and in some cases had preferred to appoint able men rather than orthodox *apostólicos*. The rebellion was soon quelled with Fernando's customary ferocity; in this he was helped by the count of España, an aristocrat of French origin (his family name was Espagnac de Ramefort), a sadistic soldier who remained as captain general of Catalonia and terrorized his subjects, who called him 'The Tiger of Catalonia'.

After three marriages without issue, Fernando married one more time in 1829. His new wife was his Italian niece Maria Cristina de Borbón. He was 45, she 23. He was anxious to have children and signed a 'Pragmatic Sanction' abrogating the French 'Salic Law' privileging the male line for hereditary rights. He thus made sure that if he had descendants they would reign. This time the marriage bore fruit: two daughters, Isabel (1830) and Luisa Fernanda (1832).

Fernando VII died on 30 September 1833. Isabel was proclaimed queen and her mother regent. Immediately Don Carlos rose in Portugal declaring the Pragmatic Sanction null and void and proclaiming his right to succeed his deceased brother. His manifesto found and echo in the Basque country and Catalonia, where small bands of *carlistas* took up arms. Spain thus followed the path of Portugal, where the ultraconservative Miguel of Bragança had been fighting his niece, queen Maria da Gloria, who was supported by the liberals.

Carlismo is therefore a movement which can be compared to *miguelismo* in Portugal and also to the French *Vendée*, a reactionary insurgence originating in poor agrarian communities which fought against the revolution in the name of strict Catholicism and absolute Monarchy. These absolutist and ultra-Catholic rebellions were reactions against the social changes that revolution and liberalism brought about. They also had an economic component: traditional peasants protested against new taxes, payable in coin and not in specie, as was the case of the traditional tithe. They also had a 'legitimist' character in that they fought for a 'legitimate' king.

In Spain, interestingly, *carlismo* took root in the area which Napoleon had tried to annex (i.e., the band between the Pyrenees and the Ebro river). The only important Carlist nucleus south of the river was in the *Maestrazgo* region, in Castellón, just adjacent. Carlists also failed to take a single large town, although they repeatedly laid siege to Bilbao. The Carlist wars have always been seen as civil wars, and so they were; but they were not only national civil wars (the Madrid governments against the insurgents); they were also regional wars, fights between liberals and Carlists in the Basque country, Navarre, and Catalonia. It is also remarkable that Carlism was popular in *foral* regions: Catalonia, which had lost its *fueros* a century before, and the Basque country and Navarre which still had them although threatened by the consolidation of the liberal state. By contrast, Galicia, where Don Carlos had planned to establish his quarters because it was close to Portugal and the nobility sympathetic, was unresponsive. In general, the popular support Carlism found in the Basque country, Navarre, and Catalonia was that of modest, but not miserable peasants attached to the Catholic Church, and averse to paying taxes in coin, something especially burdensome in a time of falling grain prices.

The persistence of Carlism in nineteenth-century politics is one more symptom of the near total stagnation of the Spanish economy and society, especially in the first half and especially in agriculture. The social composition and outlook of the peasantry changed little for a long period. And even in Catalonia, where industry and trade developed, the interior remained quite static. Something similar could be said about the Basque Country, whose coastal area developed commercially and late industrially, while the interior remained backward. It was in the mountainous hinterlands of Catalonia, the Basque Country and Navarre, plus the also mountainous Maestrazgo, that Carlism thrived.

The Slow Establishment of the Liberal System

By the Quadruple Alliance of 1834 Britain and France supported the liberal governments in Portugal and Spain in their struggle against *miguelismo* and *carlismo*. The alliance put an almost immediate end to *miguelismo*, and brought about financial and even logistic and military support to the cause of María Cristina, the Spanish queen regent. Under the umbrella of the alliance, the Rothschilds (both the British and French branches) lent some 380 million *reales* (about 3.8 million pounds sterling) to the Spanish governments with the guarantee of the Almaden mercury mines between June 1834 and December 1840 (López Morell, 2013, pp. 100-101). In spite of this substantial support, plus the efforts and sacrifices of the Spanish people, the Carlist War was prolonged until July 1840, when Ramon Cabrera, the last *carlista* warlord, called by friend and foe the *Tiger of the Maestrazgo*, harassed by the liberal troops of general Baldomero Espartero, crossed the Pyrenees from Catalonia. Almost a year before, in August 1839, the war was ended in the North with the 'Embrace of Vergara', when Espartero and the troops of the *carlista* general Rafael Maroto, agreed on a capitulation whereby the *carlistas* deposed their arms in exchange for a compromise of the Madrid government to respect the *fueros* in so far as they did not contradict the Constitution (the new, less radical Constitution of 1837) and to admit the officers of the *ex-carlista* army into the regular Spanish army with their equivalent ranks.

Carlism was able not only to keep Spain in a state of civil war for almost eight years (1833–1840), but to fight again between September 1846 and May 1849 mostly in Catalonia (Second Carlist War), and between April 1872 and February 1876, mostly in the Basque country and Navarre (Third Carlist War). Civil war, therefore, was endemic during the central decades of the century, although the second and third wars were shorter and had a more opportunistic character.

Espartero was the great winner in 1840. He joined the Progressive party and soon found himself at odds with the queen regent, who clearly favored the Moderate party. Their disagreement became evident when the Moderates submitted a bill on municipal administration to the Cortes. The bill proposed to leave the appointment of mayors to the Crown, instead of to popular election. Espartero and María Cristina were in Barcelona, where the general was received with delirious enthusiasm after the defeat of Cabrera. The demonstrators also showed their rejection of the municipal bill. The Moderates had a majority in the Cortes, so they had the bill approved anyway, something which provoked angry protests in Madrid. María Cristina correctly interpreted these demonstrations as evidence of her unpopularity and decided to resign and flee to exile, leaving her infant daughters in Spain. Espartero was soon elected regent by the Cortes. He lasted three years in the post, where he showed himself as politically incompetent as María Cristina, throwing away his political capital, and managing to unite Moderates and Progressives, Catalans and Castilians, against him. By 1842 Barcelona was demonstrating again, but this time against Espartero, and when he lost the elections in 1843 and tried to force new ballots, there were riots and a military rising which forced him to flee to exile, just as María Cristina had done three years before.

The victorious anti-Espartero coalition found itself faced with a puzzle: Isabel was still a child of 13, and the two regencies which took care of government during her minority had ended in failure. There were no suitable and generally acceptable candidates in sight for a third regency, so a desperate measure was taken: Isabel was declared of age in November 1843. The consequences were terrible. A child-queen was liable to be controlled by whatever adults took care of her; a tug-of-war developed immediately between the Moderates, who were in close contact with the queen mother in exile, María Cristina, and the Progressives, who had appointed the personnel near Isabel when Espartero was regent. The French and British ambassadors actively supported the parties, the French the Moderates, the British the Progressives. The Moderates finally won: the civilian head of the Progressives, Salustiano Olózaga, was (wrongly) accused of '*lèse majesté*' and forced to escape into exile. María Cristina wanted to come back and take care of her queen-child, but there were serious problems in letting her back because she was extremely unpopular. Aside from her own political clumsiness, her private life left a lot to be desired.

Sexual scandals had plagued the Bourbon royal family from the times of Charles IV. Queen María Luisa, his wife, became infatuated with a member of her husband's guard, Manuel Godoy, who became a sort of stepchild of the royal couple and all-powerful minister, to the jealousy and rage of the crown prince Fernando. This conflict greatly facilitated Napoleon's machinations about the Spanish throne in 1808. The royal *ménage-à-trois* was popularly despised, and Fernando became the idol of the masses (they called him *el Deseado*, the desired one). This explains his delirious reception in Madrid in 1814. However, be it a case of poetic justice or of elective affinities, María Cristina, Fernando's last wife, fell for the charms of a royal guard as her mother in law had previously done. She married her paramour in not very decent haste, after Fernando's death, during the period of mourning; so the marriage had to be in secret. But she had a series of children with Fernando Muñoz, her second husband, something quite difficult to hide from the public. Later on, finding good posts, sinecures, and advantageous marriages for her children by her second marriage became one of her main occupations, together with ennobling and enriching her morganatic husband.

In spite of her unpopularity, she returned in March 1844, soon after her daughter became officially queen, and as she took matters in hand, María Cristina made what was the greatest blunder of her lackluster political career. Traditionally the Moderates were Francophile and the Progressives Anglophile. María Cristina not only sympathized wholeheartedly with the moderates, but during her exile in France she had become a close friend to king Louis Philippe of Orleans, who helped and protected her. In addition, while in France she had also been in constant contact with the Moderate conspirators, headed by general Ramón Narváez, who schemed to oust Espartero, something they managed to do, in cooperation with a majority of Progressives, in 1843.

With the persecution of Olózaga, the Moderates became masters of the situation. Whoever controlled the queen controlled the Cortes, because she had the power to dissolve them and appoint the provisional government to oversee elections; and thanks to political bossism and 'rotten boroughs' (*caciquismo*), the party in charge of elections was practically sure to win. With María Cristina near her daughter and the Moderado personnel in the Royal Palace, Isabel was sure to keep the Moderates in power. Thus started the 'Moderate decade' with Ramón Narváez, the conservative strongman, either in government or in control of the situation most of the time.

The next important political problem was the marriage of the queen. There were many possibilities, and María Cristina finally chose the worst possible one: that was her great blunder. Isabel wanted to marry a cousin, Don Enrique, duke of Seville, but he was too liberal for the queen mother and for the Moderates. There were a series of other possibilities: one was another cousin, the son of Don Carlos. This was more to the liking of the conservatives, and it would probably have definitively solved the Carlist problem. But the Progressives were adamantly opposed. Then there were the sons of Louis Philippe, but the British opposed this; in retaliation, the French vetoed a prince of the Saxe-Cobourg house, related to the British royal family. In the end, the worst possible candidate was chosen: Don Francisco de Asís, brother of Don Enrique, but very different from him: he was almost a cripple, impotent, homosexual, politically reactionary, and an insignificant but devious character to boot. Isabel disliked him and the more so after knowing him intimately. They married in 1846 and not only the relations of the newlyweds were strained from the beginning, the relations of the queen with her mother also became more distant, as Isabel blamed María Cristina for her disastrous marriage. From then on Isabel had numerous extramarital affairs which the Court and governments tried to cover up with little success. The same day Isabel married Francisco de Asís, her sister Luisa Fernanda married the duke of

Montpensier, son of Louis Philippe, to the displeasure of the British government. Until the end of his life Montpensier intrigued to have Isabel replaced by Luisa Fernanda, his wife.

One of the consequences of all these scandals was that both the queen and her mother became personally and intimately dependent upon the Catholic Church. They needed the Church's help to have their sins pardoned and, in the case of María Cristina, to have her secret marriage recognized and sanctified. This gave the Church enormous power over Spanish politics, and it used it, especially in matters concerning Church property, taxation, civil law, education, relations with other confessions, etc. These simple family matters, which seem no more than gossip material, turned out to be of paramount importance during the lamentable reign of Isabel II and contributed powerfully to put an end to it when she was 38 years of age (Burdiel, 2010, esp. Chs. 3 and 4).

In the political situation described, the Progressive party became a pariah, de facto ostracized and rejected beyond the pale. It could not govern because the queen would never give it the charge of overseeing elections. Its only real possibility of reaching power was through a military *pronunciamiento*, a coup. This is one of the reasons why it depended so much on generals. Another consequence of this situation is that, as the only party of government, the Moderates were divided into numerous factions, from the extreme right to the center left, or almost. During the early 1850s the 'leftwing' Moderates coalesced with tepid Progressives to form the Liberal Union, a center group which hoped to reach power and carry out reforms without the total opposition of the Court and the Palace. The brain of the Unionists was Antonio Cánovas del Castillo, a young journalist, and its star general was Leopoldo O'Donnell. In the summer of 1854 O'Donnell and some fellow military staged a coup in Madrid hoping to rally support from centrists of both parties. After a brief indecisive skirmish in Vicálvaro, outside Madrid, with loyalist troops, the rebel column moved away. Cánovas then wrote a manifesto in Manzanares, a town in La Mancha, which succeeded in gaining the support of the Progressives. The coup finally succeeded, and a new government was formed with Espartero as president and O'Donnell as minister of defense. Two years of uneasy cooperation ensued, with the Unionists resentful of having been elbowed aside from center stage by the Progressives and these busily enacting their ambitious reform program. Thanks to the new legislation, the economy was revived after the depression which followed the crisis of 1848. But cohabitation lasted only two years (historians call it 'the Progressive Biennium'); Espartero's political maladroitness and naiveté made it easy for the queen to force his resignation in the summer of 1856; the Progressives were ousted and O'Donnell and Narváez alternated in power for the next twelve years.

After 1864, however, things started to go sour: a fearsome crisis shook the Spanish economy after railroads, and banks became insolvent and budget deficits mounted. There were riots and police and army brutality in the episode called 'the night of St. Daniel', when the police indiscriminately shot students and passersby in Madrid. O'Donnell resigned and Narváez assumed power to repress discontent by any means. A group of Unionist and Progressive military men (led by generals Juan Prim, a Progressive, and Francisco Serrano, a Unionist, and admiral Juan Francisco Topete, a Unionist too), with the support of civilian politicians and intellectuals, prepared a new *pronunciamiento*, which took place in September 1868. Narváez had died of natural causes a few months earlier, which probably made things easier for the conspirators. The coup (known as the '*Gloriosa Revolución*') was successful. Isabel left Spain never to come back. She had been respected in her post in 1854, but after her tricks in 1856, the revolutionaries, whose motto was '*España con honra*' (Spain with honor), did not want to see her or any member of the Bourbon dynasty on the throne again.

The revolutionaries inherited a very difficult situation, with the crisis raging and the Treasury's coffers empty. They undertook a courageous reformist program, which achieved what the Progressives had initiated in 1854. The economic team was almost the same as then, with economists Laureano Figuerola and Pascual Madoz as the most distinguished members. The monetary reform making the peseta the center of the system, and the tariff reform introducing a gradual lowering of duties deserve special mention and were the work of Figuerola as minister of Finance. The tariff law contained a series of basic principles, called bases instead of articles. The number 5 basis contained the gradual rebate principle, and it became the nemesis of protectionists. But it was the budget problem, with a gaping deficit and a galloping increase of the public debt, which remained intractable. The political problem also became a nightmare. A new, democratic constitution was enacted in 1869, which kept the monarchy at the apex of the state; the problem, however, was to find an adequate monarch. Meanwhile, Serrano became regent and Prim president. But then the centrifugal tendencies recurrent in Spanish history surfaced again: by the time an Italian prince of the Savoy house (Amedeo duke of Aosta, son of king Vittorio Emmanuele II of Italy – who became Amadeo I) had been elected, Prim was assassinated in 1870, probably at the instigation of Montpensier. A secessionist rebellion raged in Cuba since 1868, and then in April 1872 the third Carlist War started. Public finances were in chaos, and Amadeo had lost Prim, who had been the mastermind of his designation and the man of maximum prestige, the only who might possibly have solved the situation. Things went from bad to worse: the revolutionary International made inroads, public disorder increased, and the situation looked so hopeless that Amadeo abdicated in 1873. An unstable Republic was voted by the Cortes in February, and pandemonium broke loose: the division between centralist and federalist republicans impelled the southern federalists to open a third front, with *cantonalist* rebellions breaking out in several towns, the most famous in Cartagena. The Republic lasted less than one year, and it had four successive presidents. On 3 January 1874 general Manuel Pavía dissolved the Cortes and made Serrano 'provisional president of the Republic'; it was in fact a provisional dictatorship whose mission was to put an end to the chaos created by the federalists. The new government obtained a big loan from the Bank of Spain with which it was able to reinforce the military in order to defeat the Carlists and the cantonalists.

The plan gave satisfactory results, but before its mission was accomplished in its entirety (the last cantonalist redoubt, Cartagena, surrendered in December 1874), a new coup, this one by general Arsenio Martínez Campos, proclaimed *Alfonso de Borbón*, son of the deposed queen Isabel, king of Spain in the early days of 1875. This was the beginning of the 'Restoration', which lasted until the II Republic was proclaimed in April 1931. If Martínez Campos was the sword which imposed the Restoration, Cánovas del Castillo was the brain that prepared the terrain and made it possible. In fact, although Cánovas did not approve of what he considered to be a rash action on the part of Martínez Campos, the general acknowledged the authority of Cánovas and let him assume full responsibility for organizing the new regime. Soon after the Glorious Revolution of 1868 Cánovas had started preparing the restoration of the Bourbon dynasty in the person of young Alfonso. He managed to take his education from the hands of Isabel and send him to England where he should learn the workings of constitutional monarchy. He also quietly reorganized the disoriented and demoralized monarchists and, above all, he obtained the abdication of Isabel, thus clearing the path for the legitimate succession of her son.

Cánovas's ideology was liberal-conservative, and this was reflected in the 1876 Constitution, which gave the king ample powers, although he needed the approval of a bicameral parliament for issuing legislation and for a series of important decisions. Cánovas abolished male universal suffrage, which had been established by the Revolution and went back to limited suffrage of males paying a minimum amount of tax. Cánovas had carefully studied the flaws of Isabel's monarchy and made a conscious effort to avoid them. Probably his greatest contribution to the stability of the Restoration system was what has been called 'the peaceful turn of the parties'. In order for this to function he collaborated in the creation of a Liberal party which would function as the opposition to his Conservative party. To head the Liberal party he found the ideal man, Práxedes Mateo Sagasta, who had been one of the main progressive ministers under Amadeo I. For the peaceful alternation of parties he made a pact with Sagasta, whereby, after a prudential time in power, if one of the parties felt a change was needed, the president would resign and recommend dissolution to the king, and new elections with the opposition party in charge of overseeing the ballot. This agreed periodical renewal would make *pronunciamientos* unnecessary and hence would eliminate the intervention of soldiers in politics. The 'peaceful turn' worked quite well as long as Cánovas and Sagasta were alive and social conditions remained what they were, but in the twentieth century all this changed. Cánovas was assassinated in 1897 and Sagasta died naturally in 1903. Economic growth gathered pace and social conditions started to change fast, the defeat in the Spanish-American war (1898) marked the end of Spain's colonial empire, Catalan and Basque nationalism developed, and new parties came to the fore. The Restoration slowly came unstuck in the twentieth century.

Catalonia's Political Weight

> We Catalans have always been very skillful in handling Tariffs and in knowing how to defend our interests. Sometimes this defense has been exaggerated and, therefore harmful and unfair. The superiority of Catalans over Spanish politicians, and even over officials, was so great that, in the tariff debate, the victory of the former was almost always guaranteed (Cambó, 1981, p. 346).

Some historians (see, for instance, Fontana, 2014, pp. 282-3; Balcells, 2004, pp. 611-2, and 1991, pp. 16-8) claim than Catalonia was sidelined by the Spanish parliamentary liberal regime in the nineteenth century. Evidence, however, does not support this statement. Catalonia, as Francesc Cambó (a lawyer from the province of Gerona who studied in Barcelona and soon became one of the leaders of conservative Catalanism) implied in the former quotation, had a substantial political weight in Spain during the whole nineteenth century (and the same goes for the twentieth), and we will devote this section to showing how true this was.

We have already seen that the social and economic structure of nineteenth-century Catalonia exhibited distinctive traits which made it different from that of the rest of Spain. These differences could not but be reflected in the political sphere. Aside from the Carlist question, Catalonia played a distinctive role in the formulation and execution of Spanish policies throughout the whole period. In all our discussion, however, we must always remember that speaking of Catalonia as a whole is only a language shortcut which considerably misrepresents reality, for one of the characteristics of this community was that it was profoundly divided, something which made for contradictory effects at several historical junctures.

When speaking about Catalan Carlism we saw that there was a great chasm between rural areas, deeply conservative and reactionary, and the cities, mostly liberal. But within liberalism there were considerable differences also. Industrial workers, not only in Barcelona but also in the countryside, on riverbank areas where many factories were located to take advantage of water power, had a vision of progressivism to the left and more prone to mutinies and demonstrations than that of bourgeois entrepreneurs, merchants, traders, and intellectuals who militated or sympathized with the same party.

We also saw that Fernando VII found in the old kingdom of Aragon the support he was searching for his *coup d'état* against the Cortes in May 1814. Nevertheless, during the first absolutism period of Fernando's reign, Catalonia gave signs of hostility to the absolutist regime. Lacy found support for his *pronunciamiento* against tyranny there, and when he was captured and condemned to death, Barcelona's guilds and industrial associations dared to ask for his reprieve, citing the 'inconceivable wisdom' with which he governed Catalonia during the War of Independence (Vicens, 1961, p. 214). And three years after he was shot, after Fernando swore the Constitution, there was a solemn funeral in his honor in Barcelona in 1820.

Catalonia took no active part in Riego's *pronunciamiento* which reinstated the constitutional regime, but it is clear that the Catalan bourgeoisie, especially those from Barcelona, were dead set against absolutism, if only because Fernando's capriciousness moved him to violate his own laws, such as, for instance, his own prohibition to import textile products, as he did in 1815 when he authorized an Andalusian company to do exactly that. There was enthusiasm in the streets of Barcelona when the Constitution was restored, especially when the *Cortes* of the *Trienio* introduced prohibitions to import wheat and textiles. 'Only this constitutional system guarantees to Catalonia the assurance of prohibitions and, with them, its prosperity and wealth', said the *Diario de Barcelona* (cited by Sánchez, 2000, p. 515).

It may seem surprising that a liberal regime should issue prohibitionist legislation, but this kind of regulation became widespread at the time due to the deflationary tendencies after the Napoleonic wars; furthermore, after losing most of its American empire, Spain lacked the resources to finance large commercial deficits. In spite of all this, Catalonia soon became disappointed with the Liberal Triennium: for the liberals, the Madrid Cortes were too centralist, and for the peasants the land tax in coin became a heavy burden. Riots and banditry returned to the Catalan countryside in support of absolutism. The cooling of constitutional feeling in Catalonia goes a long way to explain why the invading French army had no problem in crossing it in 1823.

The return of absolutism and the terror it inspired quieted tempers for a while, but soon the most reactionary forces in Catalonia rebelled against Fernando VII in 1827 because they thought he was leaning toward liberalism. This was the brief 'War of the Aggrieved', where the rebels were defeated and harshly punished. Although their insurrection not only failed but was counterproductive (Fernando became suspicious of extreme reaction in his last years), it shows how extreme Catalonia's conservatism was. Probably as a punishment, Catalonia remained submitted to the cruelty of the count of España for several years after the quelling of the rebellion.

Things improved when España was replaced in 1832 by general Manuel Llauder, a somewhat liberal soldier and a native from Catalonia. He soon connected with the more enlightened circles in Barcelona and decisively contributed to make the regime evolve from absolutism toward liberalism. In December 1833, three months after Fernando VII's death, he wrote a memorandum to the queen regent asking for liberal reforms and especially for a summoning of the Cortes. This decided María Cristina to remove the last absolutist government and replace it with a moderately liberal cabinet, where Llauder held the Defense portfolio.

But Llauder did not last long, and it was disturbances in Catalonia which prompted his resignation. The divisions within Catalonia now became too evident. Carlism raged in the countryside. The urbanites were all against Carlism, but they were divided between moderate and radical liberals. These last ones hated Llauder whom they viewed as one more absolutist. The summer of 1835 was a very hot one in Catalonia and particularly in Barcelona. While Llauder was in the field combatting the Carlists, the rabble in the city rioted, burned convents, factories, and tax offices, and assassinated a general sent by Llauder with the mission of pacifying the city. The Barcelona turmoil caused the fall of the Toreno ministry and the assumption of power of Juan A. Mendizábal. Mendizábal was the more energetic and clear-headed politician in the Spain of the 1830s (for a short description of his record Tortella and García Ruiz, 2013, pp. 32-3). His name is forever linked to the word *desamortización.*

In Catholic countries the Church and the nobility owned very large amounts of land, a legacy from the Middle Ages. In Protestant countries the Church had been dispossessed in the sixteenth century, and the land problem there was perhaps not as acute. The French Revolution expropriated the lands of the Church and sold them to sustain a bankrupted state. Most other continental countries imitated France in this issue sooner or later. In Spain, since the mid-eighteenth century, the growth of population had made the land problem more pressing. Church and noble owners were called *manos muertas* –'dead hands', or mortmain – because most of their lands were entailed and could not be sold. Specialists in the topic spoke about *tierras amortizadas*. Since the eighteenth century enlightened and liberal thinkers had called for the 'disamortization' of these estates. Some timid steps were taken in this direction, most notably by Godoy. But it was Mendizábal who in 1836 carried out a systematic program of 'disamortization' of Church lands, with a triple objective: first, to facilitate access to land ownership to people of certain means who would manage their property better than priests and monks, and therefore, increase crop output; second, to produce a flow of funds to the Treasury, which would pay for the military expenditure needed to win the war; and third, to make the new owners enthusiastic supporters of the government in its fight against the Carlists, who were dead set against 'despoiling' the Church. Of course, these lands were not confiscated; compensation was paid, but it was paid in public debt bonds for the most part. Nevertheless, from that time on the state guaranteed the support of the Catholic Church.

Mendizábal found strong backing for his program among Catalan progressives and especially among factory owners. As Vicens (1961, p. 232) put it,

> Even those men who [. . .] were offended in their Catalan dignity by the burning of convents on 25 July in Barcelona, did not feel the least

> hesitation in acquiring vast ecclesiastical estates. One could say that, at that moment of expansion of industry in Barcelona, each factory owner had in mind a convent where he could install his looms.

A good example of Catalonia's, and especially Barcelona's, power was the episode we already referred to, when María Cristina resigned her post and Espartero replaced her as regent in the summer of 1840. Aside from her political incompetence, the decisive factor was the enthusiastic endorsement Espartero received when he entered the city and for several days thereafter, enthusiasm that degenerated into violence, which frightened the queen regent and finally determined her to flee in October. It is true that Madrid rioted also after the municipal law was passed. But Barcelona was the first and most important scenario, where Espartero was even solemnly named 'National Hero'. By then, according to Vicens (1961, pp.243), a euphoric Catalonia saw itself as the redoubt from where the Catalan liberals 'could exercise a decisive influence over the rest of Spain, whose pulse did not beat at the same rhythm. This would be a constant idea of nineteenth-century Catalan liberalism: Catalonia, land of freedom, would make Spain to become liberal'.

Disappointment soon set in, however. Espartero, as the head of the Progressive Party, was in close contact with the British embassy, and was under its pressure to lower tariffs. France, on the other hand, hosted Maria Cristina, who conspired to return with the help of the Moderate Party, one of whose factions plotted a failed coup in 1841. In order to curry British favor Espartero passed a new tariff that same year which, although still very protectionist and including outright prohibitions on the importation of textiles, grain, iron goods, etc., was very badly received in Barcelona. The former Catalan support for the 'National Hero' quickly turned into hostility, all the more so since there were rumors that the Spanish and British governments were negotiating a commercial treaty. The rumors were accurate, but the treaty was never signed. The truth is that Catalan textile producers were not ready to make the slightest concession to Spanish exporters of wines and fruits, which were subject to British retaliation for the Spanish protection of textiles. So that was how Catalonia, 'land of freedom', was making 'Spain to become liberal': by sacrificing Spanish exporters for the convenience of textile industrialists. It should be clear, however, that there were Catalans who decried this egoism, economists mainly, people such as Figuerola and Joaquín M. Sanromá, perhaps the most acute critic of the mill owners' selfishness.

Another issue which poisoned relations between Espartero and Barcelona was that of the Citadel which had been built on orders of Felipe V after the War of Succession in a razed area north of the city. The Citadel was seen by many as a symbol of oppression, and there were plans to tear it down at the government's expense. For a soldier as Espartero, the destruction of an army fortress was anathema; so when a municipal officer organized a symbolic ceremony of pulling out of a first stone, the municipal junta was disbanded and the organizers of the ceremony persecuted. This increased the hard feelings toward Espartero. In November 1842 all these ill feelings in Barcelona exploded in the form of riots against excise taxes. There were attempts to negotiate with the leaders of the rebellion, but Espartero was inflexible and ordered the bombing of the city from the southern castle of Montjuic. The firing lasted for eleven hours, some twelve people were killed, about thirty houses destroyed, and about 300 damaged. The rebels surrendered; some fifteen of them were summarily shot, and the city was compelled to pay for repairs of the Citadel and for all damages caused by the gunfire. In fact, the city paid only a part.

Espartero thought he would be received in Madrid as a hero, but he was badly mistaken. He read the omens wrong (a contemporary historian and politician, Francisco Pi y Margall, wrote that 'he read no newspapers') and called for new elections hoping to win by a landslide. He did not get a majority, could not form a government, and tried to dissolve the Cortes and call for elections again; this was just too much. Moderates and Progressives coalesced against him and a series of rebellions took place in numerous important cities along the Mediterranean coast. In Barcelona the leaders were two generals, Juan Prim and Francisco Serrano, who now was treated in Barcelona with the same effervescence as Espartero had been just three years before. The Barcelona Junta (a semi-official body of Progressive notables) appointed him 'Universal Minister'. The first act of the 'Universal Minister' was to issue a decree demoting Espartero from his post of regent. 'Barcelona then was back in its role as the center of Spanish politics' wrote a distinguished Catalan historian (Soldevila, 1959, VIII, pp. 164-5). Narváez landed in Valencia and rode to Madrid at the head of a small army, finding little resistance; the troops supposedly faithful to Espartero joined Narváez in droves. After a few months, the Moderates were in full control; thus started the long *Moderate Decade* under the aegis of Narváez, who soon became duke of Valencia.

The Moderate Decade started under hopeful economic signs: the end of the Carlist War and the disamortization had produced a hefty *peace dividend*: the Treasury's coffers, if certainly not overflowing, were in better shape than they had been for decades, the stock exchange was booming, banks and companies were being established, and the first plans for building a railroad network were being blueprinted. In 1845 a profound reform of the tax system introduced order and transparency in the public accounts, contributing to inspire confidence. In Madrid and Barcelona two important banks were established in 1844, the *Banco de Isabel II* and the *Banco de Barcelona*, respectively. The construction of three railroad lines (in Barcelona, Madrid, and Asturias) started at around this time. At that time two financiers stood out, one in Madrid, José Salamanca (Bank of Isabel II), one in Barcelona, Manuel Girona (Bank of Barcelona). Both were probably the most outstanding in their field in the whole nineteenth century, with the possible exception of the Urquijo family. In many ways, Salamanca and Girona personify the characters of their countries of origin. Salamanca, an Andalusian established in Madrid, was daring, dashing, adventurous, ostentatious; Girona, always established in Barcelona, was sober, prudent, cautious, discreet, self-effacing (Tortella and García Ruiz, 2013, pp. 36-46).

The postwar boom of the mid-1840s ended abruptly with the crisis of 1848, which provoked a stock-exchange crash and many bankruptcies. In Spain, unlike in several other European nations, there was no revolution: Narváez was in power and mercilessly suppressed any attempt at rebellion. Only in Catalonia the Second Carlist War, which took place almost exclusively there and counted with the collaboration of Cabrera, who came back from exile, occasioned scenes of savagery on both sides, and posed a threat to the government; it ended when Cabrera was defeated and wounded in 1849 and had to re-cross the Pyrenees, this time forever. He established himself in England, where he married a rich lady, admired the British constitutional system, and abandoned his Carlist principles. During the Third Carlist War he recommended to those who consulted him to accept Alfonso XII and the constitutional monarchy.

The bitter atmosphere after the Second Carlist War and the sequels of the 1848 crisis favored the *pronunciamiento* of O'Donnell in the summer of 1854. Cánovas's manifesto of Manzanares contained a series of concessions to well-known wishes and tenets of the Catalan progressives (a promise to do away with 'centralization', to favor the creation of 'Juntas', and of course a call for new elections) which found their echo in Barcelona, where troops and people took to the streets supporting the manifesto and jeering the government. Other cities followed, and even in Madrid, three days later, a multitude assaulted the houses of the prime minister and of Salamanca, who escaped disguised as a railwayman. There was a national clamor against the government, but, as Vicens pointed out, Barcelona led the way in provoking its fall.

The *Progressive Biennium* only lasted two years, although these were years of intense legislative activity: the most important laws enacted were those relative to General Disamortization (i.e., affecting not only the lands of the Church but also those of the nobility and the public domain), Railroads, and Banks. Unfortunately the tenure of the Progressives was too short, so they did not enjoy the opportunity to administer their legislation. Suffice it to say that thanks to their policies foreign capital was imported, national capital was mobilized, the basic railroad network was built, and the economy in general received a big push. However, a series of factors, both domestic and international, brought about another big crisis which destroyed a large part of what the Progressive legislation had built (Tortella, 1977, Ch. VII; Tortella and García Ruiz, 2013, Ch. 4).

There can be no doubt that the 1864–1868 crisis was the main cause of the Glorious Revolution of 1868. Although the locus of the revolution was Cadiz, it had an immediate echo in most of Spain. There was a brief battle near Córdoba (at the bridge of Alcolea) which the revolutionaries led by Serrano won, thereby finding opened their way to

Madrid, where the revolutionaries had already taken over and the loyalists had fled (the queen was spending the holidays in the Basque Country and from there she crossed into France). Meanwhile, in Barcelona the revolutionaries were also in control. According to Vicens (1961, pp. 273-6), after the discomfiture of 1856, the Barcelona workers had moved to the left and they favored a shift toward democracy. The middle classes were in a 'bad temper' after losing their savings in the crash of 1866. General Prim was now the idol of Barcelona workers and bourgeois alike, the link between Catalan revolutionaries and the 'plotting generals'. In the elections of February 1869 (the first ones in Spain by universal male suffrage) the federalist republicans of Francisco Pi y Margall won clearly in Barcelona.

In fact, says Vicens, after 1868 there were two capitals in Spain, Madrid and Barcelona. Madrid was liberal and centralist, Barcelona democratic and federalist. The discrepancies between the two cities were sharp: *Madrileños* resented that Barcelona should be disputing the political monopoly they had enjoyed since the seventeenth century (when Madrid definitively became the capital). Especially after the Republic was proclaimed, the Madrid newspapers complained that the government was being invaded by Catalans. And he adds: 'Catalonia [. . .] was the great propeller of the September revolution. The Catalans were the beneficiaries of that movement and they tried to impose their desired regime on the rest of Spain. They were bitterly wrong in thinking that the other Spaniards were in agreement with them'.

Here the great historian is simplifying a little. Neither the Catalans nor the rest of Spaniards were of one mind. The revolution unleashed a torrent of energies and ideas, but also a pandemonium of controversy, dissent, and contention in all spheres and regions. It is true that Republican federalism was popular in Catalonia, but so it was, and in extreme form, in the whole Mediterranean coast south of Catalonia. And when in Andalusia, Murcia, and Valencia there were the 'cantonalist' rebellions, many Catalan republicans were horrified, and the Catalan bourgeoisie thought that things had gone way too far. It happened with the 1868 revolution something similar to what had happened at the time of the Espartero regency: some Catalans brought it about and other Catalans brought it down. Vicens himself agrees (1961, p. 279): 'The Bourbon Restoration won because the

Catalan bourgeoisie wished to put an end to the last act of the September [1868] revolution: the First republic [. . .] Some Catalans had made possible the subversive explosion of 1868, and other Catalans brought things back to where they were before . . .'

Arsenio Martínez Campos, appointed captain general of Catalonia by the Republic, had fought the Carlists in the mountains and the radical republicans and internationalists in Barcelona, thus winning the support of the local bourgeoisie and middle classes who now longed for an end to republican chaos. On 29 December 1874 he, at the head of a group of generals in Sagunto, near Valencia, proclaimed support for *Alfonso de Borbón*, Isabel II's son, as the new king of Spain. Martínez Campos's *pronunciamiento* found the support of the majority of military commanders and the tacit approval of a majority of the population. Alfonso, a boy of 17, was recalled from his school in England. It is symptomatic that he landed in Barcelona, where he was received deliriously, especially by the businessmen and business associations. The Catalan industrial and commercial circles for one moment had hoped that Amadeo I could have imposed order. Bitterly disappointed, they then pinned their hopes on a Bourbon restoration. They also wished that the new regime would abolish the mildly liberal Figuerola tariff and its impending first round of tariff rebates (the Fifth Basis), and that the rebellion in Cuba and the Carlist war should be ended as quickly as possible. This explains the almost unanimous support of the most distinguished Catalan industrialists and businessmen for the Bourbon restoration (Cabrera and del Rey, 2002, pp. 24-5). It is telling that the Sagunto *pronunciamiento* should have taken place six months before the time for tariff rebates (July of 1875) arrived, and that one of the first measures taken by the new minister of Finance, Pedro Salaverría, was to suspend the application of the Fifth Basis.

The success of the Cánovas government in solving the problems left over by the revolutionary regimes was remarkable. The last redoubt of cantonalism, Cartagena, had already capitulated in 1874. The Carlists, who had been wiped out of Catalonia by Martínez Campos in 1875, were definitively defeated in the Basque Country in January 1876. The suppression of the Cuban rebellion took three more years, and it was achieved with the financial support of the Barcelona business circles headed by Antonio López (marquis of Comillas), a very wealthy Santander businessman established in Barcelona, and Manuel Girona, of the Bank of Barcelona, who jointly created the Banco Hispano Colonial to make a large loan to the Spanish government in 1876, an advance earmarked for the military operations in Cuba.

But Catalan businessmen remained uneasy because the Figuerola Tariff Law was not abolished, and the Fifth Basis hung over their heads as Damocles's sword. Their mistrust was confirmed when in 1881 the recently created Liberal Party came to power with Sagasta at the helm, and one of the first measures its Finance minister took was to reinstate the Fifth Basis. Catalan deputies were indignant, and even more so when the Cortes received the draft of a commercial agreement with France. In order to placate them, the application of the Fifth Basis was adjourned for ten years; but the greatest concession was the 'Law of Commercial Relations with the Antilles' (1882), which introduced gradual rebates in the duties that Spanish exports to Cuba and Puerto Rico had been paid until then. These islands thus became protected markets for Spanish exports, because imports from other countries remained subject to Spanish tariffs. In retaliation, the United States, whose exports to the Spanish Antilles were badly hurt by the new law, gradually raised its sugar duties, which in turn damaged the interests of Cuban planters. As one can see, many interests were being sacrificed to those of Catalan textile producers. There is a clear coincidence of these tariff wars and the new Cuban rebellion which broke out in Cuba in February 1895 and ended with the defeat of Spain in the Spanish-American War of 1898, the 'Disaster' as it is known to Spanish historians. Nadal (1975, p. 217) suggests that, without the Law of Commercial Relations, 'the *Disaster* of 1898 might not have happened so soon'.

Be it as it may, the Catalan campaign against the mild liberal reforms of the Tariff and commercial treaties continued unabated. In 1877 the government reformed the Tariff and lowered many duties. This was done to compensate for the fall in prices, since these duties were specific (i.e., fixed, not proportional to prices). The price of cotton textiles, in particular, had been falling continuously, both in Spain and in the international markets, since the 1860s, so the lowered duties only brought the level of protection to that of those years, which was already very high. But the Catalan deputies, Conservative as well as Liberal, were up in arms against the reduction of duties, however justified. M. Cabrera and F. del Rey (2002, pp. 88-9) point out that 'Catalan deputies and senators very often acted as a clique, no matter their belonging to the Liberal or the Conservative Parties, to the point of breaking the discipline established by their national executives'. This conduct, according to Cabrera and del Rey, would explain why these members of parliament were rarely promoted to top political posts: their behavior inspired little trust in their own parties. Nationalist historians have frequently complained about what they consider to be discrimination and exclusion, but it would appear that the exclusion was self-inflicted by the deputies and senators themselves.

It was at this time that a group of Catalan writers and politicians submitted a manifesto commonly known in Catalan as *Memorial de greuges* (Memorial of grudges), voicing a series of complaints (about the Catalan language and civil law) the most important of which was about the commercial policies of the Liberal Party. The *Memorial* included the following rhetorical question: 'How can our weak and mistreated industry compete with the robust, triumphant industry of the British nation?' This, as we shall see, was the typical argument of Catalan protectionists. It is interesting that protection of the textile industry was the kernel of the Memorial, which has been considered as the first expression of political Catalanism.

The fight of Catalan businessmen against free trade proceeded relentlessly, and in the end they attained their ends. All kinds of arguments were used to prevent the lowering of tariff duties. One of the favorite topics of the manufacturers was the 'artificial and pretended symbiosis of interests with their workmen' by appealing to the supposed common interest of all 'producers' (Cabrera and del Rey, 2002, p. 120).

The protectionists were helped by the conditions in international markets. The agrarian depression of the late nineteenth century, due largely to market integration facilitated by better communications (transport and information) and by the cultivation of new lands in the Americas and the Russian Empire, pushed agricultural and raw material prices down, something which benefited consumers but hurt producers, especially in Europe. This led to a concerted effort by producers to pressure governments and legislators to hitch up tariff duties. Since Spain was still a mainly agricultural country, falls in agrarian incomes and employment constituted a very serious problem which had numerous ramifications, notably on consumer industries, such as textiles, whose demand was bound to be affected. The clamor for protection became widespread if not unanimous. At that time the main objective of the Catalan bourgeoisie, 'the better organized and most persistent pressure group' (Serrano Sanz, 1987, p. 131), was to reach an alliance with other protectionist groups, that is to say, Castilian grain growers, Basque iron smelters, and Asturian coal miners. How favorable the atmosphere was to protectionism became evident when an official Commission was formed to study 'Tariff Reform and Commercial Treaties'. Although its president was a supporter of free trade, the Commission was packed with protectionists, so the conclusions were openly favorable to raising duties in most fields. The president's protests were to no avail.

Another omen of the times was the return of Cánovas to power in July 1890 and the publication of a booklet by him in 1891 entitled *How and why I became a doctrinal protectionist.* In it he explained that, as a liberal-conservative, he had always been a free-trader; but that the circumstances and nationalist conviction had made him change his mind and embrace protectionism. And so it was that on 31 December 1891 the queen regent (a new María Cristina, very different from her predecessor) signed a totally new Tariff law, which tried to be *integrally* protectionist (i.e., to protect all sectors, something which is theoretically impossible but which was an idea in vogue at the time). The immediate effect of what has been called the 'Cánovas tariff' was a hefty rise in the domestic price of wheat. But probably the commodity whose duties increased most in the new tariff was cotton textiles. Once more, the pressure groups of the Catalan bourgeoisie, this time helped by Castilians, Basques, and Asturians, had obtained a significant triumph in Madrid.

The Beginnings of Industrialization

Slow Recovery

The only industrial nucleus in Spain at the beginning of the nineteenth century was Catalonia, with the cotton textile industry as the most important sector. The total number of spindles in the country at the time is estimated at some 106,000, of which 86 percent were manual and 14 percent mechanical. Catalonia had 90 percent of all spindles, of which 86.5 percent were manual and 13.5 mechanical (Nadal, 2003, p. 55, Fig. 1.1.2.7). The concentration of the cotton industry in Catalonia could be explained in part by the textile tradition of the region, but the most powerful factor no doubt was the strict protection it received since the times of Felipe V and its privileged markets of colonial America. By the mid-eighteenth century, the Spanish empire occupied about one half of all colonial land surface of the world, and about 70 percent of the colonial population (Carreras and Tafunell, 2005, I, p. 19, n. 8).

This scheme collapsed when the Spanish empire fell down. Fourteen years of war between Miguel Hidalgo's rebellion in Mexico in 1810 to the battle of Ayacucho in Peru in 1824 put an end to Spain's continental empire in the Americas. Meanwhile Spain was fighting its own War of Independence against the French Empire (1808–1814), suffering the yoke of Fernando VII's absolutism (1814–1820), forcing him to accept the Constitution (1820–1823), and suffering a second French invasion which restored absolutism in 1823. It seems almost a miracle that a country battered by such invasions and turmoil could have fought against the independence movements at the other side of the Atlantic. The explanation is, of course, that the wars of American Independence were really civil wars between creoles (people of European descent) and native populations and other groups (mostly blacks and mulattoes). In these wars the Spanish armies backed or led the side against independence.

Although Spain did not effectively recognize the independence of its former colonies until 1836, its economic effects were felt much sooner, even before 1810, because since Napoleon imposed the 'continental blockade' in 1806 Britain was able to seriously disrupt communications between Spain and its American territories, which became economically independent *de facto*. The effects of independence on the everyday life of average Spaniards was probably small because the great majority were subsistence peasants, but commerce was greatly affected, with considerable repercussions for the commercial and industrial middle classes. This was the moment, Nadal (1999, p. 217) has remarked, when the Catalan economy 'went from looking outwards to looking inwards'. In other words, after losing the colonial markets, the Catalans latched on to the domestic market. This was especially the case with the textile industry. From then on cotton mill owners devoted more attention to lobbying for higher tariffs than to cutting costs. They were successful with the prohibitionist legislation of the Triennium. At any rate, the turbulent years of Fernando VII's reign were not very good for the industry, if for no other reason, because the economy was so depressed. It is remarkable, however, that neither the War of the Aggrieved in the late 1820s nor the Carlist War (1833–1840) were harmful to the industry. It was in the 1830s that the cotton industry started importing British machinery (mostly second hand), an unmistakable sign of prosperity. This dichotomy of a warring countryside and prosperous industrial cities tells us much about the division of Catalan society into two separate worlds.

The end of the Carlist War benefited Catalan industry. The consumption of cotton textiles increased in Spain, displacing the other fibers. According to David Ringrose's calculations (1987, p. 136), in Madrid cotton tissues were 5.7 percent of total textiles consumed in 1789, while in 1847 they were 73.2 percent. Roughly, the first half of the nineteenth century was the period when cotton became king in the Spanish market and better border inspection reduced the amount of smuggling: all this signally favored the Catalan cotton industry.

All in all, this industry, which was the great protagonist of Catalan industrialization, grew along the century, albeit at diminishing rates, which is logical, and with only one large interruption: the years 1855–1865. The series of raw cotton imports (the best indicator of industrial activity, since cotton imports were used almost in their entirety as raw material for spinning and weaving) shows a trough during those years. There were two main probable causes for this: first, the Progressive legislation during the Biennium stimulated investment in banks and railroads at the expense of industry; and, second, the American Civil War (1861–1865) caused two serious unbalances, the one at its beginning, the other at its end. At the start, the fall in American production and exportation of cotton (to which the Northern side's blockade of Southern ports contributed significantly) caused a 'cotton famine' in international markets and a sharp increase in prices. At the end, the opposite phenomenon took place: the fall in cotton prices as markets discounted an increase in American exports produced a change in parameters which ruined many bankers and businessmen, especially those who had invested in cotton fields in relatively marginal countries such as Egypt or Brazil.

A smaller fluctuation, a decrease in the rate of growth, took place as a consequence of the 1882 general fall of the prices of raw materials. In Catalonia, however, this fluctuation marked the end of the period of euphoria which followed the Bourbon Restoration, a boom that contemporaries called *febre d'or* (gold fever), and which inspired one of the first modern novels (with the same title) in the Catalan language, by Narcís Oller. The end of the 'gold fever' was the occasion for a renewed offensive by the millowners against what remained of the Figuerola Tariff. In reality, the figures show that that Tariff was not at all harmful to the industry, but the industrialists kept painting a bleak picture of their predicament and maintained their pressure until they got, in succession, the suspension of the Fifth Basis (1875, 1882), the Law of Commercial Relations with the Antilles (1882), and the Cánovas Tariff (1891), which abolished the Figuerola Tariff definitively and raised duties to levels unknown in Spain since the beginning of the century.

Thanks to this continued policy of tariff protection the cotton industry (overwhelmingly Catalan: in 1856, 99 percent of manual spindles and 95 percent of mechanical spindles in Spain were in Catalonia) and the textile industry in general (the wool industry was second to cotton) had turned Catalonia into the 'Factory of Spain' (*la fábrica de España*), as Catalans liked to say then. It was, however, a factory of modest proportions. By 1913 the output per capita of the Spanish textile industry was worth 31.9 German marks. Comparable values for other countries were much larger: 129.7 for Britain, 90.6 for France, 73.8 for Germany, and 41.4 for Italy (Nadal, 1999, p. 196). This was all the industry had to show after almost two centuries of protection.

In a now classic work, Nadal (1975, pp. 215, 216, 218, 242; for a shorter English version, Nadal, 1973, esp. p. 612) called this situation a 'failure' and blamed it on 'the dramatic inelasticity of domestic demand'. In other words, if the Catalan textile industry was comparatively modest it was because the Spanish market was narrow, due to backward agricultural conditions. If this were so, one wonders why Catalan industrialists did not look for wider markets abroad. Be it as it may, Nadal himself, in a later work (1991, pp. 78-85), reproduced statistics showing that in reality the Spanish market was not particularly narrow. Spanish consumption of cotton per capita in 1913 was almost exactly equal to the European average, and was ahead of consumption in Italy, Austria-Hungary, or Norway. So perhaps the problem of the textile industry could not be blamed on 'the dramatic inelasticity of domestic demand'; perhaps it was more a problem of supply. For a complex series of reasons, notably an excess of tariff protection, the Catalan cotton industry depended exclusively of a national market whose narrowness it decried, but to which it clung desperately, clamoring for protection while renouncing to compete internationally.

Everything suggests, therefore, that Catalan businessmen became accustomed to working snugly behind tariff barriers and did not try contend in foreign markets. They linked their destiny to the Spanish economy of their own volition. A relatively recent study (Prat and Soler, 2002) lays the blame for Catalan entrepreneurial conservatism on financial and organizational factors. These authors claim that in the second half of the nineteenth century Catalan textile factories were technologically advanced enough to be able to compete in international markets, but that they lacked financial backing and also an adequate commercial network. This may well be true: commercial and financial credit networks are essential and difficult to improvise. But other national textile industries were able to develop those networks that apparently were missing in Catalonia. Tariff protection probably discouraged Catalan entrepreneurs from assuming the risk and expenditure of creating such networks.

For one thing, we know that the Catalan banking system left a lot to be desired; at least Catalan businessmen and writers repeatedly complained about it (Sardà and Beltran, 1933; Sudrià, 2007). But the problems of Catalan banking could hardly be blamed on Madrid. The third incorporated bank in Spanish history (after the Bank of San Fernando and the Bank of Isabel II) was the Bank of Barcelona, authorized by the government in 1844. When, after the 1848 crisis there was thought of granting the Banco de San Fernando (soon to become the Bank of Spain) the monopoly of issue, the government decided not to in order to avoid harming the Bank of Barcelona. One had to wait for the anomalous circumstances of 1874 to see the monopoly of issue finally granted to the Bank of Spain (Tortella and García Ruiz, 2013, pp. 73-6).

Catalan banks underwent numerous ups and downs in the second half of the nineteenth century. They enjoyed a great boom under the banking laws of the Progressive Biennium, but they followed the current trend and invested more in railroads than in the textile industry. Then the crisis of the 1860s sank many of the new institutions. The extremely prudent Bank of Barcelona took advantage of the crisis to get rid of its former competitors. After the political and economic turmoil of the 'Revolutionary Sexennium' (1868–1874), Catalan banks were mostly involved in colonial loans related to the Cuban War. This coincided with the 'gold fever' period. After this episode, which in Catalonia showed a dramatic boom and bust alternation, the whole Catalan banking system went into a long period of slow decline (Tortella and García Ruiz, 2013, pp. 80-6). In Barcelona especially, commercial banks were more attentive to stock-exchange operations than to exports of textiles. A book by a Catalan economist (Tallada, 1944, pp. 70-4) offers a picturesque description of the relation banker-borrower in late nineteenth-century Barcelona:

> The industrialist asking for a loan showed up in a somewhat contrite attitude at the office of Mr. Domingo Taberner [...] Mr. Taberner pronounced a severe admonition, on occasion even scolding the visitor if he thought his entrepreneurial performance was not up to par, but in the end he granted the credit.

Tallada adds that many Catalan businessmen felt guilty in asking for a loan or issuing bills of exchange, practices they considered almost dishonorable. This old-fashioned paternalistic banker-customer relationship helps to explain the peculiarities of the Catalan banking system. And this goes a long way back. Catalonia lacked even a rudimentary banking system before the Bank of Barcelona was founded. In other words, all the industrial growth of Catalonia in the eighteenth century up to the mid-1840s was carried out on the basis of credits among merchants and industrialists or by means of reinvested profits (Tortella and García Ruiz, 2013, pp. 38-9). On the face of the evidence, it would seem that the main cause of the relative underdevelopment of Catalan banks was the mistrust and reluctance of industrialists toward banking and credit.

The growing difference between the industrial and commercial structure of the Catalan economy and the more traditional, agrarian structure of the economy of the rest of Spain started attracting the attention of politicians, journalists, and scholars and a series of essays were written on the topic. One of the questions which lent themselves better to a quantitative approach was that of the commercial balance between both communities. In particular, there were two questions which attracted attention: one was the nature of the exchanges. The a priori hypothesis was that Catalonia should sell manufactured products to the rest of Spain and buy food and raw materials from there. The second question was the sign of the commercial balance: would one of the regions be in deficit, and the other, naturally, in surplus? Figuerola had published a book (1849) collecting most of the available figures about Barcelona. Since Barcelona was the main commercial hub of Catalonia (and of Spain) Figuerola's figures could offer fairly satisfactory answers to those questions, and these answers are as one could have expected. Catalonia exported manufactured goods and imported food and raw materials. As to the second question, the balance was fairly even, perhaps with a small deficit for Catalonia. Other calculations based on other sets of figures tended to confirm these impressions. Another obvious conclusion from these studies was that 'Catalonia is the largest market for the rest of Spain [and . . .] the largest market for Catalonia lies in the rest of Spain, to the point that, if they separated, they would be ruined economically and financially' (Maluquer, 2001, p. 377).

The Rhetoric and the Cost of Protectionism

The linchpin of the close interdependence of both regional economies was, of course, the high tariff protecting Catalan industry from foreign competition. Catalan entrepreneurs and their associations were very conscious of this, and unceasingly reclaimed the continuity and, if possible, elevation of this protective barrier. Here are a few examples of their utterances and demands. Most of these texts are extracted from two official enquiries on the tariff question (*Información*,1867, and *Reforma*, 1890). The *Fomento del Trabajo Nacional* (Promotion of National Work, the main professional association of textile entrepreneurs) said in 1890:

> Several pamphlets have demonstrated that the cost price of cotton textiles in Spain is between 40 and 41 percent higher than in England and, even if we should admit that the English fabrics must sustain transport and other expenditures larger than domestic fabrics, and that this excess should be between 6 and 8 percent, depending on their destination, there still is a difference of between 32 and 34 percent, which at least for the time being makes it impossible to compete with English products, except for the coarsest qualities, unless the present tariff duties are increased or at least sustained.

The manufacturers, therefore, were admitting that their products were one third more expensive in Spain than English products and that, 'at least for the time being', they could not compete unless heavily protected by tariffs. 'For the time being' was a really ironic expression since this inferiority of Catalan fabrics had existed for almost two centuries.

In the opinion of the Industrial Institute of Catalonia, Spain was 'under the domination of a school fond of everything English' and, as a consequence, the Institute wanted to warn that the country was in danger and that it was necessary to 'save the Spanish society from a cataclysm'. This statement is interesting, because it reveals the mentality and the strategy of those businessmen; one can find no calls for an improvement of productivity or a lowering of costs in these texts. The Institute thought that the only solution to the problems of the textile industry was in obtaining ever increasing tariff protection, rather than in achieving competitiveness.

It is also remarkable that the manufacturers viewed the gradual lowering of the duties in the Law of Commercial Relations with the Antilles as an excellent device which had permitted an extraordinary increase in 'our exportation to those prosperous regions and attenuated the industrial crisis' Spain had suffered, but they considered odious and 'absurd', as 'inspired by a scholastic fanaticism [. . .] the existence of a legal precept which, with destiny's inflexibility, with mathematical exactitude, marks that a certain degree of protection should be lifted for each industry at fixed terms, as though the legislator had the power to fathom the future's vicissitudes [. . .]'. In other words, the decreasing scale that was 'very satisfactory', according to the Barcelona Committee for Agriculture, Industry and Commerce, in the Law of Commercial relations, was abominable and 'inspired by scholastic fanaticism' in the Figuerola Tariff Law, according to the Industrial Institute of Catalonia.

Of course the tariff protection the manufacturers so strenuously demanded favored them, but at the same time, by forcing higher prices upon the consumers, constrained them to subsidize to a considerable extent the manufacturers' business. An estimation of the cost, or the price the Spanish society paid for the protection of the cotton textile industry, is possible. The basic idea is simple: the cost is a function of the difference between the price Spanish consumers paid and the price they would have paid if there had been no tariff, in other words, the difference between the domestic price and the price in international markets. This price differential multiplied by the actual consumption of textiles in Spain would give us the figure we are after. This figure divided by national income (Gross Domestic Product, GDP) would give us the cost in relative terms.

The idea is simple. The major difficulty, however, is that textile production offers a myriad of different qualities, whose prices differ greatly and in many cases are impossible to establish, let alone compare. This difficulty has been resolved by referring to a few qualities which were the most consumed. The process of obtaining the relevant figures is detailed in Appendix A of the Spanish version of the present book (Tortella, et al., 2016).

The main conclusion of our calculations is that in 1860 the price of protecting the Spanish cotton industry was 0.940 percent of GDP and in 1865 it was 0.598 percent. This considerable fall was due immediately to the *cotton famine*, a consequence of the Civil War in the United States. The *cotton famine* not only did push prices up but it also diminished the price gap between Spanish and international (British) prices. Furthermore, it also caused an international recession: this recession plus the hike in the price of cotton textiles pushed down the quantity of these goods consumed. The smaller price gap together with the fall in cotton textiles purchased explains the fall in the cost of protection in 1865. The rough conclusion of all this is that in the 1860s the protection to cotton textiles cost Spain between 0.5 and 1.0 percent of GNP.

These calculations are derived from a cross-section estimation, based upon the analysis of detailed samples which are available from official Spanish documents (*Información*, 1867, and other cited in Tortella, et al., 2016). It would be interesting to extend these conclusions to more years by means of time-series analysis. Fortunately, this is possible because there are available time series of prices of cotton textiles both for Spain and for Britain (British prices were the main component of international cotton goods prices) for the second half of the nineteenth century. Aside from permitting us to estimate the cost of protection in the second half of the nineteenth century, the time series analysis is a good check on the validity of our cross-section estimations – and vice versa. The results of the time series estimation are reflected in fig. 5.1.

The main conclusions from the time-series analysis are as follows. First, the average extra cost paid by Spanish consumers over the whole period was 0.478 percent of GNP. Second, the series has two phases: from 1850 to 1885, the average extra cost was 0.692 percent of GNP; after that date the average extra cost fell rapidly, and it reached negative values for the period 1892–1900 (except in 1895). Third, during the 1860s the extra cost was of about 0.586 percent of GNP, close to the lower end of the interval established by the cross-section analysis. This dip was due basically to the low values of the years 1865–1868 when the effects of the recession were most acutely felt in Spain; after the 1860s, the extra cost returned to normal levels until the mid-1880s, when the declining trend set in. Fourth, this persistent decline was due, at least in part, to the relative tariff moderation under the liberals, which gave rise to bitter complaints of the manufacturers, as we saw earlier. Decline became faster from 1890 on; this was due to a fall in the value of the peseta, whose convertibility in gold was *de facto* abandoned in the early 1880s. This devaluation provided an extra protection to domestic products since as the quotation of the peseta declined, the price of imported

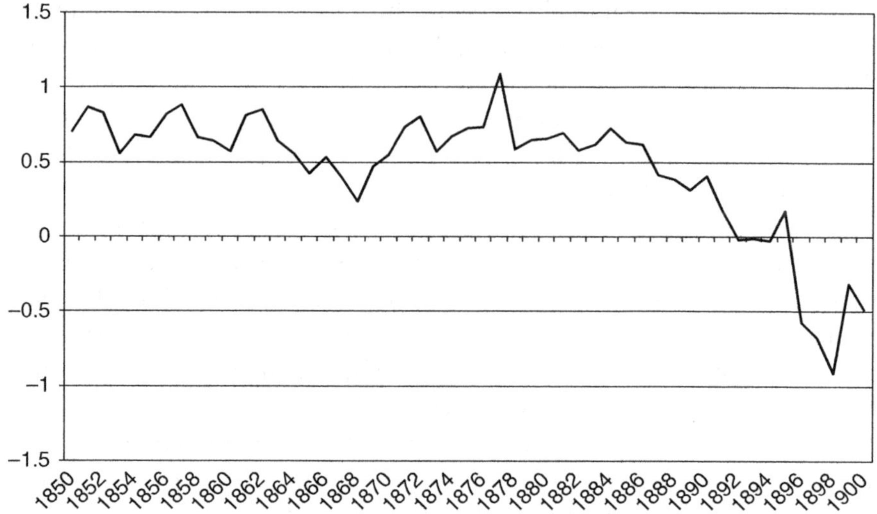

Fig. 5.1 Extra Cost due to Price Differential between Catalan and English Textiles s (% of GNP)

Source: Tortella, García Ruiz, Núñez and Quiroga, p. 495

goods went up. The gradual fall of the peseta became faster since the earlier 1990s and became precipitous when the last Cuban War broke out in February 1895. Thus, although one would have expected that the extra cost of protection should have been reflected in our series (Graph 5.1) after the Cánovas Tariff of 1891, the price increases were masked by the devaluation of the peseta, which, in fact, provided an additional across-the-board layer of protection for all domestic commodities.

Fifth, another factor contributing to the decline in the extra cost in terms of GNP was the growth of this macroeconomic magnitude. Overall it grew at nearly 1 percent per annum in the second half of the nineteenth century. This growth of course tended to lower the weight of each of its components. While this would explain the declining trend of the extra cost in the second half of the nineteenth century, it would also imply that this extra cost should have been higher during the first half of the century; unfortunately, we cannot carry out the necessary calculations to sustain this assumption for lack of data.

That the extra cost of tariff protection to cotton textiles to the consumer should have amounted to about 0.5 percent of GDP during the second half of the nineteenth century may not seem much. There are a few considerations to bring to mind. One, this average includes the dip in the 1860s, which in reality did not bring an improvement in the welfare of Spanish consumers, just a fall in textile consumption and a fall in relative British prices. Strictly speaking, the apparent decrease in cost is just a statistical mirage. Two, the same must be said about the fall of the cost in the 1890s. The fall of the peseta did nothing for the welfare of the consumers of Spanish textiles. If we could construct a more sophisticated index of consumer welfare the upshot would probably be a higher cost than is reflected in our very simple estimate. Three, another imperfection of our estimate which biases it downward (i.e., underestimates the cost to the consumer), is that we assume the demand is inelastic; in reality, if Spanish cotton textile prices had been lower, consumption would have been higher. Spanish consumers were hurt not only because they paid more but also because they consumed less. In summary, our estimated cost to consumers is less than that what they really lost due to tariff protection.

Another fact that we must take into account is that not all the cotton textile industry was located in Catalonia; the largest part was, though. In terms of workers, 73 percent of textile workers were located in Catalonia by 1910. According to the fiscal data reproduced by Nadal (2003, p. 140), the Catalan cotton industry produced 94.1 percent of cotton textiles in value terms in 1856, and 91.0 percent in 1900. All in all, therefore, it was Catalan businessmen and workers who benefited from this extra cost at the expense of the rest of Spaniards.

The Catalan 'Renaissance'

The first stirrings of Catalan nationalism appeared around the final quarter of the nineteenth century. They were inspired by the example of Italy and the *Giovane Italia* (Young Italy), which had been founded by Giuseppe Mazzini in 1831 and successfully imitated in Germany and Poland.

In 1859 a medieval tradition had been revived in the celebration of the *Jocs Florals* (literally, Flower Games) a yearly poetry contest in the Catalan language. Later on, in 1870 an organization calling itself *Jove Catalunya* (Young Catalonia) was founded by a group of intellectuals. It did not have the expected echo and was dissolved five years later, but it issued a review called *La Renaixença* (The Renaissance) which lasted for about thirty years and gave name to this chiefly cultural movement trying to revive the interest in the Catalan language, which had been losing ground in the urban and cultivated circles for centuries.

In 1880 the first 'Catalanist Congress' took place in Barcelona, and a *Centre Català* was created in 1872. The *Centre* organized a second 'Catalanist Congress' which in 1885 produced the so-called *Memorial of Grudges* that was submitted to king Alfonso XII. The text of the *Memorial* opened with a disclaimer: its purpose was not to 'debilitate, much less attack, the glorious unity of the Spanish fatherland'. It just wanted greater consideration for the Catalan language, for the Catalan civil legislation and, especially, more tariff protection for the textile industry, which it considered almost intrinsically Catalan.

Gradually, however, from purely cultural, Catalanism became more political. In 1884 the *Centre Català* was dreaming of becoming a political party and running in elections. Rifts appeared soon, however, especially between right and left. Most Catalanists were bourgeois, deeply religious and conservative; they mistrusted the leader of the *Centre*, Valentí Almirall, a left-wing republican. The *Centre* split into two. The conservatives were the most powerful wing, and they created the *Lliga de Catalunya* (League of Catalonia). They also supported the *Universal Exhibition* in Barcelona in 1888, sponsored by the state, which the Almirall group had opposed. They also approved of the presence of the queen regent at the *Jocs Florals*, although they profited the occasion to submit to her a petition for more autonomy. A series of related activities took place during those years. A *Centre Escolar Catalanista* was established with the objective of spreading Catalanist views among scholars so they could reach schools and colleges. The *Centre Escolar* was inspired by the leading Catalanist intellectual of that era, Enric Prat de la Riba, conservative but tireless in his work for the cause. A blueprint for the 'new Catalonia' was published under the title '*Bases de Manresa*', Manresa being the town where the delegates met, presided by the bishop of Vic, to write down the document. The Bases tried to revive an almost medieval Catalonia, but its most remarkable feature was the proposal of making Catalan the sole official language in Catalonia. Nothing came out of the Bases of Manresa, but the meetings and proposals proliferated. One of those proposals was to unify (*mancomunar*) some provincial assemblies so as to create a sort of Catalan autonomous institution.

The watershed for Catalanism, as for many other questions in Spain, was the year 1898, the year of the 'Disaster' which involved the loss of Cuba, Puerto Rico, and the Philippines after the defeat in the Spanish-American war. For many in Catalonia the 'Disaster' eroded the prestige of the Spanish state, whose power appeared greatly diminished. For the industrialists it meant losing the colonial markets, which many of them considered one of the key advantages of being part of Spain. These disappointments augmented the will to become autonomous, if not independent.

We may ask why did this Catalanist movement emerge at this time. One factor, of course, was the 'Disaster'. Another factor was language. The Catalan language had ceased to be a tool of thought and culture since the end of the Middle Ages, and at the beginning of the nineteenth century it was almost only spoken in the countryside and rarely written. According to Balcells (2004, p. 649 and 1991, p. 21), 'political nations were first cultural nations and in Catalonia, during the nineteenth century, an effort was made to turn the vernacular spoken language into a modern cultivated language by means of a long and difficult process. The *Renaixença* appeared much earlier than political Catalanism'. The wish to revive and resuscitate the language certainly was the first step. But the Catalan language had been dormant for centuries. Why the wish to recuperate it in the nineteenth?

One factor was, of course, the desire to imitate the romantic nationalist movements of the post-Napoleonic era in Italy, Germany, and Poland. We already referred to that. But there are other factors closer to home. The dissensions and frictions between Catalonia and the rest of Spain became ever more evident and uncomfortable after the 1850s. We have already seen the constant struggle of the Catalan bourgeoisie to obtain a privileged situation on the economic field; although it attained its objectives, this steady battle contributed to arouse a conscience of separation, a view of Madrid as a hostile city which had to be convinced and conquered, which in turn fostered a feeling of alterity: the *madrileños* were different and controlled political power. The visits of Catalan lobbyists to Madrid at the turn of the century were ably described in the novels by Ignacio Agustí (1947, pp. 104-6), a Catalan novelist who wrote in Spanish: 'Several months beforehand the bourgeois of my city had got together to form a solid block before the Madrid governments'. And so they heard the president of the Spanish government address them like this: 'May the Catalans speak their dialect in peace, but let them not try to make even our economic policy speak Catalan'. And the Barcelona industrialists answered: 'We are coming to make a proposal with the best intentions that our region can cherish. You can be sure there will be no germ of separatism in the Catalan land. Unless, of course, this germ were deposited by the government itself, due to negligence or malice'. Obviously, there was no mincing of words, at least in Agustí's fiction.

These scenes of Agustí's novel take place in Madrid immediately after the 'Disaster' of 1898, but there can be little doubt that this sort of dialogue was held earlier in the century. Separatism was used by the Catalan bourgeoisie as a means of pressure, which explains why autonomism first, nationalism afterward, found such strong support among Catalan business circles. This would also explain the somewhat paradoxical fact that those same businessmen who fought so strenuously to monopolize 'the Spanish national market' should at the same flirt with separatism.

There is another factor, more cultural than political. The difference between Catalonia and the rest of Spain was evident, owing largely to the economic differences. In the second half of the nineteenth century and well into the twentieth, until around 1930, the distance in per capita income between Catalonia and the rest of Spain widened considerably, due, as we know, to the political protection to the textile industry. Barcelona was a prosperous city, and so were many other Catalan cities, in contrast to the poverty of Castile and the parochialism of Madrid. Let us revisit Agustí's novel, whose protagonist, Rius, finds, in reaching Madrid, 'a swarm of young boys hanging from the windows of the narrow carriage' which was taking the commissioners to their hotel. Rius

> watched, on the way, the crowd of onlookers, of street vendors, of loafers with a cigarette butt on their lips. Clothes were hanging from balconies and the sun played on the leafy and elegant treetops in the Paseo del Prado. 'This is proper of a great city' suggested Jorge Cavestany, ready to point out the virtues of his place of residence. Moixó and Rius assented. 'Yes, but you leave this out and what is there left?'

For many people from Barcelona, Madrid still was a dreary La Mancha town, and they preferred to imitate Paris or London. They considered Spanish a second-rate language and compared contemptuously its literature to that in English, French, or German, something which in the mid-nineteenth century could be justified. It would not be so if one adopted a longer time perspective, as the *Renaixença* Catalans liked to do, and took into account the literary and even scientific production of the Golden Century, or that of the late nineteenth and early twentieth centuries.

It has also been argued, with some reason, that Spanish nationalism was very weak in the nineteenth century. The capital, financial and human, the Spanish state devoted to education was comparatively paltry; illiteracy was still quite high in the early twentieth century. Compared to the assimilation and education effort carried out in France, for instance (Weber, 1976), the labor exerted by the Spanish state was modest indeed. Among the reproaches addressed by the Catalanists to the Madrid governments and Spain in general was their narrowness and inefficiency, the passivity and indifference of traditional society. This is reflected in a curious way in the *Memories* of Francesc Cambó, the foremost leader of Catalanism in the early decades of the twentieth century. He points out the lack of response, the indifference of the Spanish people after the 'Disaster' of 1898. In contrast, 'among the Castilian intellectuals, those who were later called "the generation of 98," it provoked a movement toward Europeanization, which meant a break with the past; in other words, *separatism* from traditional Spain'

(Cambó, 1981, p. 63, italics added). For Cambó here *separatism* means rupture with what is traditional and retrograde.

It should also be mentioned that while Catalanism criticized Spanish traditionalism, it tried its best, with remarkable success, to resuscitate the past to build up a victimist and nationalist version of a distant Catalan history, of past, and somewhat rusty, glories. While the feats of Spanish history, brought about by the feeble and pale Spanish nationalism, were considered rancid and old-fashioned (for instance, the Cid, the Catholic Monarchs, the discovery of the New World, Felipe II's empire, the fight against Napoleon, the Cortes of Cádiz, etc.), the deeds and heroes adduced by Catalan nationalism (Wilfred the Hairy, Ramón Berenguer IV, Jaume I the Conqueror, the Aragonese Mediterranean empire, Pau Claris, Rafael Casanova, etc.) were considered to be illustrious and resplendent. Late nineteenth- and early twentieth-century Catalanism was busy inventing traditions and building monuments to all these past glories and others, and composing hymns and songs purported to be genuinely traditional but in fact of recent manufacture.

Nationalism and the 1898 Crisis

In February 1895 a new insurrection flared in Cuba under the leadership of José Martí, a Cuban poet and intellectual, son of Valencian parents, who spent several years exiled in New York. Martí died in an early skirmish, but his lieutenants carried on for three years, never really threatening Spanish control of the island, but creating a tense atmosphere of violence and insecurity, domestically and internationally. In April 1898 the American battleship *Maine*, anchored in the Havana harbor, mysteriously exploded. This became the *casus belli* of the American intervention against Spain, which led to a crushing defeat after four months of mostly naval war in Cuba and the Philippines. In the subsequent Treaty of Paris Spain ceded Cuba, the Philippines, and Puerto Rico (which had surrendered without fighting) plus other minor possessions, to the United States in exchange for a compensation in cash.

On 12 June, while the war raged, *Unió Catalanista*, one of the budding political groups active at the time, issued a manifesto which said in part that 'since the center of government was established in Madrid, the dismemberment of Spain's possessions has never ceased', something that was due to a foreign policy which threatened 'with death all the achievements of the Catalan genius'. The document added that it was essential that 'Catalonia should govern its domestic interests and should have an influence over foreign policy in proportion to its strength'. As Rodrigo (2009) has pointed out, the *Unió* manifesto, which has been attributed to Prat de la Riba, implied that Catalonia had been kept out of colonial policy, something simply untrue. Prat certainly maintained the vituperative tone after the end of the war; according to him Spain was a 'disorderly bunch of African tribes' while Catalonia was 'the main representative of European civilization'. If Spain wanted to stand up 'it should appeal to the ideals, the strength and the government traditions of the Catalan lands'.

On the centennial of the 'Disaster', nationalist historians, such as Agustí Colomines (1998), supported Prat de la Riba's former strictures. According to them, the definitive loss of the American empire was attributable to Spain's misgovernment, something with which Catalonia had absolutely nothing to do. Fortunately Rodrigo (2009) has unearthed numerous evidences of Catalonia's involvement in the several wars of Cuban independence and of the widespread support these wars found in the Catalan population.

Soon after the Glorious Revolution of 1868, Carlos Manuel de Céspedes, a Cuban lawyer and landowner, declared for independence at the head of a small army. Thus started the Ten Years War, which would end with the defeat of the rebels (Céspedes died in an encounter in 1874). Early in 1869 a group of more than one hundred Catalan businessmen, worried by the damage to their interests the rebellion might cause (the number of Catalans doing business in Cuba was quite large), asked for support from the Barcelona authorities and soon a battalion of Catalan soldiers, wearing the typical *barretina* (a distinctive Catalan floppy red beret), sailed to Cuba in support of the Spanish army's fight against the rebels. The volunteers carried the Spanish flag (not the Catalan flag, the *Senyera*, which exhibits the same colors but with several narrower red and yellow stripes). Two more battalions were formed later that traveled to Cuba to 'save the lives and the fortunes of 130.000 *peninsulares*' (in Spanish America the Spanish-speaking whites were divided into *criollos*, born in America, and *peninsulares*, born in Spain).

Several associations were created in Barcelona to support the government policies in favor of keeping Cuba Spanish, among them the *Círculo Hispano Ultramarino* de Barcelona (Hispanic Overseas Circle of Barcelona, founded in 1871), whose president was Joan Güell i Ferrer, leader of the Catalan cotton textile manufacturers, and whose vice-president was the marquis of Comillas. Both Güell and Comillas had made their fortunes in Cuba with the slave trade among other businesses. The *Círculo* was active promoting conservative causes, among others, the maintenance of slavery in Cuba, which was nonetheless abolished in 1888. The *Círculo* also made public manifestations in support of the new king, Alfonso XII (he had been crowned in 1875). It was at that time when Cánovas decided to send a strong army to Cuba to put an end to the rebellion. He found firm support in the *Círculo*, and we know that Comillas organized the subscription of a large government loan for whose managing he founded the Banco Hispano Colonial, which became the largest Catalan business bank in the late nineteenth century.

There was always firm Catalan support to the Spanish government in colonial matters; for instance, when in 1885 there was an international conflict about the Caroline Islands in the South Pacific, there was a large demonstration in Barcelona in support of Spanish diplomatic efforts to keep them against German encroachment. Something similar occurred eight years later, when there was a little war around the Spanish city in Africa, Melilla, which was besieged by Moroccan irregulars. The Spanish government found solid support in Catalonia for its military operations to defend the city against a far more numerous army. The same support for the policies of the Spanish government in Cuba was shown when general Valeriano Weyler, a hardened soldier, was sent to Cuba as captain general in 1896 and was given a multitudinous farewell at the port of Barcelona.

All these manifestations of Catalan support to the unionist policies in Cuba and the Philippines, but especially Cuba, make sense because of the high number of Catalans who emigrated to Cuba, some making great fortunes there, others just getting ahead. But just the importance that Catalan businessmen attributed to the Law of Commercial Relations with the Antilles of 1882 flatly contradicts the writings of Prat de la Riba and his modern followers about a pretended disregard for Catalan interests and advice by the Madrid governments in this matter. Cuba, Puerto Rico, and the Philippines were bound to become independent sooner or later. Let me remind the reader of Nadal's remark cited before that, without the Law of Commercial Relations, 'the *Disaster* of 1898 might not have happened so soon'.

Conclusions

The late nineteenth and the early twentieth century are probably the period when the breach between Catalan society and that of the rest of Spain was widest. While economic growth in Spain proceeded at a slow pace, all sectors of the Catalan economy expanded vigorously. The gap in growth rates, whose origins undoubtedly go back to the eighteenth century, was the cause of the breach, which in turn caused a growing dissatisfaction to many Catalans, who felt tied to a society and a government that were excessively traditional. Hence the malaise which led to autonomist aspirations, in turn favored by language and customs problems.

Things were more complex however: the breach involved serious contradictions and paradoxes. The main paradox was the continuous dependence of the Catalan economy of Spain as a whole. The industrialization of Catalonia was based on the textile industry, and this sector had renounced to competing in international markets and had bet on obtaining from the Spanish state stiff protection from foreign competitors in the Spanish market. In order to obtain this protection the Catalan manufacturers built up a powerful lobbying machine which continuously pressured the state not to lower tariff barriers and, if possible, to raise them.

But this protection to the textile industry came at a price, a price paid by the rest of the country, those who did not work for the industry. In the first place, it harmed consumers, who were obliged to buy their clothing at higher prices, and in many cases worse qualities, than those prevailing in the international market. In the second place, it affected exporters, especially those in fruit and vegetable agriculture, wine production, and food processing, who were subjected to commercial reprisals in such large markets as those of England, France, Germany, and the United States. It is true that among those hurt by those reprisals were Catalan farmers, wine makers, and distillers, but these sectors were sacrificed to the interests of the all-powerful textile lobby.

The undeniable sacrifices which the rest of the Spanish economy underwent in the benefit of the sacrosanct textile industry were not mentioned in the famous *Memorial of Grudges* of 1885, nor in the Bases of Manresa of 1892, nor in the numerous writings and addresses that Catalan politicians and businessmen published during this period. There were Catalan liberal economists who pointed these problems out, but these were accused of belonging to 'a school fond of everything English' or of being 'inspired by a scholastic fanaticism'. There were several of those distinguished Catalan scholars, but the favorite object of the protectionists' invectives was Laureano Figuerola, the author of the only moderately free-trade tariff in all that century.

Of course this artificial and over-protected textile industry employed thousands of workers, among them many immigrants from other regions of Spain, whose most likely alternative occupation would have been agrarian disguised unemployment. This fact was frequently mentioned by the protectionist literature. These authors omitted to say, however, that the relatively high wages of those industrial workers, of which they often complained, were high due to the high prices of clothing and bread, induced by high levels of tariff protection to textiles and grain.

Keeping those tariffs high all the century long was possible because of the political clout of the manufacturers, most of them Catalan. The complaints of writers and pundits, then and now, about a supposed sidelining of Catalan politicians are almost totally unfounded. There were four presidents of the Spanish government who were Catalan during the nineteenth century. This is not an outstanding figure, but put Catalonia among the regions with the highest standings in the matter. It is true, though, that, albeit respectable, Catalonia could have attained a more numerous representation in the higher echelons of Spanish politics. This relative underrepresentation may have been due, as Cabrera and del Rey suggest, to the auto-exclusion of Catalan deputies in the Cortes, who as a rule behaved more as Catalans and businessmen than as ordinary members of their respective parties.

Other myths which should be subject to scrutiny are those relative to a monolithic unity of Catalonia and the almost total identification of this region with the textile industry. As a mature community, Catalonia is, and has been, a multifaceted and complex society, with different and at times divergent groups, opinions, and even languages. We have seen how Catalonia was able on many occasions to bring about the triumph of a party or even a political regime and afterward to bring it down with the same decisiveness. This happened with the Glorious Revolution of 1868 and the successive regimes and governments, but something similar happened three decades before with the regency of Espartero. This changeability is an indication of the deep divisions of the Catalan society, but also of its political muscle, since a sector of that society could build up a political regime and other sector of that same society could tear it down afterward. This evidence just makes one doubt about these widely accepted myths: the powerlessness of Catalonia in Spanish politics and the total single mindedness of its population. The division between an agrarian and highland, conservative and reactionary country, and an urban liberal and progressive sector became evident during the Carlist wars, but in turn the Catalan urban world evolved into a series of groups: businessmen, middle classes, workers, with different political fractions representing them: liberals, progressives, democrats, republicans, socialists, anarchists, communists, federalists, centralists, etc. It seems evident that in the nineteenth century the upper classes, clustering around the textile manufacturers and the bankers and merchants, became paramount: they supported Martínez Campos's in his *pronunciamiento* and the Bourbon restoration orchestrated by Cánovas; Sagasta's moderate free-trade policies, however, brought about the first stirrings of autonomism and nationalism, which developed after Cánovas's death, the loss of the last remnants of empire, and the gradual breakdown of the Restoration regime in the early twentieth century. It is true that ethics, let alone gratitude, play a negligible role in politics; it is surprising, anyway, that those groups, and even individuals, who enthusiastically supported the colonial policies of the Restoration in the name of the progress and unity of the Spanish fatherland, once those policies were defeated militarily, reneged wholesale of them and of the Spanish fatherland they had fervidly invoked just a few months before.

References

Abelló, Teresa and others (1998), *La resposta catalana a la crisi i la pérdua colonial de 1898*. Barcelona: Editorial 62.

AGUSTÍ, Ignacio (1947), *El viudo Rius*. Barcelona: Ediciones Destino.

Anes, Gonzalo, ed. (1999), *Historia económica de España, siglos XIX y XX*. Barcelona: Galaxia Gutenberg.

BALCELLS, Albert (1991), *El Nacionalismo Catalán*. Madrid: Historia 16.

BALCELLS, Albert (dir.) (2004), *Història de Catalunya*. Madrid: La Esfera de los Libros.

BURDIEL, I. (2010), *Isabel II. Una biografía (1830–1904)*. Madrid: Taurus.

CABRERA, Mercedes and Fernando del REY (2002), *El poder de los empresarios, política y economía en la España contemporánea (1875–2000)*. Madrid: Taurus.

Calatayud, Salvador, Jesús Millán and Miguel Cruz Romero, eds. (2009), *Estado y periferias en la España del siglo XIX*. Nuevos enfoques. Valencia: Universidad de Valencia.

CAMBÓ, Francesc (1981), *Memòries, 1876–1936*. Barcelona: Alpha.

CARRERAS, Albert and Xavier TAFUNELL, eds. (2005), *Estadística históricas de España, siglos XIX–XX*. 3 vols. Bilbao: Fundación BBVA, 2005.

Cipolla, Carlo M., ed. (1973), *The Emergenc of Industrial Societies, Part Two, Vol. 4.2 of The Fontana Economic History of Europe*. London and Glasgow: Collins/Fontana Books.

COLOMINES, Agustí (1998), 'Catalunya-Espanya, descentralitzatió, regeneracionisme i catalanisme', in Abelló *et al.*, pp. 15–27.

FIGUEROLA, Laureano (1849), *Estadística de Barcelona en 1849*. Barcelona: Imprenta y Librería Politécnica de Tomás Gorchs.

FONTANA, Josep (2014), *La formació d'una identitat, una historia de Catalunya*. Vic: Eumo Editoral.

Germán, Luis, Enrique Llopis, Jordi Maluquer and Santiago Zapata, eds. (2002), *Historia económica regional de España, siglos XIX y XX*. Barcelona: Crítica.

INFORMACIÓN *sobre el Derecho diferencial de bandera y sobre los de aduanas exigibles a los hierros, el carbón de piedra y los algodones presentada al gobierno de su majestad por la comisión nombrada al efecto en real decreto de 10 de noviembre de 1865. Tomo IV, Algodones* (1867). Madrid: Imprenta Nacional.

LÓPEZ-MORELL, Miguel A. (2013), *The House of Rothschild in Spain, 1812–1941*. Farnham: Ashgate.

MALUQUER DE MOTES, Jordi (2001), 'Cataluña, avanzada de la industrialización', in Germán, Llopis, Maluquer and Zapata, pp. 357–389.

Moret y Prendergast, Segismundo. *[La] REFORMA Arancelaria y los Tratados de Comercio* (1890), Madrid: Establecimiento Tipográfico Sucesores de Rivadeneyra. 6 vols.

NADAL, J. (1973) 'The Failure of the Industrial Revolution in Spain, 1830–1914,' in: Carlo Cipolla, (Ed.), pp. 532–626.

NADAL, Jordi (1975), *El fracaso de la revolución industrial en España, 1814–1913*. Barcelona: Ariel.

NADAL, Jordi (1991), 'L'indústria cotonera' in Nadal *et al.* (1988–1994), Vol. 3, pp. 13–85.

NADAL, Jordi (1999), 'Industria sin industrialización', in Anes, pp. 183–222.

NADAL, Jordi (Dir.) (2003), *Atlas de la industrialización de España, 1750–2000*. Barcelona: Fundación BBVA y Crítica.

Nadal, Jordi, et al. (1988–1994), *Història econòmica de la Catalunya contemporània*, 6 vols., Barcelona: Enciclopèdia Catalana.

PAYNE, Stanley G. (1973), *A History of Spain and Portugal*. In Two Volumes, Madison, Wisconsin: The University of Wisconsin Press.

PÉREZ MOREDA, V. (1987), 'Spain's Demographic Modernization, 1800–1930', in: Nicolás Sánchez-Albornoz (Ed.), pp. 13–41.

PRAT, Marc and Raimon SOLER (2002), 'La formación de redes comerciales y el fracaso de la penetración internacional de los tejidos catalanes, 1850–1930', *Revista de Historia Industrial*, 21, pp. 201–225.

RINGROSE, David (1987), *Imperio y península. Ensayos sobre historia económica de España (siglos XVI–XIX)*. Madrid: Siglo XXI.

RODRIGO, Martín (2009), 'Cataluña y el colonialismo español, 1868–1899,' en Calatayud, Millán and Cruz Romero, pp. 315–356.

Sánchez-Albornoz, Nicolás, ed. (1987), *The Economic Modernization of Spain, 1830–1930*, New York and London: New York University Press.

SÁNCHEZ, Alex (2000), 'Los inicios del sistema fabril en la industria algodonera catalana, 1797–1839,' *Revista de Historia Económica*, 3, pp. 485–523.

SARDÀ, Joan and BELTRAN, Lluc (1933), *Els problemes de la banca catalana*. Barcelona: Institut d'Investigacions Econòmiques.

SERRANO SANZ, José María (1987), *El viraje proteccionista en la Restauración. La política comercial española, 1875–1895*. Madrid: Siglo XXI.

SOLDEVILA, Ferran (1959), *Historia de España*. 8 vols. Barcelona: Ariel.

SUDRIÀ, Carles (2007), 'La banca catalana en los años de entreguerras y el debate sobre la decadencia. Una revisión', *Revista de la Historia de la Economía y de la Empresa*, 1, pp. 269–287.

TALLADA, José M. (1944), *Barcelona económica y financiera en el siglo XIX*. Barcelona: Dalmau.

TORTELLA, G. and J. L. GARCÍA RUIZ (2013), *Spanish Money and Banking. A History*. Basingstoke and New York: Palgrave Macmillan.

TORTELLA, G., J. L. GARCÍA RUIZ, C. E. NÚÑEZ, and G. QUIROGA (2016), *Cataluña en España. Historia y mito*. Madrid: Gadir.

Tortella, Gabriel (1977), *Banking, Railroads and Industry in Spain 1829–1874*. New York: Arno Press.

VICENS VIVES, Jaime (1961), *Cataluña en el siglo XIX*. Madrid: Rialp.

WEBER, Eugene (1976), *Peasants into Frenchmen. The Modernization of Rural France, 1870–1914*. Stanford, California: Stanford University Press.

6

The Twentieth Century (1900–1975)

Spain in the Twentieth-Century Crisis

It is well known that the twentieth century was a period of unprecedented turmoil and violence the world over, especially its first half, from the assassination of archduke Franz Ferdinand, heir to the Austro-Hungarian empire, in Sarajevo, Bosnia, in 1914, to the end of World War II in 1945. The Sarajevo assassination was the prelude to World War I, and this war was the harbinger to profound changes in European and world politics. It put an end to what some call the *belle epoque* and others the *first globalization period*. From an economic and political standpoint, the First World War marked a watershed. It put an end to no less than four empires in central and eastern Europe (German, Austrian, Russian, and Ottoman), forcing a complete redrawing of the map in that area; it gave birth to numerous new nations (some reborn, like Poland) and brought about the erection of new borders, thus putting an end to the relatively free trade that had prevailed before. But maybe the most momentous political change that took place during the Great War and immediately after was that socialism in its two

G. Tortella, *Catalonia in Spain*, Palgrave Studies in Economic History, DOI 10.1007/978-3-319-54951-4_6

versions (communism and social democracy) burst into first stage in Europe and, by indirection, in the whole world. Communism took over Russia in 1917 after a violent revolution and became well entrenched there after a cruel civil war. Meanwhile, social–democratic parties came to power peacefully in Europe, helped by the exigencies of war and by the spread of universal suffrage. The emergence of democratic socialism entailed a new way of carrying on politics and contributed to the growth of what is known today as the Welfare State, a set of policies protecting the citizenry from a series of serious contingencies, such as sickness, unemployment, and old age, and providing for widely felt needs such as education and housing.

The victories of socialism in its two versions (communist and democratic) were seen as fearful threats by many groups around the world, but especially in Europe, and most especially in its southern fringe, where the middle classes were weaker than in the north, and democracy therefore was less solidly established. Thus were born extreme right-wing parties that intended to fight socialism, especially in its most extreme, communist version, with its own weapons: mass movements, party dictatorship (as an alternative to the Marxist 'dictatorship of the proletariat'), nationalism instead of communism, totalitarianism, revolutionary jargon, flags and emblems, etc. No wonder 'fascism' was invented by an Italian ex-socialist (Benito Mussolini) in the postwar, when Italy was in danger of a communist takeover. The only northern country where fascism triumphed (under the name of 'national-socialism' and the leadership of Adolf Hitler) was Germany, the great loser in the Great War, and another country which had been on the verge of a communist takeover and the first where a socialist had become prime minister just after the war, and later was president.

This turmoil produced deep intellectual confusion. The increase in public expenditure which the budding welfare programs entailed required not only hefty increases in taxation but also considerable pressure on the banking systems to finance the growth in expenditure. Most politicians and economists did not realize the strain all this entailed on the old liberal economic model prevailing in the nineteenth century, when public expenditures were relatively small, and the gold standard maintained prices stable. Unaware of the implications of the new realities, the public and the politicians wanted a speedy return to 'normalcy' (President Warren Harding's immortal neologism), that is to say, to the *status quo ante bellum* (i.e., things as they were before the war).

Now this was impossible, because the order of things had changed too drastically. New parties and programs ruled, socialists were replacing liberals—as they did paradigmatically in Britain—public expenditure increased, and, on top of it all, prices had skyrocketed as a consequence of war-induced inflation. This made it very difficult to reinstate one of the economic pillars of the *belle epoque*, the gold standard, which had been suspended during the war. The same happened with the other two pillars, balanced budgets and free trade. Another typical feature of *belle epoque* economics, price and wage flexibility, had also largely vanished, chiefly because the labor unions were now much more powerful and fought tooth and nail against any attempt at lowering wages. If wages did not go down, prices could not go down either. Unaware of these very serious problems, politicians, with the acquiescence of the mainstream academic profession, went on bravely on the assumption that the old economic model was still valid and that the old remedies should be applied when needed. The only economist of note who realized that the changes just cursorily described precluded the use of the old remedies was John Maynard Keynes who, when told during the turbulent postwar crisis that in the long-term equilibrium would be reached, wrote that oft-quoted phrase: '*In the long run* we are all dead' (2000 [1923], p. 80). But he was not listened to until it was too late. As he wrote years later, his warnings were heard like 'the croakings of a Cassandra . . . ' (1963 [1931], p. v). When his advice was most necessary, it attracted little attention. In the second postwar, however, Keynesianism became a sort of new Gospel, and its formulas were overused until they became ineffective. This is how social science progresses, unfortunately. But let us go back to our narrative.

The Great Depression (1929–1939), in large part the consequence of the malfunctions just described previously, affected all national economies, but in different degrees. In general, the more developed countries, with the exception of Germany, were able to weather the storm with more or less difficulties. The semideveloped tottered, and a considerable number capsized, that is to say, their democracies sank and were replaced by one type or other of dictatorship, often totalitarian. The Russian revolution only made matters worse because it polarized politics in democracies: on the one hand, it heightened the radicalism of working-class organizations and, on the other, it hardened the political outlook of the high and middle classes who in numerous cases, opted for confronting communism with its own weapons, creating totalitarian regimes and parties: the archetype was fascism, as we just saw. Such was the case of Italy, Germany, Spain, Portugal, Austria, Romania, and some other related cases; in some of those, the new dictatorships were more military than fascist, such as in Greece or Hungary. Europe thus became a powder keg which exploded in September 1939, the onset of World War II.

How did all this social turmoil affect Spain? In general terms, it behaved as one more southern European country. Male universal suffrage had been established there relatively early, with the Glorious Revolution of 1868. Although it was abolished by Cánovas, the liberals restored it in 1890 and from then onward it remained on the books save during the two dictatorships, of Primo de Rivera (1923–1930) and of Franco (1939–1975). In 1932, during the Second Republic, women were enfranchised; not very early, but certainly before French or Italian women. As happened in other countries, in Spain, until the Second Republic, democracy was partially circumvented by bossism and ballot stuffing (*caciquismo* and *pucherazo*), especially in rural areas. Urbanization contributed to dilute this evil. With or without universal suffrage, *caciquismo* plagued elections in the nineteenth century. As in other countries, in twentieth-century Spain, the composition of parties changed: the classic conservative–liberal dichotomy evolved into a congeries of new parties, which in Spain presented two distinctive traits: anarchism became very strong (as in Italy and Russia) and regionalist parties also gathered momentum.

Cánovas was assassinated by an Italian anarchist in 1897, and Sagasta died naturally in 1903. The passing away of the two leaders of the Restoration coincided with the beginning of the decomposition of the old party system: republicans, radicals, reformists, socialists, anarchists, and nationalists of various stripes, burst into the scene, while liberals and conservatives lost support and divided. The semideveloped character of the Spanish economy and society, and the country's traditional isolation, helped in a certain measure by geographical factors, explain that the chronology and the historical periods in Spain should be somewhat *sui generis* within the general European scheme. For most European countries, the divide between the nineteenth and the twentieth centuries was 1914, with the start of the Great War. In the Spanish case, the clear turn of the century took place in 1898, when the 'Disaster' erased the last vestiges of the 'Empire where the sun never set' and degraded Spain from second- to third-rate power. All in all, however, the 'Disaster' had some positive aspects, in that it convinced leaders and citizens that the time had come for the country to live within its means and forget about faded glories, to come down to brass tacks and reform moderately but firmly. 'Regeneration' became the word of the day. In the literary sphere, *regeneracionismo* was identified with the 'generation of 98,' a group of novelists and essayists who preached spiritual and material renovation and who left a deep imprint in the national consciousness. In the educational and scientific sphere, the main inspiration and also the main achievements came from the *Institución Libre de Enseñanza* (ILE). 'La Institución,' as it was commonly called, had been founded in 1876 and was a private association of professors, scientists, and intellectuals in general who protested against the ultramontane principles that the Cánovas government dictated to public universities. It renovated teaching methods, promoted scientific research free of religious prejudices, and gathered a select group of the best minds in most fields of knowledge. Its first president was Laureano Figuerola, its guiding spirit Francisco Giner de los Ríos, and several of the 'generation of 98' actively collaborated with it. In the early twentieth century, the *Institución* gained increasing influence and official support, so it could create a series of education and research institutions that were the best in the country and attained international recognition. Franco abolished it outright.

The economic expression of *regenerationism* was the Stabilization Plan of 1899–1900 designed by the conservative Finance Minister Raimundo Fernández Villaverde. The plan stopped the inflation which the Cuban war had caused and, above all, put an end to the long series of budget deficits which had characterized Spanish finances in the nineteenth century and which had considerably debilitated the Spanish economy. The plan was greatly assisted by the flow of capital repatriated after the loss of the colonies and which contributed to the recovery of the peseta and to the creation of a wave of new banks. This compensated for the budget restrictions of the plan and permitted a new process of expansion and diversification of industry: electricity, petroleum, chemicals, metallurgy, machinery, cement, and house building, all sectors which had been undeveloped suddenly became active. So the 'Disaster' had some positive effects after all.

Catalan industry diversified also, so textiles lost relative weight. The three main industrializing regions, Catalonia, the Basque Country, and Madrid, became poles of attraction for migrants from agricultural backward areas: Andalucía, Murcia, Extremadura, Old Castile, Galicia, etc. The rate of migration, both internal and external, increased in the first decades of the twentieth century. For Catalonia, the 'Disaster' also marked a political watershed: the loss of the colonial markets provoked a sort of collective shock, a disappointment with 'Spain,' and the definitive accolade to political Catalanism. A new party amalgamating older institutions was founded in 1901 under the twin leadership of Prat de la Riba and Cambó: the *Lliga Regionalista* (Regionalist League). It immediately obtained good electoral results and from then onward in Catalonia it drew votes away from the traditional parties; soon another party, more to the left and not Catalanist, became a competitor there for the popular vote: this was the Radical Republican party, drawing on the immigrants' support and led by the Andalusian Alejandro Lerroux.

Another great historical difference between Spain and its neighbors was that Spain took no part in either of the great World Wars. In exchange, of course, it had its own civil war and before suffered the turbulences of the first postwar with remarkable intensity: it was subjected to a military dictatorship inspired in fascism (Primo de Rivera, 1923–1930), saw the monarchy fall down in 1931 and be replaced by a republic which lasted 5 years and 3 months and whose tensions and ups and downs led to a long and ferocious civil war from July 1936 to April 1939. The civil war was won by the rebels led by General Francisco Franco, whose ensuing 36-year dictatorship only ended with the dictator's life in 1975. Franco's dictatorship had fascist traits, but it essentially was a military regime personally controlled by the dictator until his death. The personal character of the regime is demonstrated by the fact that it did not survive Franco. In its initial years, the Franco regime imitated many features of the fascist dictatorships in Italy and Germany; but after the end of World War II, it evolved toward an authoritarian personal regime with pretensions of being monarchical rather than fascist. Its more enduring features were its personal and authoritarian character, and its anticommunism. Its long duration can be explained by its being issued from a civil war that physically destroyed a substantial part of its natural enemies and exiled most of the rest. The liberals and leftists who remained were totally disorganized, were not politicians, and were subjected to an implacable repression, which in time was softened somewhat, but by no means abandoned. The anticommunism of the regime came to its help during the postwar years of East–West confrontation and 'cold war.' Furthermore, the dictator dexterously combined the stick of repression with the carrot of economic development through a process of gradual and limited economic liberalization after 1950.

Spain, therefore, suffered intensely the crisis of the first half of the twentieth century, although with different rhythms and consequences from the rest of Europe. While the fascist dictatorships of Mussolini and Hitler, who helped Franco to power and inspired him, were defeated in 1945 and replaced by democratic regimes, staying out of World War II allowed the Franco dictatorship 30 more years of life.

***

Staying out of World War I did not save Spain from the social tensions and political repercussions that war scarcities and inflation produced, nor from the postwar crisis that ensued. Among other effects, the tensions and repercussions entailed a deterioration of the relations of Catalonia with the rest of Spain and also within Catalonia. The antagonism between capitalists and workmen flared up in the '*Canadiense*' strike in 1919 (see later), which explains, at least in part, the support the Catalan bourgeoisie lent to Primo de Rivera's coup in 1923. We must keep in mind that it was around this time that the economic gap between Catalonia and the rest of Spain was wider. Nevertheless, the fact that Catalonia, being more industrialized, suffered more in the war and postwar crises does not mean that the region was mistreated by the Spanish governments, as some writers have stated.

This allegation has been formulated especially as regards the Franco dictatorship. Some Catalanist writers are of the opinion that Catalonia was the main victim of the Spanish Civil War and of the oppressive policies of the Franco dictatorship. This is flatly absurd. The Franco regime was detestable, but it showed no enmity to any region per se. Its repression was, so to say, geographically neutral. As stated before, its main enemy was communism, as the regime proclaimed time and again; the fascist dictators whom Franco imitated also proclaimed their anticommunism (in Hitler's case, however, the Jews were even worse enemies than the communists), as pertained to their historical role. In addition to communism, the Franco regime had a long list of other enemies, such as republicanism, freemasonry, atheism, anarchism, socialism, political and cultural liberty, regional autonomism, separatism, secularism, and so on. Some of these enemies were mostly or exclusively Spanish, others were universal. To sustain that Catalonia belonged in the long list of enemies of the regime, therefore, would be misleading. In reality, Catalonia, as a more developed region and with some autonomist proclivity, possessed a high number of the traits that were inimical to the regime, such as, for instance, republicanism, anarchism, and separatism, to cite the most obvious.

More discriminated than Catalonia could be considered to have been the Basque provinces of Biscay and Guipuzcoa, that were deprived of their *fueros* for being considered separatist and disaffected, unlike Alava and Navarra, whose *foral* regime was respected. As to the Catalan language, another often mentioned proof of discrimination, it is true that it was repressed by Franco, but so were other regional languages such as Basque and Gallego (Galician), this in spite of Franco himself being of Galician origin.

Furthermore, contrary to what some have stated, Catalonia was not mistreated economically by Franco; rather, the opposite is true. The Catalan economy not only benefited from a series of discretionary measures (Barcelona's free port, the automobile company SEAT which was located there, an important nuclear station which was located in Vandellòs, near Tarragona), but the autarkic policies of the first decades of the regime favored industry, and hence Catalonia, whose industry had the Spanish market more to itself than ever. It was after the Stabilization Plan of 1959 that the economic gap between Catalonia and the rest of Spain started to narrow, but this was not due to Catalan stagnation, far from it, but to the rapid development and industrialization of other areas. Later on, the process of relative deindustrialization, quite common in advanced economies, affected more directly Catalonia and the Basque Country, but this could not be attributed to deliberate policies of any sort.

Spanish economic growth benefited especially from two broad political decisions: first, the Stabilization Plan of 1959, which introduced a measure of liberalization in economic policies, and succeeded in promoting the highest rates of economic growth registered in Spanish history; second, after a second round of liberalization during the period of transition to democracy (1976–1984), Spain acceded to the European Unión (then the European Community) in 1986, and this was also followed by a burst of growth which, with a few bumps, lasted until the Great Recession of the twenty-first century interrupted it in 2007. All in all, it has been a long half century of economic growth and improvement of standards of living starting around 1959, which, among other favorable effects, reduced inequality, both at the individual and at the regional level. Regional convergence, of course, has reduced the weight of the Catalan economy within the total, as reflected in Fig. 6.1. In the years between 1940 and 1980, Catalonia's GDP went from being around 60 percent to around 20 percent above the Spanish average.

Catalanism in the Happy Twenties

The *Lliga*: Catalanists in the Spanish Government

After the Cánovas Tariff, the Spanish state took a turn not only toward radical protectionism but also toward an active intervention in economic affairs and in particular in stimulating industrialization. Thus, a new Tariff

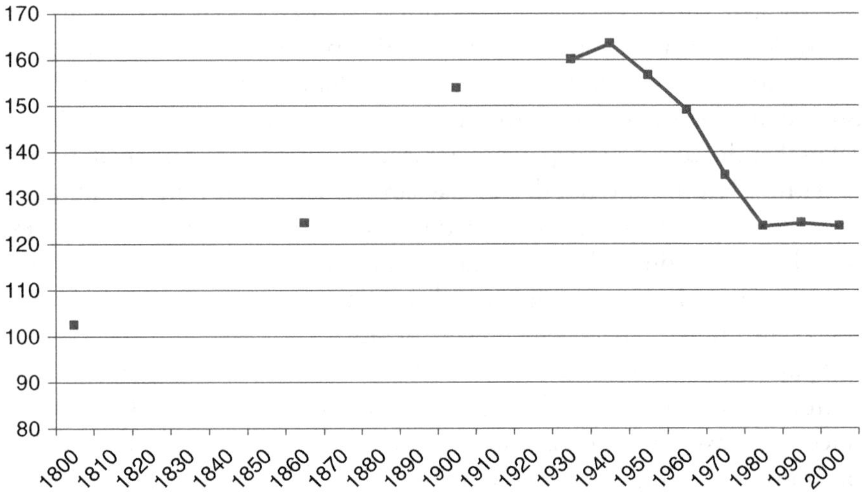

Fig. 6.1 Catalan GDP Relative to Spanish GDP (1800–2000) (Spanish GDP = 100)

Source: Carreras and Tafunell (2005), III, pp. 1372-3, Table 17.27

in 1906 pursued, rather than 'integral' protectionism, a more selective policy of targeting industrial sectors for growth through protection or favorable duties to inputs. Soon afterward, under the leadership of the conservative Antonio Maura (an energetic ex-liberal who became the star of conservatism in the early decades of the twentieth century), a more active policy of 'economic nationalism' by means of subsidies, cheap official credit, and government purchases was adopted as a complement to tariff protection.

This had been the type of policy that many in Catalonia had been advocating for years, which may explain the cordial relationship that was established at this time between Cambó and Maura. Cambó actively cooperated with Maura and was a minister twice in the latter's governments, once in 1918 with the *Fomento* (Development and Public Works) portfolio, and a second time as minister of Finance in 1921–1922. His tenures were short, slightly less than 8 months each time, but his achievements were remarkable. He was an excellent writer and in his memoirs and other works described his political work in and out of the Spanish government. He had been one of those elected on the *Lliga* ticket in 1901, and from then on he became the undisputed leader of that party, especially after Prat de la Riba died in 1917. Cambó, however, was not the only, not even the first, Catalanist in Spanish governments. This honor befell to one of his closer collaborators, Joan Ventosa i Calvell, who became the finance minister in 1917; another *Lliga* man, Filip Rodés i Baldrich was minister of education and fine arts soon afterward.

Barcelona became one of the most violent European cities, if not the most violent, in the early decades of the twentieth century. Anarchism was popular there and, while not all anarchists were violent, there were factions within the party that advocated politics by deed. Other groups of the left, but also of the right, believed in terror and assassination as political weapons. The proletariat and lumpen-proletariat of the city developed strong anticlericalism, antimonarchism, and antimilitarism; many who were not anarchist admired anarchism's methods and principles. This sort of tinderbox exploded in the last week of July 1909, in a movement that started as a strike of protest against the embarking of troops to a war in Morocco which left wingers considered a sacrifice of human lives in defense of the possessions of rich Spaniards there. The problem was mishandled by the police and the army so riots turned extremely violent, with a clear anticlerical slant: convents were burned and desecrated, and street fights broke out for several days. The government finally called upon the army to put down the riots. In the end, there were eight policemen and more than 100 civilians dead; after the days of terror, the police rounded out almost 2,000; severe punishments were meted out, including five death sentences. Among those shot was Francesc Ferrer, the slightly cranky founder of a 'Modern School' devoted to teaching republican and libertarian principles. He was accused of being the instigator of the revolt and condemned without a shred of evidence. His death caused the international discredit of the Spanish government, presided by Maura, who had to resign.

The so-called Tragic Week (Ullman, 1968) alarmed the Barcelona bourgeoisie; the *Lliga* clearly sided with the Maura government, and this coincidence facilitated its political collaboration with the conservative party, which developed in the following years. One of the first proposals of the *Lliga* to the Spanish government was the creation of a *Mancomunidad* (*Mancomunitat* in Catalan), which would coordinate the four Catalan Provinces (Barcelona, Tarragona, Lérida, and Gerona). It would be a sort of autonomous government carrying out common policies for the four provinces, especially in matters of infrastructure, education, and culture. After considerable discussion, the *Mancomunitat Catalana* was established in March 1914, with Enric Prat de la Riba as its first president. At his death in 1917, he was replaced by another *Lliga* man, Josep Puig i Cadafalch, thus confirming the *Lliga*'s hegemony in the world of Catalanism. Under the leadership of Prat de la Riba, the *Mancomunitat* channeled and coordinated investments for transportation projects and also for the improvement of provincial and municipal cultural and educational means. Its work was commendable, but the *Lliga* considered it just as a stepping-stone toward more genuine political autonomy.

In the turbulent year of 1917, an unofficial 'Assembly of Members of Parliament' was created by a group of Catalan and republican deputies to try to offer solutions to the acute social and economic problems that were being posed by war-induced inflation and scarcities, and also by the political questions of autonomism itself and the breakdown of the two-party system. Cambó was the soul of the assembly, and took advantage of this situation to put forward his proposals, which included the project of an *Estatut d'Autonomia de Catalunya* (Statute for the Autonomy of Catalonia), submitted in 1919. There was no hiding that this proposal was made in the wake of US president Woodrow Wilson's defense of the 'self-determination' of subjected peoples. No matter that Catalonia could not be considered subjected, since it was not a colony, did not belong to a multinational empire, nor was subjected to any sort of oppression; the issue of the statute was a good pretext for autonomist agitation. Furthermore, the conservative *Lliga* found in it a way of deviating attention from the social and political problems which another international movement, Bolshevism (Russian communism), was raising. Cambó says in his Memoirs that the idea originated with the king, Alfonso XIII, who summoned him to the Palace in November 1918 and said that he was afraid a revolutionary movement could develop in Catalonia, fostering anarchy all over Spain. The only possible solution he could see was to grant Catalonia its demands so that Catalans would abandon their revolutionary ideas and feel monarchical again. However *naïf*, these ideas appealed to Cambó too, since they could help to put a stop to coronel Francesc Macià, a left-wing Catalan nationalist who was a deputy in the Spanish Cortes, where he had expressed his wish that Catalonia should adhere to the League of Nations which Wilson was promoting (Spain did join in 1919).

Cambó's was not the only project of a Catalan statute being proposed; he himself had made an agreement with the then president of the government, the count of Romanones, so the government would put forward another project drafted by a committee presided by Antonio Maura. According to Cambó, it was Maura's own idea to revive the old name of *Generalitat* and apply it to the projected autonomous government of Catalonia. Cambó thought that having two *Estatut* projects would increase the probabilities of having one approved. Unfortunately, the whole plan was waylaid by the strike of *la Canadiense*. This was the name commonly used to design the 'Barcelona Traction, Light and Power Company,' belonging to the Pearson group whose headquarters were in Toronto (hence its designation). *La Canadiense* was the supplier of electricity and water to the city of Barcelona, so its stoppage in February and March 1919 had serious consequences. To adapt to the postwar depression, the company had lowered some wages: the anarchist union called the strike against the reductions and the firing of some protesters. It was a long and bitter struggle, but the government, alarmed that the strike might cause sympathy movements in other areas and cause further disturbances, pressured the company to yield. So the strikers finally won; among other conquests, the victory brought about the 8-hour workday to Spain. But the commotion caused by the stoppage was such that the Cortes adjourned and the *Estatut* remained in limbo.

As was the case with the Tragic Week, the strike of *la Canadiense* alarmed the men of the *Lliga*. Cambó decided that to maintain social peace in the strained postwar circumstances was more important than to proceed with the autonomist program. So he accepted Maura's proposal to become finance minister in 1921. Although his tenure was short, Cambó left an impressive legacy of his mandate. His two salient contributions were a Banking Law and a Tariff Law. The Cambó Banking Law (*Ley de Ordenación Bancaria*) was very innovative in that for the first time an attempt was made to regulate the whole banking system and to establish the relationships between the Bank of Spain and the rest of the system. Cambó was a lawyer interested in economic and financial topics, so he knew exactly what he was doing: he increased the control over the Bank of Spain by the government and let a wide leeway to the private banking sector to regulate itself with only distant government supervision. His Tariff Law was a rather Catalan instrument in that it followed the principles of the 1906 Tariff in discriminating between finished manufactures and inputs, to heavily tax the former and lightly the latter. It was clearly an industrialist's tariff.

Catalanism and the Primo de Rivera Dictatorship

The effects of the First World War on a neutral country such as Spain were ambiguous. On the one hand, it produced an export boom, as the European powers involved in the conflict curtailed their production of peacetime goods and reduced their sales abroad while they multiplied their imports. This boosted profits and employment and caused a balance of payments surplus which filled the coffers of the Bank of Spain with gold. On the other hand, the scarcities provoked by the war fostered inflation, which, though a little less steep in Spain than in the neighboring belligerent countries, affected the standard of living of those of modest means and provoked serious social tensions and strikes.

Barcelona continued being the largest, although by no means the only, focus of violence and terror in Spain. Street gunfights between hoodlums in the pay of industrialists and union-affiliated thugs became more and more frequent. In 1920, General Severiano Martínez Anido, well known for his ruthless methods in defense of law and order, was appointed civil governor of Barcelona. He established brutal practices, such as the so-called *ley de fugas* (evasion law), which justified killing detainees on the pretext that they were shot while attempting to escape from custody. This well-known practice stimulated violence rather than discouraging it: in 1921, President Eduardo Dato was assassinated in Madrid, in part in retaliation against Matínez Anido's savagery, and street violence between unions and employers continued unabated, especially in Barcelona.

To complicate matters further, Spain's position in Morocco was becoming difficult. Under the aegis of the UK, Spain and France had constituted a protectorate over Morocco in 1912, where France controlled most of the country, but Spain kept the northern coastal strip, a mountainous area populated by rather bellicose tribes. In 1921, a local chieftain, Abd-el-Krim, who had been educated in Spain, organized a general rebellion, defeated the Spanish troops at Annual, and constituted and presided a Republic of the Rif (name of the northern mountain chain), Spain's effective control being reduced to the narrow coastal areas. The defeat of Annual increased the unpopularity of the army in Spain, and also that of the king, who was suspected of having been involved in the military operations. A government committee headed by a general (Juan Picasso, not related to the painter) was created; part of the government stalled in giving evidence to general Picasso, which only increased the widespread suspicions of guilt in the top political spheres. Before the Picasso report was made public, on 13 September 1923, General Miguel Primo de Rivera, an Andalusian at the time captain general of Catalonia, staged a coup, whereby he became the president of a 'military directory' in charge of government but subject to the approval of the king. In Primo de Rivera's manifesto, separatism, public disorder, and corruption were the main evils the dictatorship was supposed to correct. Martínez Anido became minister of the Interior, thus making clear that the new regime proposed to deal severely with problems of public order.

Primo's coup was rather favorably received by the Catalan bourgeoisie. Cambó in his *Memòries* (1981, pp. 373-5) attributed it to 'the inability of constitutional powers to accomplish their mission' and to the lack of representativeness of the traditional political parties. Primo de Rivera, while he was captain general of Catalonia, announced to everybody that he was going to put an end to that shameful situation. People liked him because he was *simpático*, cordial, and had a remarkable ability to make friends. He spoke Catalan, liked to hear and watch *sardanas* (the traditional local dance), and showed affection for the *senyera* (the ancestral regional flag). 'When he met me—generally at the *Liceo* [the Barcelona opera house]—he took my arm and was full of kindness and friendly expressions [. . .] it is not surprising, then, that when he made public a manifesto against a hated and despised government he should have found not only support among the garrison, but also the sympathy of almost everybody in Barcelona.' Most historians agree that Primo found firm backing in the Catalan upper and middle classes.

Meanwhile, the Moroccan problem became so embarrassing that Primo himself assumed the post of Spanish Comissar (the top civilian echelon) in Morocco. At that point, however, Abd-el-Krim, thinking himself invincible, made the error of his life: he moved south and attacked French positions. He made deep strides and threatened the city of Fez, but this alarmed the French and induced them to sign an alliance with Spain. In September 1925, troops of both nations attacked the 'Republic of the Rif' from north and south in a pincer maneuver. Abd-el-Krim resisted fiercely but in May 1926 he had to surrender to the French and was exiled to the island of Réunion in the Indian Ocean. He never came back to Morocco, not even after this country's independence.

Primo de Rivera boasted of his good rapport with the notables in Catalonia, but in the end he blundered badly and managed to alienate all Catalanists, right and left alike. He disbanded traditional democratic institutions while trying to preserve the power of some *Lliga* men, but this was done so clumsily that even those who had originally supported him adopted an attitude of passive resistance when not open hostility. The dictator overhauled local institutions, basically reinforcing municipalities at the expense of regional institutions. One of his purposes was to combat *caciquismo* and in this he was successful. But in this overhaul, one of the main casualties was the Catalan *Mancomunitat*, which was the apple in the *Lliga*'s eye.

The abolition of the *Mancomunitat* was an egregious blunder. Its president, Josep Puig i Cadafalch, was among the most enthusiastic supporters of Primo's coup, but this did not save him from being dismissed in January 1924 and replaced by Alfons Sala, also an unconditional supporter, but who saw his powers and resources pared down until the *Mancomunitat* was abolished in March 1925 and he was offered another post. Deeply humiliated, he refused and retired from politics. Between summer and winter of 1923, Primo de Rivera had radically changed his political program for Catalonia: from a mild sympathizer of autonomism he became its implacable enemy, offending his former allies, moderates and conservatives, without gaining any support from the left, whose popularity increased as the *Lliga*'s dwindled. No wonder that the first act of Francesc Macià after the Republic was proclaimed in 1931 was to declare Catalonia's independence. As Manuel Azaña, the second president of the Second Republic, wrote in his memoirs (1967, III, p. 507), 'Primo de Rivera always boasted about having solved the "Catalan problem". There is evidence that he aggravated it. So it turned out that in the elections of 1931, hurt catalanists took revenge and the left-wing republicans of Catalonia became nationalist without exception.' Niceto Alcalá-Zamora (1977, p. 135), the first president, concurred in Azaña's condemnation of Primo de Rivera's policies in Catalonia.

In addition to all this, the dictatorship forbade the exhibition of any flag but the Spanish, even prohibited the public manifestation of regionalist sympathies, and imposed the exclusive use of the Spanish language in all official and religious meetings and public acts; these measures were applied strictly, and severe penalties were applied to offenders. A gaping breach opened between Catalan society and the dictatorship. Even close collaborators with Primo de Rivera, such as José Calvo Sotelo (1974, pp. 54-5), who was his finance minister for several years, was astounded by Primo's '*unitarianism* [. . .] after his regionalist fervor,' and wrote a letter to him stating that a 'policy of strength, of intransigence, is fruitless.' To no avail. Primo remained adamant.

Historians have wondered about the causes of this about-face which Primo himself admitted in one of his 'office-notes,' the frequent short articles about his political musings he published in the press. González Calbet (1987, p. 181) suggests that the Moroccan problem and Primo's subsequent immersion in military circles made him 'commune one hundred percent with military ideology: the unity of the fatherland above all.' In fact, the dictator totally turned around in his opinions about Catalonia and about the Moroccan question after taking power. Immediately after Annual, Primo de Rivera had been in favor of Spain abandoning Morocco. But it appears that while gathering support from his comrades in arms he had to switch his position in order to gain their backing. It is possible that he also had to concede secretly to them on the Catalan question. After the French–Spanish operation against Abd-el-Krim became his most popular success, he probably felt he could not carry out policies of compromise with autonomism in Catalonia, which were abhorrent to the overwhelming majority of army officers. According to Ben-Ami (1983, pp. 195-6), a dictator cannot dally with decentralization and power-sharing.

If victory in Morocco boosted the popularity of the dictatorship, its economic policies, which initially seemed to be its strongest point, in the end brought it down. In its early years, the dictatorial government carried out a policy of economic nationalism which seemed to yield good results. Entrepreneurs invested confidently knowing that they were shielded against foreign competition. The nationalist economic program was completed with state investment in infrastructure (roads, ports, public buildings, etc.) and military modernization (weapons, battleships), all of which contributed to the growth of basic industry. Of course, the financing of this program entailed large expenditures which brought about budget deficits. Calvo Sotelo, who became finance minister in 1925, cleverly managed to camouflage the deficit by running a sort of parallel budget, so confidence remained and the peseta, propped up by the large gold reserves in the Bank of Spain, remained strong in international markets. An excess of confidence made Calvo-Sotelo assert publicly and repeatedly that a strong peseta was the proof of the soundness of government policies. But he committed a great error: quite in line with his nationalistic principles, he decided to subject petroleum to a state monopoly. Spain did not produce any petrol, so it had to be a distribution monopoly. After 1927, only a state chartered company (Compañía Arrendataria del Monopolio de Petróleos Sociedad Anónima [Corporation Holding the Lease of the Petrol Monopoly], CAMPSA) could sell petroleum products in Spain. He thought this would curtail the power of the oil giants in Spain and increase state revenues, but in the end his scheme backfired.

In order to create the monopoly, the Spanish government had to expropriate the assets of the private companies which had been operating in the Spanish petroleum market; the most important of them were Shell and Standard Oil. Indignant for what they considered arbitrary and shabby treatment by Calvo Sotelo, they dumped on the markets the pesetas they had received for their expropriated assets; thus started a downturn in the quotation of the peseta which left Calvo Sotelo in a difficult position. Cambó, who had gone into business and temporarily retired from politics, published a series of articles denouncing the unsoundness of Calvo Sotelo's policies. Suddenly by the late twenties, everybody had become impatient and fed up with the dictatorial regime. Calvo Sotelo fought back by creating a committee to sustain the peseta and also sought advice from Spanish and foreign experts about what to do with the peseta. His idea was to make it convertible into gold at a time when it seemed that the gold standard was the epitome of monetary respectability. However, both domestic and foreign experts said that in order to make the gold standard viable in Spain, the first priority should be to put public finances in order. This was a medium-term proposal, while the slide of the peseta continued. Calvo Sotelo resigned in January 1930, and so did Primo de Rivera himself a week later. This was the end of the dictatorship and in its fall it carried down the monarchy.

The king, however, fought desperately to forestall the inevitable: he had become extremely unpopular, and his obvious support of the dictatorship had alienated the politicians. He appointed another general, Dámaso Berenguer, to see whether he could find a way of returning to normal, but his base was too narrow and the republicans were plotting openly to overthrow the monarchy. In the fall of 1930, the main republican groups (many monarchists had recently become republican) got together in the so-called Pact of San Sebastián, sketching a program of government for after the Republic was established. There was a republican military rebellion in Jaca, a garrison city in the Pyrenees, which failed, and the plotters were summarily shot; they became instant martyrs and their executions increased the antimonarchy and antimilitary popular feeling. Berenguer resigned in February 1931 and a caretaker government prepared municipal elections for April. Although the majority of the councilors elected were monarchists, the republican and left-wing parties won in all large cities; the results were received with spontaneous pro-republican demonstrations. The king, fearing violence and bloodshed if he tried to impose order, and after consulting with police and military chiefs, fled from the country. The Republic was proclaimed on 14 April.

The Second Republic

The Catalan Statute of Autonomy

On the same day, the Spanish republic was proclaimed in Madrid, an ephemeral Catalan republic was born in Barcelona. Francesc Macià announced the birth of the new republic as part of an inexistent

'Iberian Federation,' and appealed to Catalans to be ready to defend it by 'sacrificing their own lives' if necessary; he also appealed to the other 'brotherly peoples of Spain,' etc. Macià had just founded *Esquerra Republicana de Catalunya* (Republican Left of Catalonia, ERC), a party whose title just pretty well defined it.

Macià's proclamation had been a spur-of-the-moment personal decision; this is shown by the fact that the second in command in *Esquerra*, Lluis Companys, an experienced lawyer specializing in labor matters, had just hoisted the Spanish republican flag in a neighboring building. Macià's decision prevailed over that of his junior partner, but only for less than 2 weeks, the time it took for Macià to hurriedly appoint a cabinet, and almost immediately to open conversations with three ministers of the Spanish government (two of them Catalan) arrived from Madrid to negotiate an arrangement with Macià whereby he would back down. It was soon agreed that the Catalan government (*generalitat*) would be a part of the Spanish government and would be charged with writing a statute of autonomy for Catalonia. A committee was appointed, which in a few months had prepared to text of the *Estatut* project. By August, this text was submitted to referendum and approved by a great majority. According to this text, Spain became a federal republic and the *generalitat* was vested with very wide powers to govern the so-called Catalan countries (not only Catalonia, but other communities such as Valencia and the Balearic islands where the Catalan language was spoken alongside Castilian Spanish). These 'countries,' according to the draft statute, could join Catalonia if they so wished. Catalan would be the only official language in the territory governed by the *generalitat*, although this body would use Castilian in its exchanges with the Madrid government.

While Catalonia was almost exclusively absorbed with the *Estatut*, in the rest of Spain there were more transcendent novelties. One of them was the accession of socialists into the government, something which had arrived only a few years before in other European countries such as Germany, the UK, or France: in Spain, the socialists held the portfolios of Justice, Finance, and Labor in the first republican government. But this did not seem enough to satisfy the masses who, once free from the repression of the dictatorship, indulged in a surge of violence against what they considered the symbols of that repression and especially those which could not easily repel their aggression, such as churches and landowners. The government was hastily decreeing religious freedom and carrying out a deep reform of the army, but violence proceeded, especially in the south. General elections took place meanwhile (28 June), giving the victory to the left. The Catalan government submitted the project of *Estatut* by mid-August, but its examination had to wait until the new republican Constitution was approved. This took place in December: it was soon evident that the *Estatut* project needed considerable modifications to make it compatible with the Constitution. Among other points, for example, article 4 of the Constitution declared that Castilian Spanish was the official language in the whole nation, although regional languages could be co-official; in any case, knowledge of regional languages could not be made mandatory. This flatly contradicted the projected sole official character of Catalan as the draft *Estatut* asserted.

The draft *Estatut* had drawn wide support in Catalonia but found serious opposition in the rest of Spain, where there were mass demonstrations against it and hostility among many politicians. An ample sector of Spanish opinion wanted its rejection outright; this was the position not only of conservatives but also of many intellectuals and liberals of prestige, such as José Ortega y Gasset or Miguel de Unamuno. In the end, it was Manuel Azaña, at the time the head of the government, who almost single-handedly managed to obtain the approval of the *Estatut*, in a considerably modified version. According to Jackson (1967, p. 75), 'Azaña staked the life of his government, and his personal prestige, on the passage of the statute.'

The final version of this text (9 September 1932) was quite different from the original draft. The 1931 Constitution did not accept the federal formula or the existence of the 'Catalan countries.' Catalonia would be an autonomous region within the Spanish republic, the Catalan language would be co-official, and all the references to sovereignty or to Catalonia as a 'nation' were eliminated. The powers of the *generalitat* were circumscribed accordingly. Although grudgingly accepted, these modifications appeared to have settled the initial discrepancies. In the local elections which took place soon after the approval of the *Estatut*, ERC came out well ahead of the *Lliga*.

In August 1932, an attempted coup was staged under the direction of General José Sanjurjo, who was the director of the *Guardia Civil*, an elite police corps, and had distinguished himself in the Moroccan war. It failed, and Sanjurjo was condemned to death, but his sentence was commuted to life imprisonment. The botched coup was a shot in the arm for the government and facilitated the passage of the Catalan statute and the Agrarian Reform Law, one of the great republican projects. The lands of many grandees were expropriated and access to ownership by modest peasants was facilitated, but this did not totally calm down agrarian resentment and turmoil.

All these conflicts contributed to the defeat of the left in the elections of November 1933. Among the factors favoring the right was that women voted for the first time in Spanish history, and it was widely agreed that they voted conservative. This was the reason why some left-wing women had been opposed to being given the vote. Another factor, of course, was that the conservatives, totally disorganized in 1931, had had time to regroup in 1933. The main conservative party was the recently founded *Confederación Española de Derechas Autónomas* (Spanish Confederation of Autonomous Conservatives, CEDA) a large amorphous group which covered an ample spectrum from Christian-Democrats to extreme rightists, bordering on fascism. Its leader, José M. Gil Robles, deliberately played upon this ambiguity and adopted some fascist-style symbols, such as being called *jefe*, chief (akin to *duce* or *führer*). There were other, smaller but noisy, overtly fascist groups such as the *Falange* (Payne, 1961), headed by Primo de Rivera's son, José Antonio, or the *Juntas de Ofensiva Nacional Sindicalista* (JONS), led by a Valladolid lawyer and a philosopher. Both groups soon merged.

In Catalonia, ERC again won the local elections in January 1934. Macià had just died, and Companys succeeded him at the head of the party.

From Revolution to Civil War

The two final years of the republic in peace were a real prelude to civil war. The shadows of the Communist revolution in Russia in 1918–1921 and of Hitler's takeover in Germany in January 1933 hovered above the

Spanish political arena as two sinister birds of prey. The conservatives saw communist conspiracies everywhere while the left prepared to combat an imminent fascist coup. The proverbial intransigence of the Spaniards was carried to limits by these recent historical episodes. The paradigm of left-wing paranoia materialized after the CEDA victory in 1934. For the left, if President Alcalá Zamora charged Gil Robles to head a government, it would be as German President Von Hindenburg appointing Hitler chancellor. Such were the warnings and the tension that Alcalá Zamora opted for charging Lerroux with heading a government. Lerroux, after having been a leftist bogeyman in his youth now had become a right-of-center political hack of the old school. Gil Robles accepted the situation and pledged his support for the Radicals, waiting for a more opportune moment to assume the post that he logically thought was his due.

The position of the Lerroux government was precarious and had to accept many impositions from the CEDA; the one that brought it down was issuing an amnesty which freed general Sanjurjo. The scandal on the left forced Lerroux to resign. He was replaced by Ricardo Samper, a member of Lerroux's party and government. Samper almost immediately was confronted with a serious difficulty in Catalonia. This was caused by a Law of Agrarian Contracts which the Catalan parliament approved in March 1934. This law tried to solve a long-standing problem in Catalan agriculture: vine cultivation was quite extended there in the nineteenth century, and usually subject to a contract of tenancy which lasted as long as three quarters of the vines standing when the contract was signed were alive, so the contracts were popularly called *rabassa morta*, dead stump, and the tenants were called *rabassaires*. Normally these contracts lasted about 50 years, but a plague of phylloxera which ravaged Europe in the late nineteenth century left many *rabassaires* at the mercy of the landowners, who squeezed them to compensate their losses. The *rabassaires* became a sort of agrarian revolutionaries, and Companys was their lawyer. So he had this law passed which permitted the *rabassaires* to acquire the land they had cultivated for 15 years on favorable terms. The landowners, logically, opposed the law and they appealed to the Spanish Supreme Court (*Tribunal de Garantías Constitucionales*) arguing that according to the Constitution only the national Cortes could legislate on contractual obligations. A divided Supreme Court ruled in favor of the landlords, but Companys did not accept the verdict. Samper, instead of following through with the law, quietly reached an underhand agreement with Companys. But a dangerous precedent had been established whereby the Catalan *generalitat* infringed the Constitution and disobeyed the Supreme Court with the acquiescence of the Spanish government.

This episode, plus general unrest in the countryside where the application of the agrarian reform had been *de facto* suspended by the conservatives, plus the Basque insistence in obtaining their own statute of autonomy and behaving as though they were autonomous already, left the Samper government on the verge of dissolution. Gil Robles thought that his time had arrived and in September demanded that CEDA become part of the government. On October 4, a new cabinet was formed with three CEDA ministers. This news provoked a general rebellion of the left, which was focalized in three places: Madrid, Barcelona, and Asturias. In Madrid, there was a general strike with hints of violence, but the situation there was rapidly controlled. In Barcelona and Asturias, things became more distressing. In Barcelona, on October 6, Companys proclaimed the constitution of a Spanish federal republic whose provisional government would be located in Barcelona. Catalonia would become, in his own words, 'the indestructible redoubt of the essences of the Republic' against the monarchical and fascist forces which wanted to betray it. The Barcelona town hall soon adhered to Companys's manifesto, but not much later the state of war in Catalonia was decreed by the Lerroux government. General Domingo Batet, the captain general, laid siege to the *generalitat* and town hall buildings. There was scattered violence in the streets of the city and some exchange of fire between the besieged and the government troops, but by daybreak of the 7th, Companys surrendered and assumed full responsibility for the rebellion. Some participants in it escaped through the sewers and reached France, an episode which became the topic of acerbic jokes. Allison Peers (1938, pp. 230-7) called them 'sewer rats.' The casualties in Barcelona were about 30 dead and more than 100 wounded. In the rest of Catalonia, there were some scuffles but no serious violence. Among those detained in Barcelona was none other than Manuel Azaña, the former president of the government, who happened to be there on a private visit and was accused of having participated in plotting the revolt. He was one of the *bêtes noires* of the right. After months of detention and harassment, he was finally exonerated and wrote an explanatory book ironically entitled *My rebellion in Barcelona.*

The situation in Asturias became even worse, among other reasons because the insurrection had more support there. Asturias, a coal-mining region, was a stronghold of the socialist party and its *Unión General de Trabajadores* (General Workingmen's Union, UGT). In preparation for the rising, the Socialist party had smuggled weapons among the miners, so they were numerous and well armed; they also used dynamite sticks as hand bombs. The insurgents took Oviedo, the provincial capital, and other towns, mostly mining centers. The Asturias insurrection had some smaller echoes in other mining regions in neighboring León and Palencia, and in some mining districts of the Basque Country. The government sent to Asturias an army contingent and the foreign legion; after 10 days of almost civil war, the Asturias rebels were subdued. The uprising left about 100 dead and double number of wounded.

Lerroux was cautious in demanding responsibilities, to the impatience of the CEDA. After the problem of what to do with the rightist prisoners of the Sanjurjo coup, now there was that of the far more numerous leftists imprisoned after the October rebellions. Companys and his close collaborators were condemned to 30 years' imprisonment. In the case of Asturias, there were several death sentences, a few actually carried out. What to do with the prisoners was a subject which deeply divided the government. While both presidents, Alcalá Zamora of the Republic and Lerroux of the government, favored leniency, the right demanded hard retribution for armed rebellion. Complicating matters further, reports of harsh repression and torture by the army on the Asturian prisoners were widespread. In Catalonia and Asturias, normal government was suspended, and they were ruled by politicians appointed in Madrid. To all this, problems of corruption were added which, while they would be considered trifling incidents today, at the time scandalized public opinion. Lerroux's Radicals had been the main culprits of these misdemeanors for many years. In 1935, a new scandal broke out which was sort of the straw which broke the camel's back: the promoter of a kind of roulette called *straperlo* frustrated because his license had been revoked, alleged that, to obtain it, he had bribed a group of politicians close to president Lerroux. Nothing conclusive was proved, but the incident put a tragicomic and dishonorable end to the Lerroux government and induced the call for new elections. The term '*estraperlo*' was adopted into Spanish and for many years became a byword of scam, swindle, or black market.

The new general elections of February 1936 were carried out in a bitter climate of revenge and hatred. The left coalesced into a Popular Front with the purpose of putting an end to what they called the 'black biennium,' which they identified with reaction, clericalism, and fascism. The right was angry that it had been deprived of power unfairly, and suspected that the left wanted to conclude the revolution which they, the right, had been able to abort in 1934. Both sides were justified in their ominous suspicions about their rivals. The Popular Front won the election, but to Azaña, one of the leaders of the Front, who was immediately to become head of the government, their victory was full of somber presages. The transitory restrictions which followed the October revolution were lifted and a wide amnesty was issued. Catalonia recovered its full autonomy and Companys, freed by the amnesty, was restored to his post as president of the *generalitat*. So were his companions and councilors. Now the situation had turned again: it was the military who had suppressed the rebellion who were threatened with legal procedures.

As a result of all those angry feelings, street violence flared again, this time mostly between Falangists and left-wing militias. In the predominant spirit of rancor, President Alcalá Zamora was forced to resign on a petty technicality and Azaña was elected to replace him. He appointed Santiago Casares Quiroga, head of an autonomist Galician party very close to Azaña's Republican Left party, president of the government, where the socialists did not participate.

The months intervening between the election and the start of the civil war on 18 July, verbal and physical violence predominated, which the government was unable to terminate. Gunfights between Falangists and leftists escalated and so did assassinations. José Antonio Primo de Rivera was detained by the police for illegal arms possession in March. This did not prevent the continuation of violent raids by the Falangists. The escalation culminated in the murder of José Calvo Sotelo on July 13 by socialist policemen and henchmen, in retaliation for the former slaying of a socialist lieutenant. Calvo Sotelo had become one of the most prominent politicians of the extreme right, and the news of his death was taken as the opportunity a group of plotters had been waiting for. The conspiracy had brought together conservatives, Falangists, monarchists, and military men. The top military plotter was General Emilio Mola. General Francisco Franco joined at the eleventh hour after months of hesitation.

The Civil War

The plotters had planned a coup to be carried out by top military men and some politicians in the main cities, especially Madrid, where they expected to be able to control posts of command and centers of power in a relatively short time. The rebels' plan as such failed in that they did not take control of Madrid, Barcelona, or most large cities save Saragossa and Seville. In Madrid, the government distributed weapons to the unions, and the rebels were bottled up in their barracks, which were eventually taken by storm amid much carnage; the survivors were taken prisoner.

In Barcelona, a considerable part of the garrison refused to join the coup and the rebels retreated. General Manuel Goded, who had taken over Mallorca for the insurgents, flew to Barcelona to head the rebel troops but fell easily into the hands of the loyal troops and was made prisoner. After some failed attempts to negotiate with the government, Goded was court martialed, condemned to death, and shot.

Although the coup had failed, the rebels still controlled about a third of the peninsula, with their strongholds in western Andalucía, Galicia, Aragon, Navarre, and most of northern Castile in the days immediately following the coup. They fell back on a plan to advance rapidly on Madrid from north and south, helped by Italy and Germany, which contributed with airplanes, weapons, and men, and to take the capital before the end of the year. They were stopped in the western outskirts of Madrid in November 1936 and in Guadalajara (east of Madrid) in March 1937.

In Catalonia, a congeries of parties and unions (anarchists, socialists, communists, Catalan nationalists, Trotskyists, and *rabassaires*) had received (or wrested) arms from the *generalitat*. Soon there were two parallel powers there: the *generalitat* headed by Companys and the 'Central Committee of Anti-Fascist Militias,' where all those parties and unions were represented. The Committee assumed matters of war and law and order (sic).

The first task of the Committee was to organize a series of columns to advance into Aragon and try to recover it from the insurgents. They also sent boat expeditions to the Balearic Islands which managed to recover Ibiza and Formentera for a couple of months. With considerable Italian support, the rebels were able to recover these islands by the end of September. Only Menorca remained faithful to the Republic until the end of the war. In Aragon, the Republican, mainly anarchist, columns did some inroads into rebel territory but captured no provincial capitals. According to Azaña in his memoirs, 'in the front of Aragon there has been no action.' The best description of the war in Aragon from a participant's standpoint is contained in Orwell's *Homage to Catalonia*, of which Ken Loach made a film, *Land and Freedom*.

The war situation disorganized Catalan industries. In an effort to subordinate industry to war needs, a Committee of War Industries was created, presided by Josep Tarradellas; the Committee expropriated about 500 metallurgical and chemical firms. The anarchists on their part were also taking over industrial factories and putting them under worker control by means of ad hoc committees. The *generalitat* tried with some success to coordinate all these takeovers and expropriations; they also did the best they could to protect people, buildings, and objects from the antireligious fury of the anarchists and others. An anecdote is told about the Communist poet Rafael Alberti in Ibiza, who confronted a group of anarchists intent on destroying images and objects from a ransacked church building. The only way to convince them not to destroy them was to point out that, because of their artistic and historical value (about which the anarchists did not care a bit), these objects could be sold and bring about money to buy food and weapons.

Tarradellas, one of the founders of ERC, who had quit for his differences with Macià and later returned, became Economics counselor (regional minister) and managed to bring together the variegated group of Catalan parties and unions under his direction. The *generalitat* was extending its powers and reach considerably beyond the limits of the Spanish Constitution and of the Catalan *Estatut*. Some thought that the exigencies of the war required this. President Azaña, however, thought otherwise (1968, IV, p. 796); according to him, the Catalan authorities 'took advantage of the July rebellion and the ensuing confusion to expand with impunity, thanks to the weakness in which the military revolt left the state.' When the Madrid government denied some credits to the *generalitat*, this body proceeded to seize the Bank of Spain branches and the Finance ministry offices in Catalan territory. On August 28, the *generalitat* awarded itself a status of nearly full independence when it established that in Catalonia only the decrees published in the Catalan legislative bulletin would have legal force. In the following months, the *generalitat* took control of all public services, including those relating to foreign trade. This was de facto independence. It did not last long.

Tarradellas became *conseller en cap* (first councilor), a sort of prime minister with Companys as a sort of president of the Catalan state in the fall of 1936, and he managed to obtain the dissolution of the Anti-Fascist Committee and the reversion of its capacities to the *generalitat*. It was a measure of rationalization, but the political crisis of May 1937 put an end to his tenure. The Tarradellas government also created a so-called Army of Catalonia composed basically of the Aragon columns. Little positive came out of this new 'Army,' largely because of the anarchists' lack of discipline.

Azaña had a rather dim opinion of Tarradellas's policies (1967, III, p. 506; 1968, IV, p. 795); he thought that the 'Catalan Army,' the creation of a separate department of Defense, and the appropriation of the war industries by the *generalitat* were all illegal and disloyal acts whose consequence was to hinder the Republic's military effort. 'The consequences of this conflict did not come to light because, when the military debacle arrived, all was buried under the rubble.'

In November 1936, while Madrid was being besieged by the rebels, the Spanish government was transferred to Valencia (in October 1937, when the Franco army secured Teruel, the siege of government was moved to

Barcelona). Francisco Largo Caballero, a left-wing socialist and former construction worker, became president and appointed four Catalan anarchists (among them a woman, Federica Montseny) ministers. In Barcelona, the tensions between the Communists, who tried to cooperate as efficiently as possible with the Republican army and who were not loath to impose strict military discipline, and the anarchists, who of course preferred anarchy, were reaching a critical point. Right after the war began, Catalan Communists and Socialists had merged into a new party, the Unified Socialist Party of Catalonia (PSUC), in what in fact was a Communist takeover. A splinter anti-Stalinist Communist party, the Workers' Party of Marxist Unification (POUM) was also founded at about this time by Trotskyists, *rabassaires*, and above all a group of intellectuals disappointed by Stalinism. The POUM was very small but had some excellent political thinkers; it tended to side with the anarchists and was the object of intense hatred from the PSUC and the Communist party.

All these tensions came to a head on 3 May 1937, when the department of Interior of the *generalitat* tried to recover the telephone company building from the anarchists who were installed there and were suspected of interfering with the communications from the government in Valencia. A gunfight broke out between the *generalitat* policemen and the anarchists inside the building. As the news spread, there was an anarchist uprising in all of Barcelona, with the support of the POUM. A sort of civil war within the civil war took place in the city, between the anarchists and the POUM on one side, and the Communists and Socialists (although some UGT men sided with the anarchist union, the CNT-Confederación Nacional del Trabajo, National Labor Confederation) on the other. Even troops from the front of Aragon joined in the struggle to defend their anarchist comrades. Orwell was in Barcelona at the time and portrayed this internecine strife in his *Catalonia* book.

Reluctantly, the *generalitat* appealed to the government in Valencia, but the response was slow, as the Republican cabinet was also split and 'the watchword issued by the rebels and accepted de facto by the *generalitat* was that it was a brawl *between Catalans*, in which nobody else should get mixed, including, *naturally*, the government of the Republic' (Azaña, 1968, IV, p. 580; his italics). Azaña happened to be residing in Barcelona at the time, in the building of the Catalan parliament, not far from the port and from the telephone building, in the thick of the fighting. Finally, Largo Caballero sent two battleships from Valencia to Barcelona, ostensibly to rescue Azaña, but in fact to land 1,500 guards and put an end to the shooting (Azaña finally returned to Valencia by plane). The political end result of this lamentable episode was that the government of the Republic recovered the control of Catalonia, whose army became a part of the Republican army. The Tarradellas government fell and the *generalitat* was reduced to its statutory and constitutional limits. Taking advantage of the circumstances, the Communists wanted to inflict punishment on the POUM; Largo Caballero opposed this and had to resign; he was replaced with Juan Negrín, a socialist doctor from the Canary Islands, who was quite close to the Communists for practical reasons: he believed only they had the means and the discipline to carry on the war and resist Franco's army (Jackson, 2008). Negrín let the Communists have their revenge against the POUM. Their henchmen arrested one of their leaders, the Catalan Andreu Nin, took him to a house they controlled in Alcalá de Henares, near Madrid, and tortured him to death. They wanted him to confess that the POUM was a nest of infiltrated Franco agents. He died heroically, but they spread this lie nevertheless and embellished it with a fabricated story that Nin had been abducted by his Gestapo or Falangist comrades: the tale came in several versions. The news of Nin's disappearance and the rumors of what had been done to him (not confirmed until the opening of Soviet archives after 1989) seriously harmed the credit of the Republic in international circles (Bolloten, 1991, Chapters 48 and 49; Jackson, 2008, Chapter 4).

Remembering those days, Azaña, the former intrepid defender of Catalonia's autonomy, now disappointed and sarcastic, wrote (1968, IV, p. 587):

> One thousand times, with bitterness and spite, I reflected on what the rumpus in Barcelona had entailed for politics and the war. The conclusion of ten months of raving incompetence, conjoined with treason! Franco's broadcasters celebrated enthusiastically [. . .] Officially, however, it was a struggle among Catalan workmen who were defending the conquests of the revolution.

He could also have added that this was one more episode, perhaps the most distressing, of the long history of division of Catalan society, which had so often surfaced in the past, from the War of the *Remensas* and the Caspe compromise to the War of the Reapers, the War of Spanish Succession, the Carlist Wars, the Tragic Week, and so many other cases that could be cited.

The anarchists also left the *generalitat.* The next month the Franco troops conquered Biscay, and the Spanish bishops (save the exiled Catalan cardinal Francesc Vidal i Barraquer) wrote a joint letter in support of Spanish nationalism. Negrín also took power away from the so-called Council of Aragon, an anarchist committee associated to the Aragon army which had been carrying out land confiscations and collectivizations in the area they controlled. In this, he followed the Communist watchword of postponing revolution and class war to concentrate on winning the war against Franco. But Negrín (who also assumed the defense portfolio) soon relinquished the idea of winning the war and focused his efforts upon prolonging it as much as possible while abandoning revolution altogether and seeking the support of the western powers to mediate and help him find a negotiated end to the conflict. In the international context of the late 1930s, the Western democracies were torn between the fear of communism and that of fascism and did not respond to his requests.

While the Republican side dissipated its forces in internal strife, the Franco side showed an iron military discipline. Franco became the official and undisputed leader in 1 October 1936. In April 1937, he created a single party by decreeing the awkward merger of the Carlists with the Falangists, in the no less awkwardly called '*Falange Española Tradicionalista y de las JONS,*' or '*FET y de las JONS*' for short. Franco handled this strange party at his will during his long tenure; there were, in addition, many more political groups and factions on his side (monarchists, recalcitrant Carlists, Catholics of several stripes, technocrats, etc.) not officially recognized, but tolerated and accepted as different 'families' within the regime.

After securing the northern coast and postponing the taking of Madrid, Franco's troops commenced a long operation of trying to cut the republican zone into two by reaching the Mediterranean at around the Ebro delta. This would separate Catalonia from the rest of the dwindling republican territory. The rebels thus moved their troops to the Aragon front. The battle for Teruel (December 1937–February 1938) was crucial; once Teruel was secure in Franco's hands, the *nationalist* (the Franco side called itself *national*, meaning that the republicans were either communists or separatists) army pushed eastward toward the sea, which they reached at Vinaroz in April. Catalonia was thus separated from the rest of the Republic. Almost simultaneously Lérida fell to the 'nationalists,' and Franco decreed the abolition of the *Estatut*. The next—and really the last—great action was the Battle of the Ebro. The Republican troops crossed the river and pushed back the nationalist army in July 1938. Slowly and gradually, the Franco troops fought back and by November they had recrossed the Ebro and recovered their positions. That was the beginning of the end. From then onward, the republican troops were on the defensive and fought a losing rearguard battle. Tarragona fell on 15 January 1939, Barcelona ten days later; by 10 February, the 'nationalists' had reached the French border and the entire Catalonia was in their hands. Many republicans had crossed the border. As Azaña wrote in his memoirs, 'once Catalonia is lost, nothing can be done in the rest of Spain.' Surrounded by Franco's troops, a second 'civil war within the civil war' flared in republican Spain. This one was in Madrid, between those who wanted to resist and those who thought all was lost and it was best to surrender. Franco's troops entered Madrid without a fight or negotiation on 28 March. Those republicans who could embarked hurriedly in Valencia and Alicante. The war was over.

Postwar Repression

What arrived in April 1939 was not peace, but victory for some and defeat for others. A Law of Political Responsibilities had been issued by the 'nationalists' in February, which was to mark the patterns of political repression typical of the Franco regime for many years to come. All political parties, except *FET y de las JONS*, were prohibited, and so were all unions except the official ones, which in fact were part of the state bureaucracy and depended on their own ministry. Having taken part in the October 1934 *subversion* or having opposed the *National Movement* (i.e., the generals's coup of July 1936) were considered serious crimes which could be punished with death. The law was applied with all rigor in Catalonia, where political purges in the best totalitarian style were carried out in earnest. The region's prisons were full of political prisoners (about 14,500); it is calculated that about 3,500 Catalans were condemned to death and there was even the case of a writer, Carles Rahola, summarily condemned and shot only for his writings. Many people lost their employment for being considered 'disaffected.' It must be taken into account, however, that the same regime of political terror was applied throughout all of the national territory, and especially in Madrid, which resisted the onslaughts of the 'nationalist' army during all the war and fell later than Barcelona.

Particularly heinous were the executions of politicians captured by the Nazis in France and handed over to Franco. Such was the case of Lluis Companys, who was shot after a summary trial on 15 October 1940. But again, there were other similar cases which have received less attention, such as that of another Catalan, Joan Peiró, who had been a minister of the republic during the war, was also hand over by the Nazis, and shot in 1942. Other non-Catalans, such as Julián Zugazagoitia, a Basque, and Manuel Cruz Salido, an Andalusian, suffered similar fates.

Catalan culture was also heavily repressed, especially in the long aftermath of the war. The Catalan language was prohibited in public and reduced to the private sphere. However, things evolved during Franco's long tenure and he adapted his repression methods to internal and external circumstances The *Institute of Catalan Studies*, founded by Prat de la Riba, was expelled from its headquarters and had to subsist in a semiclandestine situation, protected by Félix Millet, a conservative Catalanist and businessman who had joined the Franco side since the beginning of the civil war. From the end of the World War, the prohibition to publish in Catalan was gradually softened. From 1951, there was a mini-boom of Catalan publications. Later on, even some newspapers of restricted circulation were allowed. Let us not forget, nonetheless, that a severe regime of censorship always existed in all of Spain under Franco.

Political repression and persecution and silencing of dissenters were consubstantial to the regime. In the last years of the regime, there were several *causes célébres* which showed how little the repressive nature of the regime had changed. In 1973, the whole committee of *Comisiones Obreras*, a union (illegal, of course) close to the Communist party, was condemned to sentences of between 12 and 20 years of prison, for no other crime than peacefully carrying out their tasks. And in 1974, Salvador Puig Antich, a Catalan anarchist who had been involved in some violent actions, among them the death of a policeman in an exchange of gunfire (serious doubts still subsist whether it was Puig Antich and not his fugitive companion, who fired the fatal shots), was garrotted to death. This case caused an uproar in Europe, where personalities such as the Pope and German chancellor Willy Brandt pleaded for the defendant's reprieve.

Anyhow, external change and social evolution brought change in the internal sphere. In the early forties, for instance, Franco collaborated closely with the Nazis, to the point that Spain had a contingent of about 50,000 men fighting in Russia alongside the German army, the so-called Blue Division. This was withdrawn in 1943 when the Franco regime adopted a more neutral position in the World War as the Axis campaigns lost steam. Spain had also signed the Anti-Comintern Pact even before the Spanish civil war was over. As the Axis star waned, however, the Franco regime became isolated; there were voices, such as that of Don Juan, son of Alfonso XIII and the official pretender to the throne, asking for political change and offering a constitutional monarchy as the best alternative to the dictatorship. The United Nations in 1946 recommended withdrawing diplomatic recognition of the Franco regime, which was saved by economic help from Juan Perón's Argentina and, later on, by the Communist takeover in China and the Korean war, which hardened the front lines of the Cold War. The regime tried to adapt to the new circumstances and to shed the fascist mantle. In 1947, a Law of Succession was approved which declared Spain to be a monarchy 'in accordance with its tradition,' but vested upon Franco the power to designate his successor either as king or as regent (he thus became a real kingmaker). In November 1950, the UN lifted the recommendation of the diplomatic boycott of the regime at the behest of the United States of America, which now saw the dictator as an ally in the confrontation with the USSR. Franco also obtained several diplomatic victories with the signature of a Concordat with the Holy See, a mutual defense pact with the United States in 1953, and the accession to full membership of the United Nations in 1955. This partial international recognition gave the regime a new lease of life and made it more confident and thereby a little less repressive.

The relative softening of the regime became evident in 1951, when a hike in the prices of public transportation in Barcelona was followed by a strike, or rather a boycott, of tramways and buses. This revealed a certain degree of organization among the strikers. There were detentions, but the government finally caved in: the fares went down, and the mayor and governor were fired. The government was faced with other serious challenges during the 1950s: there was intense agitation in the universities, street demonstrations in Madrid and Barcelona, and strikes in the coal mines of Asturias and factories in the Basque country and Catalonia. In 1956, France suddenly granted independence to Morocco without even consulting Spain, whose government was forced to follow suit, losing face with its own military, with the population at large, and also in the diplomatic sphere (Trythall, 1970, pp. 241-7; Payne, 1987, pp. 427-9). The economic situation also became alarming, with high inflation, chronic balance of payments deficit, and almost total depletion of gold and dollar reserves. After considerable hesitation, the response of the regime to these difficulties was directed toward limited liberalization. In 1957, a new team joined the cabinet: the new stars were two economic ministers (Alberto Ullastres and Mariano Navarro) belonging to the modernizing religious group Opus Dei inclined to economic liberalism and political moderation. This group was led by a Barcelona professor, Laureano López Rodó, and a Catalan banker, cousin of Félix Millet and long established in Madrid, Luis Valls Taberner. Under the inspiration of this group, plus some independent economists, such as the Catalan Joan Sardà and the Castilian Enrique Fuentes Quintana, the 1959 Stabilization Plan was implemented, which steered the Spanish economy (and thereby, to a limited extent, politics) toward the western European model.

Economic Stabilization and Development

Politics in the Twilight of Fascism

Sardà was a Catalan economist who had emigrated to Venezuela after the civil war. He was an economist of moderate convictions and returned to Spain at the behest of Mariano Navarro to head the research department at the Bank of Spain and from there help in preparing the Stabilization Plan of 1959. Although he had no political sympathy for Francoism, he believed that by scrapping as much as possible the many vestiges of fascism left over in the Spanish economy two goods would derive: one, economic development; and, two, the way would be paved for an easier return to democracy. I myself heard him say so at table in my house (he was a lifelong friend of my father; they had been schoolmates at the University of Barcelona before the civil war). I was a student at the time and was not totally convinced by his reasoning. Of course, he was right on both counts. Thanks to Sardà, among others, the Spanish economy became more open and similar to the economies of its western European neighbors and experienced the fastest growth in its history during the 1960s. Spanish society became more open and modern, more conscious of the advantages of the Western democratic paradigm, so that, as we shall see, the demise of the dictatorship was made much easier, as the vast majority of Spaniards were impatient for change when the time came. In a second phase, after the Plan started to yield growth and welfare, the French model of flexible planning was adopted. Even the French terminology was copied so that the ministry of development was called the Commissariat of the Development Plan with López Rodó at the helm. The end result of the Development Plans was mixed; according to Fuentes Quintana's bon mot, the Stabilization Plan produced development, while the Development Plans contributed to stabilize an economy that was growing in a somewhat disorderly manner.

As we saw before, the Franco regime was not really a one-party system. There never was a purely *FET y de las JONS* cabinet, and the political weight of the Falangists dwindled gradually as the Axis powers crumbled down and Spain had to step up its interaction with the Western world.

After 1957, the Opus Dei, a secular religious order, was the mainstay of the Franco cabinets, although it never totally monopolized power. There soon developed a bitter rivalry between the Falangists and the *opusdeistas*, although there always were ministers of both groups in the cabinet. Franco was master at keeping a balance between rival 'families,' who remained faithful to him in the hope that he would give them more power in the next government reshuffle. The rivalry between the two groups came to a head with the *Matesa* case, where this firm, belonging to a Catalan entrepreneur close to Opus Dei, was found receiving enormous credits from the Bank for Industrial Credit, an official bank. These were supposed to be credits for exportation, but Matesa really was selling to its own foreign branches. The case could be economically justifiable, but the Falangist press made a big scandal of it. This was happening at a crucial moment, in the summer of 1969, when Franco was about to appoint Juan Carlos de Borbón (the son of Don Juan, the royal pretender) his successor as the next king of Spain, according to the 1947 Succession Law. This was a carefully prepared operation, with the decided support of the *opusdeistas*. The Falangists hoped that the Matesa affair would discredit the Opus Dei and derail the nomination of Juan Carlos, but their plot backfired. Franco appointed Juan Carlos and in the ensuing government reorganization of the cabinet the *opusdeistas* almost monopolized the portfolios.

Nonetheless, Franco again proved past master at creating division among his allies, because the nomination not only riled the Falangists, it also created dissension among the monarchists, since the legitimate pretender to the throne according to the rules of succession was not Juan Carlos, but his father Don Juan, and many old monarchists, starting with Don Juan himself, were angry at seeing Franco interfering with the monarchy's own precepts and priorities. But there was little they could do; furthermore, this arrangement had one advantage for them: they had two horses in the race.

Those were the years when everybody sensed that the dictatorship was approaching its end, when politicians started to think of their role in the post-Franco era and to make bolder moves. Street demonstrations and strike activity intensified. In Catalonia, opposition to the regime was closely related to autonomism and to Catholicism. In 1961, *Omnium*

Cultural was founded; it was—still exists—a cultural institution with strong Catalanist overtones and solid financial backing: Félix Millet was one of its founders. Political protest was active in Catalonia. The abbot of the Montserrat shrine near Barcelona was forced to abandon Spain in 1965 for criticizing the dictatorship in the French newspaper *Le Monde*. In the following year, more than a hundred Catholic priests demonstrated in Barcelona in protest against police torture of political prisoners while Jordi Pujol, the future long-serving president of Catalonia, launched the slogan 'We want Catalan bishops' (hence preaching in Catalan), and a democratic student union was founded in the sacred precinct of a Capuchin monastery so as to prevent police interference. In 1968, the singer Joan Manuel Serrat refused representing Spain in the Eurovision contest because he was not allowed to sing part of his song in Catalan. All in all, however, Catalan anti-Franco resistance was relatively peaceful. Police action was more forceful in the north (Asturias and the Basque country), where opposition was more violent. However, as we saw before, there was occasional violence and drama in Catalonia in the last years of the dictatorship of which the capture and execution of Salvador Puig Antich was the clearest example.

Catalan opposition soon had an ad hoc organization in the *Assemblea de Catalunya*, which was created in 1971 as a wide platform of opposition to the regime comprising many disparate elements: communists, socialists, the group of Jordi Pujol (later called *Convergència Democràtica de Catalunya*, CDC), Christian-democrats (*Unió Democràtica de Catalunya*, UDC), plus all sorts of groupings of students, professional organizations, citizen movements, religious movements, etc. The *Assemblea*'s only distinctive ideology was Catalanism. Its slogan was *Llibertat, amnistia i Estatut d'Autonomia* (Liberty, Amnesty, and Autonomy Statute). Amnesty, of course, referred to political prisoners. They also proposed to restore the *Estatut* abolished by Franco in 1939.

After Franco's death, the street demonstrations, most of them organized by the *Assemblea*, became massive, and its slogan very popular. The political parties united in the *Assemblea*, however, soon left it as they wanted to recover their liberty of action and the Assemblea practically disappeared. Many years later, it was revived as a separatist institution. Correspondingly, it was now called *Assemblea* ***Nacional*** *de Catalunya*.

Economic Development in Spain and Catalonia

There is little doubt that, from a long-term standpoint, the economic performance of Spain in the first three quarters of the twentieth century was one of success. The relatively high standards of living in 1975 go a long way to explain the rather easy, peaceful transition from dictatorship to democracy which followed the death of Franco (Tortella and Núñez, 2011, p. 561). All available series show that growth accelerated in the second half of the century. Does this mean that this growth should be attributed to the dictatorship? The answer must be in the negative. The process of growth predated the civil war, and the evolution of the Spanish economy is clearly related to that of its European neighbors. It could even be argued that Francoism was rather an obstacle to growth and that a freer Spain could have developed faster after the Second World War. What is undisputable, however, is that the economic policy of the dictatorship left its imprint on the Spanish economy.

What was the role of Catalonia in this process of growth? Fig. 6.1 shows that in the nineteenth century Catalonia passed from having a per capita income only slightly higher (1.05 percent) than the Spanish average to having a much improved position in 1900 (1.53 percent) and an even better position in 1930 (1.87 percent); from then onward, this relative position has declined somewhat and by 2000 it was around 1.30 percent. Today it is closer to 1.20. It is true that some of the figures underlying these calculations are not as robust as one would wish, but the empirical descriptive evidence seems to confirm the evolution of the series.

In the first decades of the twentieth century, Catalonia was still able to go on taking advantage of the economic policies of the Spanish state, much as it did in the previous century. After the civil war, Catalonia was still favored by the policies of the dictatorship, no matter how distasteful this regime might have been to its bourgeoisie. However, other regions such as Madrid, the Basque country, the Balearic Islands, Aragon, Navarre, and Valencia also benefited from the boom, especially after the Stabilization Plan of 1959. The tourist boom of the second half of the twentieth century, although affecting especially the Mediterranean coast, scattered its blessings wide. As a consequence, a process of convergence set in and this explains the partial regression of Catalonia toward the mean.

Industrialization and State Intervention

The Spanish economy during the period we are studying clearly favored industry, something quite normal as this pattern has been common historically. In the early stages of development, industry is usually the predominant sector. However, after the inception of the oil crisis of the mid-1970s, a certain reversion took place, something again common in later stages of development. This had already been diagnosed much earlier by Colin Clark (1957, p. 493; his italics): 'As real income per head increases, it is quite clear that the *relative* demand for agricultural products falls all the time, and that the relative demand for manufacture first rises, and then falls in favour of services.' As this phenomenon became more and more common, it became widely studied under the name of *deindustrialization*.

Catalonia had become the 'factory of Spain' during the nineteenth century, thanks to tariff protection. In the twentieth century, as textiles lost importance, Catalonia found protection for other industries, such as, for instance the automobile. *Hispano-Suiza* was the result of cooperation between a gifted Swiss engineer, Mark Birkigt and an enterprising Catalan businessman, Damiá Mateu. Barcelona became a budding center of this industry, with, in addition, two assembly lines of Ford and General Motors, and several tire and parts factories. The industry received support from Primo de Rivera's government in the form of state purchases, tariff protection, and the construction of a modern road network complete with state hostels, intended to promote motoring tourism. Nevertheless, market and labor problems contributed to the relocation of Hispano-Suiza in France. The depression and the civil war devastated the industry.

The military mentality predominating under Franco was extremely favorable to industrialization. In 1941, the *Instituto Nacional de Industria* (INI) was established. The preamble of its foundational law contained a scathing criticism of Spanish private entrepreneurs, deemed unable or unwilling to undertake 'the required amount of investment that the making of certain products demands.' Of course, this criticism was unwarranted or at least exaggerated. But some Catalan historians have tilted to the other extreme and forgotten that INI had a strategic role in the reindustrialization of Catalonia after the civil war. One of the best Catalan economic historians today, Jordi Maluquer de Motes (prologue to Cabana, 2006), has decried the 'almost total absence of public enterprises in Catalan economic growth in the last two hundred years.' It is surprising that such a fine scholar should forget that INI created the SEAT automobile company in the Freeport zone of Barcelona, and that this company, which became the most important in the sector, on top of being public, enjoyed all sorts of privileges granted by the Franco regime, among them the consideration of 'model enterprise.' It thus enjoyed tariff protection and privileged access to official credit.

Historians and entrepreneurs have blamed the lack of coal in Catalonia as a drag on its development. However, it has good hydraulic resources from the Pyrenees. *La Canadiense*, the electric company of the Pearson group, was established to profit from the power generated by the Pyrenean Mountain rivers. The INI founded the *Empresa Nacional Hidroeléctrica del Ribagorzana* (a river) commonly called ENHER to compete with *la Canadiense*. The government was striving to put as much of the power generating system in national hands as possible, and if public, the better. The *Canadiense* was subsequently the object of political, economic, and judicial harassment which in the end put it in the hands of Juan March, the Majorcan businessman who was the wealthiest man in Spain, had contributed to finance Franco's war effort, and liked to call himself 'the last pirate of the Mediterranean.'

Contrary to what nationalist historians say, Catalonia was one of INI's preferred areas of investment. By the end of the dictatorship, about 20 percent of INI's assets were in Catalonia. Of the other regions, only Asturias (where the government made a tremendous effort to make the coal mines viable by building a gigantic steel plan in Avilés) could compare. Another massive investment of INI in Catalonia was the oil refinery of Tarragona which was created in 1971 when Claudio Boada, a leading Catalan businessman and manager, was INI's president.

Catalan politicians and businessmen often complain that the Spanish government does not invest enough in Catalan infrastructures. This is at least debatable. But what is not debatable is that the Franco dictatorship built infrastructures in Catalonia way ahead of the Spanish average. Only Castile-León, the largest region in terms of land surface, three times the extension of Catalonia, had a larger railroad stock measured in pesetas. The same can be said about highways: by 1975, Catalonia had 45.5 percent of all highways built in Spain.

One may wonder why the Franco regime showed such marked favoritism for Catalonia, the richest region at the time. There are several possible reasons why Franco, notwithstanding his hatred of separatism, may have favored Catalonia economically: his military mental makeup favored industrialism, and Catalonia was the most industrialized region of Spain. For somebody as keen on industrialization as he was, Catalonia offered a ready field of investment. It had the capital, the labor, the infrastructure for it. Also, he may have wanted to placate a region where there was hostility to his regime; a prosperous Catalonia should be less dangerous to the regime than an impoverished one. In the third place, there was hostility in Catalonia toward Franco, but there were many Catalans who supported him. We have seen how many of the *opusdeistas* who supported him were Catalan; there were many others. Books have been written about this, listing how many relevant members of Catalan society, especially businessmen, supported him (Riera, 1998; Molinero and Ysàs, 1990). And there could even be Catalanists who supported Franco, such as somebody we have encountered several times already: Félix Millet.

The Problems of Catalan Banks

A surprising trait of Catalan economic development is the relative weakness of Catalan banking institutions, a phenomenon which has been pointed out by economists, politicians, and businessmen (Cambó, Sardà and Beltran, Tortella and Núñez, Sudrià), and which we already examined in the previous chapter dealing with the nineteenth century. After the First World War, the largest, most respected and long-lived Catalan bank, the Bank of Barcelona, suspended payments and never recovered. Other smaller institutions, such as the Bank of Tarrasa and the Crédito Mercantil, also disappeared. The Bank of Catalonia, which had had a meteoric rise in the twenties, also went under in 1931. The Banks of Barcelona and Tarrasa were the victims of the first postwar crisis and of speculation in German marks; the Catalonia was hurt by the onset of the Great Depression, and by the enmity of the republican government, which considered it a creature of the Primo de Rivera dictatorship (to a large extent it was). The trouble, however, was that no other important Spanish banks closed their doors in the interwar period save a 'mining bank' in the Basque country, affected by the fall of metal and coal prices after the war and by some shady practices. In addition, the only remaining large bank (savings banks excepted) in Catalonia, the *Banco Hispano-Colonial*, had lost its old vigor and become little more than a holding company. It was acquired in the 1930s by a Madrid bank, the *Banco Central*. It is difficult to pinpoint the causes of the weakness of Catalan banks, but it seems clear that they were exclusively Catalan.

The voids left by Catalan institutions were filled in by outsider banks, from Madrid, the Basque country, and foreign countries, mainly France and Germany. The most important bank in Catalonia before the civil war was the largest Spanish bank, the *Banco Hispano-Americano* of Madrid. Other Madrid banks also enjoyed a prominent position in Catalonia, such as the *Banco Español de Crédito*, commonly called *Banesto*, or the Central, operating mostly through the Hispano Colonial. The main Basque bank operating in Catalonia was the *Banco de Vizcaya*. These banks took an active part in financing the Catalan automobile industry, for example. Banesto was the banker of Hispano Suiza and Hispano-Americano of General Motors in Barcelona. After the civil war, the large Madrid banks advanced even more in Catalonia: the Hispano Colonial acquired a series of medium-sized banks there and finally, in 1950, was absorbed by the Central. Banesto and Hispano-Americano also made substantial acquisitions. The only reverse case was that of Banco Popular, a Madrid bank which was largely taken over by a Catalan group led by the omnipresent Félix Millet, who in a few years would be replaced in the presidency of Popular by his cousin Luis Valls-Taberner.

The debility of the Catalan banking system has continued until the present day; more recent examples are the rise and fall of Banca Catalana, which we will examine in the next chapter, plus the discomfiture of nearly all Catalan savings banks (excepting *La Caixa*, the largest Catalan savings bank, which recently became a commercial bank under the name *Caixabank*) in the crisis of 2007. The only other Catalan bank of importance today is the *Banco Sabadell*, a local bank established in 1881 with the main object on financing the woolen textile industry of that city and which only during the last decades became a bank of national stature.

At this point, we may ask what the long-term consequences were of this seemingly congenital weakness of the Catalan banking system. A study of interregional flows (García Ruiz, 2003 and 2007) suggests that they were not too serious. If the Franco regime invested public monies in Catalonia massively, so did the outsider banks, which poured in the region more funds that what they absorbed from there in the form of deposits. All in all, the financial services that Catalonia demanded were available from non-Catalan banks. There did not seem to be a pressing need for a genuinely Catalan bank, in the wake of the Banks of Barcelona and Cataluña. Nevertheless, in 1959, a new bank headed by Florenci Pujol, a stock exchange operator, and his son Jordi, soon became Banca Catalana, whose story we will examine in the next chapter.

Commercial and Fiscal Balances: The Early Studies

The economic relations between Catalonia and the rest of Spain constitute a fascinating topic for Spanish economists today and no wonder since it is a crucial question for nationalists. Furthermore, the economic differences between Catalonia and the rest have been evident since at least the mid-nineteenth century and it is logical that economists and politicians should have tried to study and, if possible, quantify them. We saw that Figuerola tried to do just that in the nineteenth century. These calculations were attempted again in the twentieth century by several scholars. One of them was Carles Pi i Sunyer, an engineer affiliated to ERC, who worked in the Spanish Ministry of Industry and Commerce during the Second Republic and used the statistics that were made available to him. According to Pi i Sunyer (1959 [1931]), Catalonia sold manufactured products (especially textiles) and bought food and raw materials, while the commercial balance was slightly in favor of Catalonia. Nothing surprising there, but Pi, a Catalan nationalist, deduced that this was proof of Catalonia's 'economic aptitude,' something that seemed to be missing in the rest of Spain.

Decades later, an Economics professor, Ernest Lluch (1962), calculated that in the interregional trade, in 1957, Catalonia had a wide commercial surplus; another novelty was that mechanical products had surpassed textiles among Catalan 'exports,' an obvious consequence of the INI's investment in the region. Later studies for 1975 (Institut d'Estudis Catalans, 1983) showed similar results.

Conclusions

The period studied in this chapter is the time when the gap between the Catalan economy and that of the rest of Spain was larger; the gap diminished gradually in the second half of the twentieth century. The growing gap in the first half of the century provoked a political distancing between Catalonia and Spain as a whole. Two forces made this distance deeper, one internal and the other external. The internal force was the socioeconomic gap; the external was the profound crisis which shook the world economy, and especially the European economy, during the first half of the twentieth century.

The economic development of Catalonia gave rise to some social strata and conflicts that were alien to the rest of Spain, whose agrarian backwardness faded away only slowly. In Catalonia, especially in Barcelona, industrialization subdivided social classes: the peasantry gradually lost weight—with the exception of the *rabassaires*, who in many aspects behaved as urban workers—while the working class and the bourgeoisie became stronger and at the same time more complex: new parties and unions were born and contended among themselves, in some cases violently; the regionalist movement of the past century now muted into nationalism, while splitting into two wings, right and left. Official Spain watched these evolutions with perplexity and incomprehension—except for a few remarkable exceptions, Azaña being, possibly, the most notable one—unable to find a solution, if such should have been possible. This does not mean, of course, that the rest of Spain remained static. The first third of the century brought about significant transformations in the largest cities, such as Madrid, Bilbao, Saragossa, Valencia, Seville, etc.; but it took many years to bridge the gap with Catalonia.

In addition, the terrible twentieth-century crisis, which started in1914 and ended in 1945, impinged upon, and rendered more acute, the problems of Spain. Although the country remained neutral, the Spanish economy followed the profound oscillations which followed the onset of the conflict: a short span of prosperity accompanied by inflation and a postwar crisis which affected gravely the conditions of employment and the standards of living. The effects of these fluctuations on Spanish politics, especially in Catalonia, were destructive and intensified the internal tensions we just described. Primo de Rivera's dictatorship was a direct consequence of the heightening of these tensions. But the superlative maladroitness of the dictator in his attempt to 'solve' the problem of Catalonia where he had initially had a favorable reception made his actions comparable to trying to put out a fire with a can of gasoline. He deserved Azaña's dictum: Primo de Rivera boasted about having solved the Catalan problem, but in reality he made it worse.

All this was too heavy a legacy for the fragile Second Republic, whose life coincided with the Great Depression, which was a chapter of the great twentieth-century crisis which had atrocious consequences in Europe. Spain was one of the main victims of this terrible upheaval. Internal tensions and dissensions were exacerbated by the repercussions of international events, both in the economic and in the political fields, and they finally exploded in the form of civil war. In this war, the divisions of the republican camp, among which those brought up by Catalan separatism were far from the lesser, contributed powerfully to the victory of the fascist rebels. Trying to keep their distance from the Spanish republic, the ERC separatists facilitated and accelerated Franco's victory and were thereby instrumental in bringing about 36 years of airtight centralism.

Some Catalanist historians have asserted recently that the civil war was something that was imposed upon Catalonia from without and that

Catalonia was only an innocent victim of this long and painful drama. Some qualifications are required here. There is no doubt that the majority of Catalan citizens were innocent victims of the war, as was the case with the majority of Spaniards. But the Catalan governing elites carried as much (if not more) responsibility for this terrible drama as the rest of Spanish leaders. The rebellions of 1934, in which Catalan nationalists played one of the leading roles, marked a decisive step toward the civil war. Furthermore, if Republican Spain had not been rent and weakened by divisions during the civil war (divisions for which Catalan separatists carry a heavy responsibility, as Azaña noted in his diaries), the war could have been prolonged a few months more and the Spanish Republic could have had a role in World War II comparable to that of, say, France. In this case, as in De Gaulle's France, democracy might have been restored in Spain in 1945. One should keep this in mind when attributing political responsibilities for the defeat in the Republican camp.

Another myth which should be put into question is the statement that the civil war was a conflict between Catalonia and the rest of Spain and that in the postwar repression Catalonia was the victim and Spain was the hangman. This horror tale does not stand one minute of scrutiny. We have seen how mixed 'the Catalan question' was in the origins of the Spanish Civil War. Furthermore, the Franco regime oppressed Spaniards with notorious impartiality; if Catalonia felt doubly oppressed because the Catalan language was discriminated, it should be remembered that other regional languages were equally discriminated, among them *Gallego*, the language spoken in Franco's birthplace. It is also true that these linguistic discriminations were gradually, though not completely, relaxed after around 1950, and that Catalan was freely spoken in the streets even in the worse years of the dictatorship.

The history of Spain (Catalonia included, of course) in the twentieth century speaks of the futility of oppressive and authoritarian policies, derived from totalitarian ideologies aiming at *national constructions* of one sign or the other, such as the ones that both sides tried to impose upon the Spanish population. In the long run, those policies not only did not attain their ends, but they produced diametrically opposite effects. The endeavors by Primo de Rivera and Franco to repress the Catalan language and the regional feeling brought about the victory of

ERC in the first case, and the triumph of *Convergència i Unió* (which in the end turned separatist, as we shall presently see) in the second case. In both cases, the effect was the opposite of what each dictator wanted. While the attempts of ERC to separate Catalonia from the rest of Spain in the 1930s contributed to the outbreak of the civil war, fatally weakened the Republic while the conflict was on, and ended up facilitating Franco's victory, an aim which, we must suppose, was far from their intentions. A clear lesson history offers about the consequences of political sectarianism.

References

ALCALÁ ZAMORA, N. (1977), *Memorias. (Segundo texto de mis memorias)*. Barcelona: Planeta.

AZAÑA, Manuel (1967), *Obras completas. III. La Recuperación del Ideal Republicano, etc.* México: Ediciones Oasis.

AZAÑA, Manuel (1968), *Obras completas, IV. Memorias políticas y de guerra.* México: Ediciones Oasis.

BEN-AMI, Shlomo (1983), *Fascism from Above. The Dictatorship of Primo de Rivera in Spain. 1923–1930.* Oxford: Clarendon Press.

BOLLOTEN, Burnett (1991), *The Spanish Civil War, Revolution and Counterrevolution.* Foreword by Stanley Payne. Chapel Hill, N.C.: The University of North Carolina Press.

CABANA, Francesc (coord.) (2006), *Cien empresarios catalanes.* Madrid: LID.

CALVO SOTELO, José (1974), *Mis servicios al Estado. Seis años de Gestión. Apuntes para la Historia.* 2ª ed. Madrid: Instituto de Estudios de Administración Local.

CAMBÓ, Francesc (1981), *Memòries, 1876–1936.* Barcelona: Alpha.

CARRERAS, Albert and Xavier TAFUNELL (2005), (Eds), *Estadística históricas de España, siglos XIX–XX.* 3 vols. Bilbao: Fundación BBVA, 2005.

Clark, Colin. (1957), *The Conditions of Economic Progress.* 3d. edn. London: Macmillan.

GARCÍA RUIZ, José Luis (2003), 'Los flujos financieros regionales en la España del siglo XX, una perspectiva desde la historia bancaria', *Revista de Estudios Regionales*, 67, pp. 15–54.

GARCÍA RUIZ, José Luis (2007), 'Nuevos datos sobre flujos regionales de la banca española en el siglo XX', *Revista de Historia Industrial*, 35, pp. 115–140.

GONZÁLEZ CALBET, María Teresa (1987), *La dictadura de Primo de Rivera, el Directorio Militar*. Madrid: El Arquero.

INSTITUT D'ESTUDIS CATALANS (1983), *Els fluxos econòmics de Catalunya amb la resta d'España i la resta del món. La balança de pagaments de Catalunya 1975*. Barcelona: Author (directed by Antoni Castells y Martí Parellada).

JACKSON, G. (1967), *The Spanish Republic and the Civil War, 1931–1939*. Princeton, NJ.: Princeton University Press.

JACKSON, G. (2008), *Juan Negrín. Médico, socialista y jefe del Gobierno de la II República española*. Barcelona: Crítica.

KEYNES, John M. (1963), *Essays in Persuasion*. New York: W.W. Norton & Company Inc.

KEYNES, John M. (2000), *A Tract on Monetary Reform*. New York: Prometheus Books.

LLUCH, Ernest *et al.* (1962), 'La balanza comercial interior de Cataluña', *Información Comercial Española*, 241, pp. 291–299.

MOLINERO, C. and YSÀS, P. (1990), 'Los industriales catalanes durante el franquismo,' *Revista de Historia Económica*, **8**, pp. 105–129.

PAYNE, S.G. (1987), *The Franco Regime. 1936–1975*. Madison, Wisconsin: Wisconsin University Press.

PEERS, E.A. (1938), *Catalonia infelix*. New York: Oxford University Press.

PI i SUNYER, C. (1959 [1931]), *El comerç de Catalunya amb Espanya*. Mexico: El Club del Llibre Catalá.

Payne, Stanley G. (1961). *Falange. A History of Spanish Fascism*. Stanford, CA: Stanford University Press.

RIERA, I. (1998), *Los catalanes de Franco*. Barcelona: Plaza & Janés.

TORTELLA, G. and C. E. NÚÑEZ (2011), *El desarrollo de la España contemporánea. Historia económica de los siglos XIX y XX*. 3d ed., Madrid: Alianza.

TRYTHALL, J.W.D. (1970), *Franco. A Biography*. London: Hart-Davis.

ULLMAN, J. C. (1968), *The Tragic Week: a Study of Anticlericalism in Spain, 1875–1912*. Cambridge, Mass.: Harvard University Press.

7

From Dictatorship to Democracy

Introduction

The most serious political problem Spain faces today is Catalan separatism. The question which immediately comes to mind on this topic is: How did this problem acquire today's dimensions when by 1980 it was decidedly a very minor question? The answer is clear: the regional governments of *Convergència i Unió* (CiU, a coalition of CDC and Unió), the party of Jordi Pujol, who won his first election precisely in that year, has devoted its best efforts to magnifying the differences between Catalonia and the rest of Spain (*el fet diferencial*, the 'differential fact' in Catalan, a phrase coined by Cambó which became one of the favorite mantras of his followers), to propagate nationalism (as Pujol announced in his inauguration speech), to harass Catalan nonnationalists and if possible hound them out of Catalonia, to discourage, even to punish, the use of the Spanish language in Catalonia at all levels and ambits, and to use all means at their reach, especially the schools and the press, but also public ceremonies, demonstrations, exhibitions, sports clubs, private associations, etcetera, to indoctrinate the population in the

G. Tortella, *Catalonia in Spain*, Palgrave Studies in Economic History, DOI 10.1007/978-3-319-54951-4_7

nationalist version of history, of culture, and of social reality in general, a nationalism which was bound to become separatism in the medium term, as effectively it did. Many features of this program openly violate the Spanish Constitution, but Spanish governments of the left and of the right have let nationalist regional governments trample freely over the Constitution and disobey Court sentences with impunity. All this created the critical mass that finally produced, some 5 years ago, the separatist explosion.

There can be no doubt about the control of the media by the *generalitat*. Some try to question to what extent it controls education, saying, for example, that all textbooks are similar in all of Spain. We will address this question subsequently. What cannot be discussed is that the *generalitat* has imposed teaching in Catalan almost exclusively in all public schools in Catalonia, on the pretext that bilingualism divides the Catalan population, something which is simply untrue: Catalonia has been a bilingual country since the Middle Ages. Its best writers wrote in Castilian Spanish, from the Renaissance poet Juan Boscán to Antoni de Capmany, to modern novelists such as Ignacio Agustí, Ana María Matute, José María Gironella, or Juan Marsé, to cite just a few (of course, economists such as Figuerola or Sanromá, or bankers such as Girona also wrote in Spanish). What the attempt to turn Catalonia into a monolingual region certainly does is to divide Spanish society and to isolate Catalonia, and in this it has almost succeeded; to widen this chasm has been one of the main objectives of the *generalitat*, with the passive assent of the Madrid governments, eager to avoid 'conflict.'

As to history textbooks, it is just not true to say that they are similar throughout Spain; in general, what prevails in them is a myopic localism: they disregard Spain as a whole and concentrate on regional histories, of limited interest to the rest of the nation and even less interest to foreign readers. Furthermore, these textbooks show a decided bias against 'centralism.' They speak more of 'the Spains' than of 'Spain,' and the word 'Spain' is often mentioned in association with the Franco dictatorship. That is to say, the task of demolishing the idea of Spain as a united nation is not exclusive of Catalan texts, even though these are far ahead in this endeavor, as will be shown later. Furthermore, books are only a part of the learning process, even at school. The Pujol governments were careful in selecting professors, especially in social sciences, among those who shared their ideology.

This aversion toward Spain in Spanish schools is no doubt a consequence of a reaction against the National Catholicism that the Franco dictatorship imposed as its orthodoxy. Both extreme attitudes are obnoxious. One of the consequences of this exaggerated feeling of rejection toward Spanish nationalism has been that the public has reacted with indifference to the permissive attitude of the Spanish governments toward the infringements of the law committed by the *generalitat*. In general, the revulsion against the centralism characteristic of the Franco dictatorship has given legitimacy in the eyes of many of today's Spanish politicians to regional nationalist ideologies, so that even, or rather especially, left-wing parties have overlooked the obvious traits of conservatism, racism, and xenophobia which these ideologies involve.

The recent spurt of separatism in Catalonia is due in a large part to economic motives. For one thing, Catalonia's indebtedness has grown enormously in the last 10 years. The reaction of the *generalitat* governments, be they CiU or tripartite (between 2003 and 2010 Catalonia was governed by a left-wing tripartite coalition—socialists, ERC, and the communist rump, called ICV—who copied the nationalist policies of CiU with a vengeance) to the 2007 crisis has been to keep up public expenditure while receipts went down with a resulting accelerated growth of public debt, which from 15.8 billion euros in 2007 went up to 72.3 billion in 2015, i.e., it multiplied by 4.6 in 8 years. In per capita terms, in that same time span the debt went from 2,158 to 9,616 euros. International ratings of the Catalan debt have plummeted; Moody's latest qualification (May 2016) was 'negative outlook,' practically equivalent to 'junk bonds.' Nobody wants to buy Catalan debt, so the *generalitat* has turned to its archenemy, the Spanish state, the source of all Catalonia's misfortunes (according to the *generalitat*), to be bailed out. In 2012, the Spanish state created a line of credit intended to help the regions cope with their financial difficulties, called Liquidity Fund for Autonomous Regions (FLA in Spanish): over those 5 years, Catalonia, with barely 17 percent of Spanish population, has borrowed 58.0 billion euros, some 30 percent of the total disbursed by the FLA. As we will see, separatists not only claim, against all evidence, that Spain 'robs Catalonia,' they also announce that the repayment of the Catalan debt should be 'negotiated' when Catalonia becomes independent.

There is another type of economic reason for Catalan nationalists to want independence. The cases of political corruption in Catalonia have been frequent since CiU took over, and CiU has been the main culprit. Pujol in particular has been rumored for years to have taken bribes for construction contracts in Catalonia, and he has recently (May 2015) admitted that he had been defrauding in his taxes and covertly sending money abroad for about 25 years. He has not been tried (who knows whether he will ever be), but some of his associates have, and some have even been sent to jail. Spanish justice treats Catalan separatists with kid gloves, but they are not totally immune. There is ample reason to believe that they would be totally immune, *legibus solutus* so to speak, if Catalonia were independent. For the Catalan political elite, an independent Catalonia would be like their own private ranch. In contrast, for the average Catalan, independence would have no material advantages, on the contrary: it would bring inflation, unemployment, and tax increases (autonomous Catalonia already has higher tax rates than the rest of Spain). But it is the political elite, plus the well-to-do in Barcelona and the largest cities and the rural areas, who support independence and who have managed, by incessant propaganda, to convert a section of the population to separatism, who are to gain from independence.

Transition to Democracy

Francisco Franco died a natural death in a hospital at age 82 surrounded by his family and faithful on 20 November 1975, after having governed Spain with an iron hand for more than 39 years (including the civil war). His body, in estate at the Royal Palace of Madrid, was bid farewell by a crowd of citizens who lined up and passed by the coffin in a popular wake which lasted several days. His succession took place as planned: the Prince of Spain, Don Juan Carlos de Borbón, his designated heir, was crowned immediately (in Spain, this is done in a very simple ceremony);

and one of his first measures was to confirm in his post Carlos Arias Navarro, who was the last president of the government under Franco.

Only very gradually were some protests heard against the continuation of the authoritarian regime which the majority now identified with Arias. The Spanish people who had endured the dictatorship silently and stoically started to stir and express their preference for a transition to democracy. The opponents to the dictatorship now manifested themselves in growing numbers and mounting impatience, reminiscent of the old Spanish adage: *a moro muerto, gran lanzada*, which could be freely translated as: 'show you courage when the enemy is dead.' They belonged to very different political groups and creeds, but the main difference at that point was that which separated *aperturistas* and *rupturistas; aperturistas* were those in favor of a gradual transition toward democracy while the *rupturistas* wanted to abolish all the institutions of the dictatorship and start from zero, so to speak.

The opposition to Franco had been stronger in the large cities (Madrid, Barcelona, Valencia, Seville, etc.) in addition to, especially, mining centers in Asturias, where repression however was easier because the working populations were concentrated in small towns; in large cities, there was more dispersion and anonymity. To these should be added, especially in the Basque country, small nuclei of violent opposition, more nationalist than democratic; the best known of those was ETA, whose terrorist activity had started in 1968. There were other smaller terrorist groups in Galicia, Madrid, and Barcelona, where the *Terra Lliure* (Free Land) band carried out some very cruel terrorist acts, especially after Franco's death. *Terra Lliure* was disbanded around 1990.

On 1 July 1976, Juan Carlos dismissed the unpopular Carlos Arias and 5 days later appointed Adolfo Suárez to replace him. This move surprised many, for Suárez was not very well known and those who knew about him identified him with the Falange party. He was, however, a man ready to undertake a policy of gradual demolition of the institutions of the dictatorship, a task for which he was well endowed, since he had held second rank but significant government posts where he had had the opportunity to know key figures of the regime and familiarize himself with the inner workings of that system; he also had a juvenile air, a pleasant persona, and considerable courage. The king trusted him to carry out this demolition task while building a new democratic state. The king had also the advice of Torcuato Fernández Miranda, another apparent pillar of the Franco apparatus, who was equally ready to contribute to the orderly dismantling of the regime he had up to then faithfully served. Fernández Miranda lacked the charm and youth of Suárez, but he was a professor of Constitutional Law, had solid credentials as a jurist, and was as familiar with the interstices of the regime as Suárez if not more. He had already shown his mettle when he managed to put Suárez's name on the short list that the Council of the Realm, a Franquist top institution, handed the king to choose the next president to replace Arias.

The method proposed by Fernández Miranda, which was the one put to effect, consisted of carrying out the transition to democracy with the least possible trauma, what he called, 'go from the law to the law,' by which he meant that the transition should be carried out without violating the laws of the dictatorship, just annulling them by using the possibilities they offered. The key to his plan was that the Franquist Cortes should vote their own demise, by calling elections by universal suffrage (never held under Franco) to elect a new, democratic Cortes. To many people's surprise, the old Cortes voted this new 'fundamental law,' with more than the required two-thirds majority. Many said the Franquist Cortes had committed suicide. In any case, such majority permitted the new law to override former 'fundamental laws' and was possible, thanks to an intense lobbying campaign masterminded discreetly by Fernández Miranda. The new law was then submitted to a referendum, where it obtained an overwhelming support of 94 percent of the vote (73 percent of those eligible to vote).

The first general elections (June 1977) were won by Suárez's party (Union of the Democratic Center, UCD), but the results in Catalonia were quite different. Although the same three parties came on top as in the rest of Spain (UCD, Socialists, and Communists), in Catalonia UCD was third, almost on a par with Jordi Pujol's party, then called Democratic Pact. In the Basque country, the results were even more different, since there the nationalist regional party (PNV) came out first, with the Socialists very close and UCD at considerable distance.

The election outcome in Catalonia (Socialists and Communists came on top) created alarm not only in Madrid but also among the center and right groups in Catalonia itself. Jordi Pujol begged Suárez not to grant autonomy in Catalonia while the left was in power because, if this were the case, 'Catalonia will have a left wing majority for many years, and that should be avoided' (Molinero and Ysàs, 2014, p. 173). Suárez agreed. Josep Tarradellas, the only surviving leader of republican Catalonia, seemed called to play a role in the transition to democracy there. Now old, moderate, and respectable, he seemed to be a safe alternative to the looming Catalan *red coalition*. The so-called *Operation Tarradellas* got under way in the summer of 1977.

He lived in France, near Tours, and had been elected president of the *generalitat* in exile in 1954. Several noted Catalans had approached him a few years back and acted as his unofficial deputies. Nobody doubted that he was destined to play a role in the passage to democracy, but what this role would be was unclear. There soon were two types of legitimacies in that territory: historical legitimacy, embodied by Tarradellas, and democratic legitimacy, embodied by the group of members of the Cortes, collectively known as the 'Assembly of Parliamentarians,' who had been recently elected in the four Catalan provinces. It would seem that the members of parliament were better qualified to represent the Catalan electorate, but in reality this was not so. Tarradellas had two aces up his sleeve: one, he had the support not only of the Madrid government but also of the whole Catalan right of center; and, two, he embodied the link between post-Franco and pre-Franco Catalonia, and this sentimental nexus had great sway in that region, where historical myths have exceptional force. A textbook of wide circulation in Catalonia (Casassas *et al.*, 2009, p. 339) proudly claims that Tarradellas's inauguration was the only act in the transition to democracy where 'the Spanish government recognized the legitimacy of an elected official of the Republic.' Furthermore, there were few republican worthies left in Spain and of these several did not want to return to politics, or were not famous enough, or others, such as the communist leaders Santiago Carrillo or Dolores Ibarruri (the well-known *Pasionaria*), were too famous (or infamous) for Suárez and Pujol. In the end, even the Assembly of Parliamentarians asked for the return of Tarradellas. Another argument in his favor was that the members of the Cortes had not been elected to negotiate the transition but simply to govern and legislate. They lacked a specific mandate to deal with the Spanish government in transitional matters.

There followed several months of tensions and political fencing between the Spanish government, Tarradellas and the Assembly of Parliamentarians. After a busy summer when negotiations were on the verge of breakdown more than once, the first *Diada* (commemoration of the fall of Barcelona on 14 September 1714, a ceremony which was celebrated for the first time in 1901 and forbidden by Franco) since the times of the republic, seen as a show of support for Tarradellas, mollified spirits and made agreement easier. In Powell's opinion (2001, p. 211), the agreement had been reached before the *Diada*. Be it as it may, early in October the government issued a series of decrees where the *generalitat* was recognized as the government of Catalonia with the immediate mission of preparing the project of a new *Estatut*, and where Tarradellas was appointed as provisional president of the *generalitat* until regional elections took place according to the rules fixed in the new *Estatut*. On the 23 October, Tarradellas arrived in Barcelona and pronounced an inauguration speech that opened with a phrase that became famous: 'Citizens of Catalonia: here I am!' (*Ciutadans de Catalunya: ja soc aquí*!'). Next day, he was solemnly invested in the presence of President Suárez.

Many thought this was the solution to the Catalan problem; it soon became clear that it was just temporary. It was very important, anyway, because the Catalan solution offered a model for the rest of regional governments, which soon would receive the generic name of Autonomous Communities. In the Basque Country, attempts were made to find an equivalent to Tarradellas. Dolores Ibarruri was the best known Basque republican celebrity, but she was too divisive a figure. In the end, a veteran Basque socialist, Ramón Rubial, was appointed head of the Basque government until the Statute was approved and regional elections took place.

The most important step in the transition to democracy was the Constitution. A seven-member committee was appointed among the Cortes deputies, trying to keep a proportion of parties. There were two Catalans, one representing the Communist Party (Jordi Solé Tura) and one representing a group of more conservative Catalan parties (Miquel Roca, at the time a close associate of Jordi Pujol).

In matters of autonomy and territorial decentralization a principle operated in that committee that we could call 'the pendulum principle,' a dangerous sociopolitical mechanism but one which is all too common in Spain. After four decades of Franco's centralism, many thought the time had come to decentralize everything, to take decentralization as the paradigm of democracy. This conviction took possession of several members of the constitutional committee. Since the Franco version of Spanish nationalism seemed abhorrent, any regional nationalism was bound to appear respectable and positive, all the more so since Catalan, Basque, and Galician nationalisms had found some form or other of support from the Republic. The strange formula of the 'nation of nations' was unearthed and found admirable among politicians and among the public at large, with very few noticing the pitfalls that this maxim involved.

Nobody apparently perceived that there is properly no nation on earth that can be clearly defined as 'nation of nations.' The term might possibly apply to the United Kingdom whose name indicates a union of kingdoms and where nobody minds calling Scotland a nation. We should readily admit, though, that recognizing Scotland as a nation poses serious problems to the integrity of the United Kingdom. Some historians have called the USA a 'nation of nations' but it really is no such thing. It certainly is a federal republic; and in its early years, it had some characteristics of a confederation, but this is no longer true. No American state calls itself a nation or pretends sovereignty. The attempt at secession by the Southern states (which called themselves 'confederate') in 1861 led to a terrible civil war, where the confederates were soundly defeated. A country which, according to its Constitution, could be defined as a nation of nations was the Union of Soviet Socialist Republics, controlled with an iron fist from Moscow while Communism lasted, but which exploded into several independent o semi-independent republics as soon as the grip of Moscow was relaxed. The same appellative could have been used to describe the Austro-Hungarian Empire or the Ottoman Empire; both disintegrated at the end of World War I after centuries of uneasy coexistence. Another more recent and ephemeral example could be the Federal Republic (formerly Monarchy) of Yugoslavia, which was one of the resultants of the demise of the Austrian and Ottoman Empires. Yugoslavia was made up of a series of states that coexisted under a king in the interwar period. After the Second World War, it adopted the form of a republic, in fact a dictatorship under Marshal Yosip Broz, better known as Tito, his nom de guerre. At his death, the republic gradually came apart and exploded into a series of civil wars, whose genocidal episodes many of us still remember. To sum up, it does not seem that the idea of a 'nation of nations' be quite common today nor that historical experience should recommend it. But in transitional Spain, the rejection of Francoism made many to embrace it with more enthusiasm than sober reflection.

To say that Spain is not a nation, but a conglomerate of nations, just makes no sense. Spain is a nation since it has been admitted as such in most international or supranational organizations, such as the United Nations, the European Union, NATO, etc. It sounds ridiculous even to be discussing a question like this, as ridiculous as this nonsensical concept of 'nation of nations.' Spain is one of the oldest nations in history. It was recognized as a geographical unit even in Antiquity; Saint Isidore, in the sixth century AD, wrote a *Laus Hispaniae* (Praise of Spain); King Alfonso X of Castile wrote a *History of Spain* in the fourteenth century. It became formally a nation (or a state, or a 'united kingdom') at the union of Castile and Aragon under Isabel and Fernando in 1479, and gradually achieved the homogeneity proper of a modern nation in the following centuries. It became a totally unified kingdom after the War of Succession and Catalonia profited handsomely from this union. We have devoted the first chapters of this book to tell this story. It is symptomatic and meaningful that the first central bank established in 1782 was called 'National Bank of Saint Charles.' The moments when Spain was prosperous were periods of political unity while the moments of disintegration (*taifa* kingdoms, seventeenth-century crisis, War of Succession, carlism, cantonalism) brought about violence and impoverishment.

The relative cultural and political weakness of Spain in the nineteenth century opened the way for the centrifugal forces of the twentieth century. The political pendulum movements of the twentieth century were the source of grievous errors. The national failure which was the 'Disaster,' the defeat in the Spanish–American War of 1898 in Cuba and the Philippines, lent force to the nationalist movements in Catalonia and the Basque Country. On top of this, the breakdown of the political balance of the Restoration and the tensions which economic growth and industrialization provoked set in motion a cycle of instability which started with the Primo de Rivera dictatorship. Primo's coup, in turn, was a reaction to the insecurity and conflicts caused by the repercussions of the First World War and its aftermath. After the downfall of the dictatorship, the pendulum swung leftward with the Second Republic, which in turn experienced shorter 2-year swings left-right-left. With the civil war, the pendulum swung all the way to the right: democracy, republic, regionalism, liberalism, and much more were suppressed by Franco under the weight of intransigent centralism. When the Franco dictatorship reached its end, the pendulum moved to the left again, but with a difference: the social question (what the Marxists called the class struggle) moved to a relatively secondary level, because the economic growth which took place in the second lap of the dictatorship took away the urgency of class confrontation. The Communist party lost ground to the socialists, while these in turn abandoned their former revolutionary pretensions (Largo Caballero, the leader of the socialist left wing in the Republic, liked to be called 'the Spanish Lenin') and adopted social democracy unambiguously, thanks to which they came to power in 1982 and stayed on until 1996. Instead of the social problem, therefore, regional nationalisms came to the fore: the class struggle was replaced by the nationalist struggle.

Unfortunately, the rebirth of regional nationalisms was reflected in the 1978 Constitution: the outcome was Title VIII, dealing with 'the territorial organization of the state,' whose multiple defects reproduce the doubts, disagreements, and reservations of the committee members. One of them (Gregorio Peces-Barba) said that this Title was the one that gave them more trouble and required the most difficult balances (Molinero and Ysàs, 2014, summarize the discussion on pp. 219-34). Among so many deadlines, requirements, enumerations, exceptions, and remissions, Title VIII contains all kinds of loopholes and ambiguities of the kind that permit clever and unscrupulous politicians to grab fragments of sovereignty and carve out little nations where none should exist according to Article 2 of the Constitution which proclaims 'the indissoluble unity of the Spanish

Nation.' The inclusion of the term 'nationalities' (*nacionalidades*), deliberately ambiguous, was the product of a transaction between two committee members (Miquel Roca and Miguel Herrero), when the former proposed to introduce the term 'nation' through the backdoor, which would have given official currency to the noxious concept of a 'nation of nations' and Herrero said 'nation no, nationality yes,' and the term was accepted.

Another error, in this case not of the Constitution, but of its application, was to deprive the Autonomous Communities of greater fiscal discretion and make them closely dependent on the national budget. Article 157 of the Constitution permits the Communities to establish their own taxes and levies, but this has been interpreted restrictively. If the state had not been so anxious to control the strings of the public purse, the Communities would have been obliged to finance their projects (some of them foolish or even disloyal) with their own taxes (or indebtedness, which should only mean future taxes). A limit could have been set to their indebtedness and all this would have made them more responsible in planning their expenditures, which, if excessive, would have made them unpopular and thus put the posts of their leaders in jeopardy. If, on the contrary, the direct financing of the communities from the national budget distributes their leaders' profligacy among all taxpayers and not only among those of their community, they have every reason to spend, since the benefits of expenditure will only be felt in their Communities, while the costs will be shared among all. Furthermore, they have a perfect occasion to paint themselves as victims of the central power: all problems with infrastructures, public health, etc., can be blamed on the stinginess of the national government, and thus justify separatist aspirations (Catalonia is the perfect paradigm of this), although of course independence would put an end to this scapegoating and compel the new state to live on its own resources. But of course in these matters logic takes a back seat.

The errors committed by the 'fathers of the Constitution' were crowned by the flagrant contradiction between article 14, which states that 'Spaniards are equal under the law, and no discrimination may prevail for causes of birth, race, sex, religion, opinion or any other personal or social condition or circumstance,' and the first 'additional clause' which declares that the 'the Constitution recognizes and respects the historical rights of the *foral* territories,' something which entails fiscal discrimination by the fact of living in certain Communities, such as the Basque Country and Navarre. The pendulum has swung to a point which clearly surpasses the reasonable. Thus, a slow fuse was left burning there, ready to produce a conflagration when the time came.

The Constitution was approved by the *Cortes* by a wide majority and ratified by referendum on 6 December 1978, by a substantial majority as well (59 percent of the electoral census), although not as large as the one that approved the Reform Law of 1976. In Catalonia, the support for the Constitution was slightly larger than the national average, but in the Basque Country abstention was so high that only 31 percent of the electorate actually supported it.

In the spring and summer of 1979, 20 members of the Catalan Parliament prepared a draft *Estatut* to be submitted to the Parliament, then to the *Cortes*, then to referendum in Catalonia, and finally to the *Cortes* again and then ratified by the king. All these filters were passed in the fall of that year. Popular support for the new *Estatut* was considerably weaker than that shown for the Constitution a year before. This was due mainly to a wider margin of abstention. This already pointed to a factor which was to be a constant in Catalan elections: voter participation is always higher in national elections than in regional ones. The average participation in national elections is around 10 percent higher than in local ones.

The obvious reason for this gap is that the average Catalan feels more Spanish than Catalan, at least as an active citizen. The consequence of the gap, however, is contradictory: while in national elections 'national' parties (most frequently the socialists, although this is no longer true) usually win, in local elections, the nationalist parties, usually conservative, as the Pujol party was, win. In 2003–2010, however, a left coalition of socialists, crypto-communists, and ERC (the *tripartite*) was in power in Catalonia, but they rivaled CiU in the intransigence of their nationalism.

A conclusion which can be extracted from 'this dual' vote pattern is that those electors who abstain in local election are those who feel more Spanish, i.e., immigrants from other regions, the natural supporters of the Socialist Party (many of them felt betrayed by the *tripartite*). The consequence of their abstention is that in local elections the Catalan nationalists win, and these in turn carry out policies which do not benefit the immigrants in linguistic matters, in education, and in economic policies in general, because they maintain the highest possible fiscal pressure (the 1979 *Estatut* gave Catalonia the highest fiscal discretion possible within the Constitution) and use those monies, plus those received from the Spanish state, not to improve the quality of public education or health, but to carry out a blatantly nationalistic policy, from opening 'diplomatic offices' in foreign countries, to subsidizing press, radio, and television in Catalan, lavishing millions in organizing monster demonstrations in the *Diada* celebrations and others, etc. The nationalists also managed to have the Catalan language officially recognized as Catalonia's 'own language' something they have used to relegate Spanish to very second place in education, and in all fields of communication. To call Catalan Catalonia's 'own language' is a patent untruth, because there are in Catalonia more native Spanish speakers than Catalan speakers, as we will see later. It is true in that it is spoken only in Catalonia (and Andorra, a tiny Pyrenean enclave). Be it as it may, this denomination is being used by a minority to oppress the Castilian-speaking majority, who try to adapt as best they can. The nationalists also obtained recognition for the *generalitat* as having 'full' or 'exclusive' capacity in matters of education, something which has had grave consequences, as we will see later.

Is Still Catalonia 'The Factory of Spain?

Crisis and Change in the Spanish Economy

The economy of democratic Spain has been confronted with two serious crises, the so-called oil crisis of the 1970s and early 1980s, and the recent 'Great Recession' which started in 2007 and has lasted, in Spain, until very recently—unemployment figures are still of crisis proportions. Even subjected to these grave difficulties, plus that of adapting the political and economic structures of the dictatorship to those of a democratic society, the overall balance has been positive, since, even with the stubborn presence of high rates of unemployment, the standard of living in Spain is much higher than it was in the last years of the dictatorship.

After the demise of the Franco dictatorship, there was a clear majority opinion in Spain in favor of taking the necessary measures to gain membership of the European Community (the future European Union). The governments of the dictatorship had already requested membership in 1970, but the request had been rejected due to the dictatorial character of the regime. In the second attempt, however, the result was favorable for democratic Spain since the political obstacle had been removed. Both Spain and Portugal (whose dictatorial regime had been overturned 1 year before the end of the Franco regime in Spain) acceded as full members in 1986.

The intervening 1975–1986 period was rather difficult in Spain because to the complications of the transition from dictatorship to democracy were added those of the 'oil crisis,' which put an end to the 'Golden Era' of European prosperity. The term 'Golden Era' refers to the nearly three decades of growth after the end of World War II. As in all the Western world, the jump in oil prices after 1973 provoked 'stagflation' and industrial crisis—the onset of 'de-industrialization'—but in Spain this was accompanied by a severe financial crisis, the first of the five national financial crises after World War II detected by Reinhart and Rogoff (2011, p. 159).

The Spanish crisis of 1977–1985 hit commercial banks much harder than savings banks. The reason was that commercial banks had been more involved in industrial finance. Under the dictatorship, protected by the characteristic banking repression, which in fact shielded those mixed banks (commercial and industrial) from sudden liquidity crises, all of the largest banks had an 'industrial group' of firms totally or partially owned, and were involved in long-term financial loans to these firms and others. The industrial crisis reached those banks at the time when the authorities were introducing liberal reforms, which the banks fought tooth and nail. They found themselves in the difficult position of trying to divest themselves of those assets when their prices were tumbling, and wanted to do it under the shelter of financial repression. But this was not possible: a measure of liberalization was necessary to opt for membership of the European Community. Between 1977 and 1985 more than half the commercial banks and about one third of commercial banking employees and assets were affected by one of the largest banking crises in Spanish history. Foreseeing this problem, the Bank of Spain had created a Spanish version of the US Federal Deposit Insurance Corporation, the *Fondo de Garantía de Depósitos* (FGD), which acquired, liquidated, or bailed out, as each case required, about one third of Spanish commercial banks. A notorious case was that of Banca Catalana, which we will examine further down.

The financial crisis and the imminent accession to the European Community convinced politicians and some bankers that the sector needed a profound shakedown. It was realized that even the largest domestic banks were too small for competition in the wide European market. Both politicians and bankers were afraid that larger foreign banks would swallow the smaller Spanish units and that the domestic financial market might fall in foreign hands. Thus, prompted especially by Carlos Solchaga, the minister of Finance, the largest banks initiated a process of mergers and absorptions in the early 1980s which two decades later had concentrated the six largest banks into two, Santander and Bilbao (now called BBVA).

The European currency crisis of 1992, largely attributable to the problems created by the reunification of Germany after the fall of the Iron Curtain in 1989, seriously affected Spain: the peseta was one of the worse hit currencies (together with the Portuguese escudo, the Italian lira and the British pound sterling). In spite of all the devaluations and realignments which ensued, European monetary unification proceeded apace, although the peseta was devalued several times until in 1998 the parities became fixed. The following *Europhoria*, the firm belief that European monetary and economic unification would be easy and would bring benefits all around, personified by the French president of the European Commission, Jacques Delors, brought about the definitive monetary unification in 2002, with the substitution of the *euro* for the currencies of most countries of the European Union (Britain being the most salient exception).

In Spain, *europhoria* was strong and seemed to be justified by the plain economic euphoria of the first years of the twenty-first century. Few paid attention to the correlative deterioration of the country's balance of payments due to the increasing indebtedness of its economic agents (banks, families, and enterprises) who were taking advantage of the easiness for these operations that the common currency introduced. A substantial share of this borrowing was invested in the hottest asset of the moment: real estate and buildings. These assets were much in demand because *europhoria* brought about higher standards of living: many people wanted, and could afford, better living quarters or a second house; tourism also required new and better buildings; and so did the immigrants who flocked in great numbers. Housing prices went up and so did the number of houses built. But the housing boom, which had lasted for more than 10 years, came to an abrupt halt in 2007 and tumbled down from 2008 onward. This was a general world recession, but Spain was one of the worse affected countries. Unemployment jumped from 8.3 percent in 2006 to 22.6 percent in 2011. The socialist government of J. L. Rodríguez Zapatero tried to counter the downward trend by devising a program of expenditure in public works: the budget deficit jumped to 11.2 percent of GNP (from a surplus of 1.9 percent in 2007) without any visible recovery of the economy.

The recession was soon reflected in a new financial crisis, this one affecting savings banks, while the commercial banks, reorganized and wary of industrial investment, were much better able this time to weather the storm. Savings banks had acquired a fatal flaw: a socialist law of 1985 had politicized them, permitting their boards to fill up with local politicians and union members, who not only were ignorant of the most elementary principles of banking but also wanted the banks to invest in politically rewarding projects (airports, auditoriums, convention centers, gymnasia, etc., which in most cases were hardly used or needed but which were inaugurated with great fanfare) or who favored investment in construction and real estate because these seemed the most secure and rewarding assets. The recession brought about the end of Spanish savings banks; the few that came out unscathed became commercial banks.

In the general elections of 2011, the socialists were booted out and the conservative Popular Party (PP) of Mariano Rajoy came to power with an absolute majority. Meanwhile, the crisis was felt in all of Europe, with Greece teetering on the verge of bankruptcy. It became evident that having a common currency without a common fiscal policy was an invitation to disaster. The European Commission passed from a hands-off policy to demanding drastic budget austerity from its members. The Spanish situation was not as bad as that of Greece, but the country had to receive help to restructure its banking sector. Crucial psychological relief came from the governor of the European Central Bank, Mario Draghi, when he stated publicly that the ECB would do 'whatever it takes' to prevent a financial collapse in Europe.

Among the discomfiture of Spanish savings banks, there was a shining exception: that of the Catalan *Caixa de Barcelona*, the largest savings bank in Spain, whose prudent policies had permitted it to come out safe and sound from the debacle of its subsector. It adopted, however, the structure of a regular commercial bank (Spanish savings banks had been owned by their depositors, which had permitted the entrance of politicians and unionists on their boards with the help of the 1985 Law) under the name *Caixabank*.

The Catalan Economy at the Turn of the Century

At the end of the Franco dictatorship, Catalonia was still the most industrial of Spain's regions. But in four other regions, Navarre, Basque Country, Madrid, and the Valencia Community, the industrial sector had grown much faster than in Catalonia, whose unofficial title of 'the factory of Spain' was becoming increasingly disputed. The 'oil crisis' hit Catalan industry harder than that of Spain as a whole. Sectors such as the textile and shoe industries were seriously affected. The only consolation was that it was the industries with a higher technical component that survived the crisis better.

The Spanish state, starting with the centrist governments of Adolfo Suárez and continuing with the socialist ones of Felipe González, carried out an expensive program of 'industrial reconversion' which benefited especially Catalonia: Barcelona, for instance, received 52 percent more funds than Madrid and more than double the figure received by Bilbao. But the policies were not all that successful, since they did not stop the process of deindustrialization. Thus, when the conservative José María Aznar came to power, the government abandoned industrial reconversion and adopted a more hands-off line. Deindustrialization proceeded, but this did not trigger a depression: the posts that were lost in industry were replaced by those created in real estate and construction. The subsequent building boom brought about momentary prosperity but ended in 2007. Catalonia evolved in this respect exactly as the rest of Spain. In Catalonia, as in all of Spain, the service sector, especially the tourism industry, has come to the rescue. When the recent crisis was universal, tourism was just an economic palliative. More recently, with the developed world in full recovery and the eastern Mediterranean in turmoil, tourism is becoming Spain's number one industry, with Catalonia in the lead.

According to Maluquer, adding up not only hotel, but all types of accommodation, Catalonia is the most important tourist region in Europe, more than the Cote d'Azur, the Riviera, Andalucía or the Balearic Islands. So Catalonia seems to have shifted from being 'the factory of Spain' to being 'the camping of Spain.' Jokes aside, in spite of deindustrialization or *tertiarization*, relative figures still show Catalonia as being more industrial than the rest of Spain, although not by much now. Catalonia is still leader in consumer industries (food and beverages, textiles, furniture, and paper), electronics, optical instruments, chemistry and pharmaceuticals and, of course, the automobile, thanks to the SEAT factories.

There is however a serious problem for Catalan industry but also for the rest of Spain: private industries show a very low rate of investment in research and development. What industrial R&D there is, it tends to be carried out by the state and public enterprise; and in this Catalonia's position is rather undistinguished: its ranking by technological capacity is low by European standards and below those of Madrid, the Basque Country, or Navarre. This is also suggested by the fact that the leading Catalan exporting firms are foreign owned: SEAT, Nissan, Sony, etc.

The *Generalitat* in Action

First Steps

Once a decentralizing Constitution was approved and the regional statutes in place, the next order of things was to proceed with decentralization, in other words, with transferring government capacities from the central state to the regional governments. Catalonia, being the first to have a valid statute, was the first to acquire new capacities in different areas. There followed a flurry of pressures, disputes, and legal appeals, about the number, extension, scope, and financing of the new attributions. For the *generalitat*, the transfers were too slow, insufficient, and miserly endowed. For the central government, the *generalitat* was exceeding its limits and demanding too much. The rationale for decentralization was to provide an administration that was closer to the citizen. But the other side of the coin is that this is more expensive. There are economies of scale in government, and to have the same services which the central administration provided now administered by 17 administrations (this is the number of Autonomous Communities in Spain) must perforce be onerous. It was inevitable that disputes about endowment should break out.

In the case of Catalonia, the tensions multiplied, because the *generalitat* wanted to assume capacities and responsibilities as close to those of an independent state as possible. It not only wanted to administer, it wanted to make policies; not regulate, but legislate. Since Pujol assumed the post of president of the *generalitat* he repeatedly demanded for Catalonia 'the structure of a state.' This put the *generalitat* in an advantageous political position, because every shortcoming of the Catalan administration (and there were many, as we will show) could be blamed on the incomprehension, the stinginess, or the enmity of the Spanish state. The fact is what structures of State Catalonia achieved were a faithful reproduction of those of the Spanish state, complete with pseudo-embassies in foreign countries.

Catalan autonomy has certainly not come cheap. It is the Community with the most Chancelleries (*consejerías*, the regional equivalent of ministries). In 2013, for example, it had 12, when the national average was 8.5. In the 'tripartite' period, it had no less than 16, for obvious reasons: there were three parties, so the number of posts needed to be enlarged. Then there are not only the 'embassies' but a myriad of new institutions, most of them devoted to extoll the virtues of Catalanism and denounce the oppression Catalonia suffers at the hands of the Spanish state, and to foster the knowledge of the Catalan language at home and abroad. Catalonia has no less than 70 offices abroad, among them 'government delegations,' the equivalent of embassies, before the EU, France and Switzerland, North America (the USA, Canada, and Mexico), Italy, Germany, United Kingdom and Ireland, and Austria. But these are the 'embassies;' other offices of Catalonia dealing with economic, cultural, and other affairs practically cover the globe. It is difficult to know what use there is in duplicating the Spanish diplomatic network, unless these offices fulfill the dual role of satisfying the political vanity of the *generalitat* and of offering attractive posts to friends and toadies. Most of these agencies on top of being extremely expensive are of dubious legality because they exceed the capacities delegated by the Spanish government and granted by the Constitution.

To what extent this gargantuan expansion of the Catalan administrative machinery has benefited the average citizen is debatable. According to a study of the European Commission (Charron, et al., 2012) which measures the quality of national and regional governments of the Union, Catalonia occupies 113th place of a total of 172 regions; it is the lowest place of all Spanish Communities. The Basque Country, for example, the best placed, takes the 55th post in this ranking, closely followed by other northern regions such as Galicia and Asturias.

The 1979 Estatut: The Beginnings of Enforced Catalanization

Catalans had a key role in the writing of the Constitution. Two of the seven-member committee who drafted the chart were Catalans; we also saw that the atmosphere at the time of the writing (and many years afterward) was favorable to radical decentralization, so that, unlike what happened in 1932, the drafters found support in the Constitution for many of their autonomy aspirations. Thus, the *Estatut* obtained advantages and capacities 'beyond what Catalonia had ever enjoyed historically' (Molinero and Ysàs, 2014, p. 288). But if Catalan politicians used to present a united front in Madrid, they showed serious differences of opinion among themselves when debating at home, as became obvious when discussing the draft of the *Estatut*. There were two very disputed subjects at that juncture: the linguistic question and the problems of an electoral law, more precisely, the problem of electoral circumscriptions.

For Popular Alliance (AP), a conservative group which later became the Popular Party, bilingualism was the obvious solution. Catalan officials should know both Catalan and Spanish, and use one or the other according to the preference of the citizen they were dealing with. The left, socialists and communists, insisted that the Catalan government should make an effort so that citizens were equally fluent in both languages, but also wanted to avoid excessive pressure upon those who spoke only Spanish. They thought the learning process would take time so that the obligation to know Catalan should not be enforced right away. For their part, the nationalist parties wanted the *Estatut* to put both languages exactly on a par, with a special clause saying that the Catalan language should have in Catalonia the same treatment as the Constitution attributed to the Spanish language in all of Spain (Article 3 of the Constitution: 'Castilian is the official Spanish language of the State. All Spaniards have the duty of knowing it and the right to use it. All other Spanish languages shall also be official in their respective Autonomous Communities in accordance with their Statutes'). In any case, putting Catalan in Catalonia at the same level as Castilian Spanish in Spain is clearly unjustified and oppressive, as in Spain practically all citizens have Spanish as their native language or at least speak it fluently, whereas this is not the case with Catalan in Catalonia, where it is not even the language of the majority. It is thus evident and understandable that the opinions about the linguistic question varied widely among Catalan politicians. In the end, the 1979 *Estatut*, while insisting that Catalan was Catalonia's 'own language,' put Castilian and Catalan on a par in Catalonia.

The other big topic of discussion was the electoral district o circumscription. The left favored the 'one person, one vote' principle, while the nationalists of the right and left, favored the regional vote by *comarcas* (counties) thereby granting more weight to scarcely populated agrarian and mountainous areas, which tended to vote nationalist. In the end, the *Estatut* established a rather rough system of elections whereby Barcelona, where nationalism has less relative support, was underrepresented, which of course was what the nationalists wanted. The province of Barcelona, which today contains 73.6 percent of the population of Catalonia, is apportioned 63.0 of the votes. The *Estatut* promised a fairer electoral law, but it was never enacted.

In spite of the continuous complaints of the nationalists, the fact is that, as De Riquer (2004, p. 401), a historian who certainly could not be accused of antinationalism, has written, after the Spanish transition to democracy, Catalonia experienced 'an exceptional historical stage [...] because it has been the stage when Catalonia has enjoyed the longest period of self-government in the modern era.' Let us see what the *generalitat* did during those years of self-government.

The Catalan elections of 20 March 1980, the first held under the provisions of the new *Estatut*, marked a watershed in Catalan history. Before the elections, the president was Josep Tarradellas, in circumstances we already know. To the surprise of many, who expected the socialists to prevail, Pujol won the 1980 election, and the mood of the *generalitat* underwent a radical change. Tarradellas had practiced scrupulous loyalty to the Spanish government and avoided confrontation with it without abandoning his principles. Pujol, whose party, CDC, soon joined forces with *Unió*, the old Christian Democratic group, which became its junior partner, announced in his inauguration that his policies would be nationalistic, and in this he was faithful to his word. Tarradellas had respected his agreement with the Spanish Ministry of Education that linguistic parity would be rigorously observed. From the moment Pujol took over, this respect for the Constitution was abandoned. The aim now was to attain the supremacy of Catalan over Castilian by all means fair and foul. Wielding the famous concession of the Madrid governments that the Catalan language was Catalonia's own, and in addition repeating two more slogans (linguistic parity will cause the disappearance of Catalan and it creates fracture in Catalan society), an incredible effort has been carried out by the Pujol governments to relegate Castilian Spanish and to force everybody in Catalonia to use Catalan all the time.

Let me make clear that the slogans constantly repeated by the education authorities of the *generalitat* are false: there is no evidence that Catalan will disappear if Catalonia follows a bilingual policy in accordance with the Spanish Constitution. We have already seen that Catalan was repressed under Franco and nevertheless survived. True, only a minority could write it correctly, but it was spoken currently in the homes and in the streets, a respectable literature was written and printed in Catalan, etc. If Catalan did not disappear after almost 40 years of repression, why should it disappear after becoming a co-official language in Catalonia? As to the fracture in Catalan society, this is a recent invention of the nationalists: Catalonia has always been bilingual and has never suffered a linguistic fracture. History shows Catalans divided by social class, by political beliefs, by regional origins, but never by language. It is the nationalists who are creating a fracture in Catalonia with their linguistic obsession: they are creating a rift in Catalonia and in Spain, by making every effort to make Catalans to use Catalan exclusively and forget Castilian Spanish. All this in detriment of Catalans themselves, because no matter how respectable and charming the Catalan language may be, it is spoken by no more than some 8 million, whereas Castilian Spanish is spoken by more than 500 million, which makes it one of the most widely spoken languages in the world. The war against Castilian in Catalonia is not only ridiculous and futile, it is divisive and harmful for the Catalans themselves, let alone for Spain as a whole.

The struggle to impose the Catalan language was based upon two laws: the Law of Linguistic Normalization of Catalonia (1983) and the Law of Linguistic Policy (1998); both were passed with the exclusive support of the nationalist parties in the Catalan Parliament. Parts of the Law of Linguistic Normalization were struck down by the Constitutional Court, so this prompted the enactment of the Linguistic Policy Law, much more radical and coercive than its predecessor. These laws were complemented with a series of decrees and administrative measures intruding into the private lives of citizens to push the to use Catalan at home, at school, at work, and in all facets of everyday life; teaching in Catalan at all levels but the university was made compulsory; a General Direction of Linguistic Policy was established in the *generalitat*; soon after a *Corporació Catalana de Mitjans Audiovisuals* (CCMA, Catalan Corporation of Audiovisual Media) was created. With the Law of Linguistic Policy, penalties were introduced for those who were not diligent enough to communicate in Catalan. Shopkeepers, for instance, are now subject to steep fines if the signs on their shops are in Spanish (it does not matter if they are in French, say, or English; Castilian Spanish is the forbidden language). The only prominent Catalan who dared to publicly criticize this oppressive linguistic policy, and he did so early, was Tarradellas, who wrote a letter in *La Vanguardia* (16 April 1982), Barcelona's leading journal, accusing 'the new government of using *victimism* as a shield to hide its political incompetence and its lack of ambition.'

A group of Catalan intellectuals and professionals, however, had published a *Manifesto for the equality of linguistic rights in Catalonia* in March 1981, with 2,300 signatures supporting it. The Manifesto was received with incredible violence and hostility in official and nationalist circles. It was accused of being 'against the official character Catalan language' (De Riquer and Maluquer, 2004, p. 375) in spite of the fact that its authors made clear that they did not oppose co-officiality, but only 'the attempt to replace, as a matter of principle [. . .] the language of those who speak Castilian with Catalan, a replacement which must be carried out voluntarily or by compulsion, or as some have even said, by persuasion, by coercion, or by imposition, according to each case.' A counter-Manifesto was published and demonstrations carried out in the 'defense of the language, the culture and nation of Catalonia.' In the ensuing collective hysteria, the terrorist organization *Terra Lliure* kidnapped one of the first signers of the Manifesto, Federico Jimenez Losantos, an Aragonese, professor of literature and journalist, who had been a student at the University of Barcelona, tied him to a tree and shot him in a leg. His life was saved by a friend who untied him and took him to the nearest hospital. In this atmosphere of terror, Jiménez Losantos and many of the signers of the Manifesto left Catalonia and went to live elsewhere.

A new tactic of the nationalist movement had been born: the mobilization of the 'civil society' at the service of the cause. From then onward, street demonstrations and other similar means of defending 'the Catalan cause' against all sorts of enemies, external and domestic, were organized by the Pujol *generalitat* to show that 'the people' supported the sacred principles. The perfect example of this was the case of *Banca Catalana*.

The Banca Catalana Affair

This case offers the most evident example of the utilization of civil society for political ends at the service of nationalism. It contributed decisively to lend force and continuity to the nationalist policies of CiU and its leader, Jordi Pujol.

As we saw in the previous chapter, even before the fall of the Bank of Barcelona in 1920, there was among Catalan politicians, economists, and businessmen a widespread dissatisfaction with the state of Catalan banks. This was later aggravated by the downfall of the Bank of Catalonia in 1931 and by the numerous takeovers of Catalan banks especially by Basque and Madrid institutions in the following decades. The worry for the inability of Catalan banks to cater to the needs of a buoyant industrial economy was no doubt a powerful factor among those which moved a small group of businessmen near Jordi Pujol, then a young doctor more interested in politics and business than in physiological topics, to buy a small local bank in Olot (Girona), belonging to the Dorca family, in 1959. The idea was to transform this small family bank into a powerful industrial promoter, capable to fulfill a role which no other Catalan establishment was fulfilling.

This group around Pujol included his own father, Florenci Pujol, a financier and stock exchange operator; Moisés D. Tennenbaum, a prosperous financier and jeweler of Polish Jewish origin established in Catalonia since the 1930s and a close associate of Florenci Pujol; and Francesc Cabana, a lawyer and historian, married to Pujol's sister, and sharing Pujol's fervent Catalanism. The rest of the group included well-known members of the Catalan bourgeoisie, in some cases linked to Republican circles.

It is worth mentioning that the three leaders of the group had problems with the law at the time. The problems of Florenci Pujol and David Tennenbaum were financial: both were accused and sentenced for illegal dealings in foreign currency. Jordi Pujol's problems, instead, were political: he was detained and judged by a military court in 1960, accused of boycotting an act in the *Palau de la Música* in Barcelona, by chanting a forbidden hymn and spreading antigovernment leaflets. He was sentenced and spent 2 years in prison in Saragossa and 1 year confined in Girona. Consequently, he could not fully join the bank until 1965, by which time it had moved its headquarters to Barcelona and changed its name to *Banca Catalana*.

Banca Catalana grew very fast in its first 20 years. It is remarkable that, although Franco had accurate information about the circumstances, purpose, and main actors of its development (as documents in archive of the Francisco Franco Foundation demonstrate), he did nothing to hinder its growth. The early times of the bank were almost clandestine and had traits of heroic determination. Cabana, the historian, went around villages on a motorcycle interviewing prospective customers, doubtless appealing to their Catalanist sentiments. One of the police reports in the Francisco Franco Foundation says that the bank operated also in Barcelona in an irregular manner because it still was a mere local bank. But it soon was able to become a provincial institution and therefore to operate legally in Barcelona. Cabana and others very successfully managed the bank in its early years. Pujol himself, however, even from the Saragossa prison and later on from Girona, where he was confined but apparently enjoying ample freedom of movement, had taken part in the direction of the enterprise. He was even able to visit Barcelona several times in the year of his confinement, before he took over officially in 1965. His main task was to widen the circle of partners and shareholders; he was successful in bringing around a remarkable number of relevant members of the Catalan upper classes. Politics undoubtedly helped Pujol in his endeavors. A substantial number of customers were identified with the bank's Catalanist purposes and were ready to entrust it with their savings and pay for its services just by virtue of what the bank meant of opposition to the dictatorship and 'defense of the land' (an expression dear to Catalanists). In the long term, however, it was politics that sunk Banca Catalana, although certainly not the career of its guiding spirit, Jordi Pujol.

The main problem of the bank was that Pujol was in a hurry to make it grow, diversify, and become a source of power and personal prestige, a firm stepping-stone on his way to the political stage. Impatient to reach his aims, Pujol pressed the accelerator perhaps too much, forgot the basic axiom in banking, which is prudence, and forgot especially the stormy history of Catalan banks, where so very often the wish to get rich quick and to mix banking and politics had yielded such terrible results. He should have remembered more often the sad ends of the Bank of Barcelona and the Bank of Catalonia.

In the early years, however, Pujol and Banca Catalana were extremely lucky. The Franquist authorities let them do what they pleased, allowed their installation in Barcelona and their change of name, adopting one that clearly reminded that their leaders were 'leftist and separatist to the core,' as a police report said. The report erred in classifying the Pujols, Cabana, and their entourage as 'leftists.' In any case, the regime did not interfere. Furthermore, the economic and political situation was favorable. Those were the years of fast economic growth and of the attempts to modernize the state by a group of technocrats many of whom were Catalans. It is possible that the presence of Catalans such as López Rodó, Fabián Estapé, or Lucas Beltrán in the government might explain the benevolence with which an openly Catalanist bank led by a man who had been jailed for subversive activities was treated. In the years following the Stabilization Plan of 1959, the dictatorship was more focused on economics than on politics. The following anecdote is telling of the situation: Manuel Ortínez, a Catalan economist and businessman who later was linked to Banca Catalana, was friendly with Faustino García Moncó, a former banker and at the time minister of Commerce. García Moncó wanted Ortínez for a high post in his economic team. Ortínez, who was one of Tarradellas's representatives in Catalonia, accepted his friend's proposal on the condition that he would not be asked to swear fidelity to the dictatorship, as was mandatory. García Moncó asked Franco whether this would be possible, and the dictator's answer was: 'If he gives a good performance the oath is immaterial.' This shows that Franco himself put economics above politics, and may explain his tolerance for the Pujol group.

The moment was propitious for a new bank bent on innovation and enterprise. The success of the Stabilization Plan spurred members of the Catalan bourgeoisie to invest in finance and industry, and many of them felt attracted by Pujol's project, which offered not only a way to work for Catalonia (*fer país* is another Catalanist expression meaning 'building the country') but also to do profitable business. Many were like Ortínez, who could work for the Franco government while marking his distance. They certainly were not revolutionaries but rather mildly liberal and certainly nationalistic.

Jordi Pujol was in a hurry and stepped on the gas pedal of Banca Catalana. This entailed not only expanding the volume of business, moving into new offices and hiring new personnel, but also buying a group of new banks, in principle complementary with the original; they formed what was called the Catalana group. Acquisition of new banks was also favored by the current government policies. Monetary policy was profoundly revamped with a Banking Law of April 1962, which not only nationalized the Bank of Spain but also put an end to the *numerus clausus* principle, which severely restricted the opening of new banks and established the separation between commercial and investment banks. In this way, the law favored the creation of banking groups. Up to then, Spanish banks had followed the lead of German and Italian banks in that they had mixed commercial, short-term loans, with industrial, long-term credit. From 1962 onward, these operations should be carried out by separate institutions; in accordance to the law, several mixed banks were split up into a commercial and an industrial bank. This is what Pujol did by founding the *Banc Industrial de Catalunya* (BIC) in 1965, whose first director was Manuel Ortínez. Later on, Banca Catalana acquired several new banks, among them another industrial outfit, the *Banc Industrial del Mediterrani* (BIM). Both BIC and BIM followed expansive policies with the purpose of 'building country' as much as making money. All went well as long as the boom continued. The group also built new headquarters in the center of Barcelona, more to impress the public than out of real necessity of space, since the building was never fully occupied. Pujol also carried out a policy of media control, imposing a Catalanist slant which in the end was counterproductive and brought the ruin of some prestigious publications such as *Diario de Barcelona*, a century-old daily, and *Destino*, Barcelona's leading weekly.

All these expansive policies were possible as long as the going was good. However, from the mid-1970s onward the boom came to an end, due to international and domestic factors. The war in Vietnam and the oil crisis put an end to the golden era; the international crisis plus the political uncertainties of the transition to democracy in Spain caused an industrial crisis which affected banks especially. Among the many banks and groups hit by the crisis there were two whose size set them apart: Rumasa and Banca Catalana.

Jordi Pujol had formally resigned his posts in Banca Catalana in 1977, but he kept a hefty package of shares and remained an unofficial authority in the bank at least until it was intervened by the Bank of Spain and was put under the surveillance of the Deposit Guarantee Fund (FGD). His resignation was due to his increasing political role in CDC, which he had founded in 1974. In 1977, the first democratic elections took place and perhaps this was the reason for his resignation. In any case, that was also the moment when the situation in Banca Catalana started to be alarming.

That the Catalana group should be seriously affected by the crisis was only normal. Its two industrial banks (BIC and BIM) found themselves before a growing list of defaulting customers as the industrial crisis spread. We should remember that, as Cabana (1988, p. 233) himself admitted, many loans had been granted more for political than for economic reasons ('were the fruit of a political will'). In other words, the banks' directors had loaned the money more according to personal or political affinity, or the attractiveness of the project, than after coldly calculating the viability of that project, or the trustworthiness of the borrower. Pujol himself had proclaimed that the BIC should play the role of a government bank in Catalonia, more interested in the nature of the projects than in their short-term profitability. The only problem was that the BIC's resources were limited and it did not have a government budget to finance it in case of trouble. The directives of the BIC made a series of mistaken bets; they thought that Catalonia needed a strong metallurgical industry and invested heavily in it; they miscalculated and the bank could not recover its outlays. Similar problems arose in plastics and in real estate. The crisis hit these sectors hard. Josep Vilarasau, general director of *la Caixa* at the time, says in his memoirs that Jordi Pujol was always ready to help Catalan firms just for being Catalan, even if hard figures recommended caution; according to Vilarasau, this was a blessing for other banks, who could thus recover their dubious credits, thanks to Pujol's generosity; the end product of all this was a lengthening list of delinquent customers for Pujol's banks.

The rumors about the situation of the Catalana group had been insistent for years when, in 1980, the Bank of Spain, which had been fighting the crisis for a few years, sent its inspectors to Banca Catalana where they detected some 'little problems.' The 'little problems' grew, especially those pertaining to BIC and BIM, but they concerned several other banks of the group too. In this respect, the book by Cabana (1988), written in the form of a diary, makes very interesting reading, because it shows its author, who had been collaborating for years as representative of middle-sized institutions with the Bank of Spain and *Corporación Bancaria* (CB, the predecessor of the FGD) in rescuing failed banks, finding himself after 1980 in the uncomfortable role of defendant on behalf of his own bank, now facing his colleagues of the Bank of Spain and the CB as prosecutors. He complains repeatedly about attacks in the press, but the fact is that they would not have been as acid and frequent if Banca Catalana had not showed so many vulnerable flanks and had not been so clearly linked with politics.

Soon there appeared strong discrepancies between the Bank of Spain envoys and the directors of Banca Catalana. The inspectors were convinced that things were being hidden from them. At some point, Cabana (1988, pp. 125, 145) admits: 'It seems to me [the inspectors] have found more things than we thought,' and says that a high officer of the Bank of Spain complained that Banca Catalana 'did not supply trustworthy information.' I myself had a conversation with the head inspector of the Bank of Spain in 1987 and he said to me that the directors of the Banca 'lied shamelessly through their beards' (an Andalusian expression).

In 1982, it became clear that the Banca Catalana group had to be radically reformed, reconstructed, and sold. Mariano Rubio the vice governor of the Bank of Spain (later governor) let the directors know: 'The situation is very serious and a solution must be sought immediately.' A few days later, he added that the Bank of Spain was wondering what to do so as 'not to politicize the problem' (Cabana, 1988, pp. 140-1). An attempt was made, at the suggestion of the men of Banca Catalana, to pursue a 'Catalan solution,' that is to say, to sell the group, or at least the main bank, to a local institution, which obviously had to be the

Caixa, the only one of an adequate size. This appeared as a possibility in 1982, but after months of indecision, the *Caixa* made an excessively low offer (according to Cabana, p. 174, they were trying to buy pesetas at sixty cents, a common Catalan expression to describe bargain hunters). The rumors about the group's insolvency became more insistent and finally the Bank of Spain put Banca Catalana in the hands of the FGD. By mid-1983, a pool of 11 banks led by the Basque Bank of Biscay acquired all of Banca Catalana and early in 1984 the Bank of Biscay absorbed Banca Catalana in its entirety.

When the report of the Bank of Spain's inspectors was known by the government, the minister of Economics and Finance, Miguel Boyer, told the Cortes in June 1983 that there were 'signs of serious irregularities in Banca Catalana' and that he had asked the Bank of Spain to submit a copy of the report to the judicial authorities to determine possible criminal responsibilities. This was done; the report was sent to the Barcelona District Attorney's Office and was assigned by lot to two public prosecutors, José M. Mena and Carlos Jiménez Villarejo.

Mena and Villarejo studied the evidence and reached the conclusion that in effect there were signs of possible crimes; they then reported their conclusions to the government attorney general, Luis Burón, who decided to prosecute. The accusation was submitted on 22 May 1984. The main irregularities detected were as follows. First, Banca Catalana used a system of double accounting which permitted the directors of the bank to ensconce substantial amounts of money (approximately 9 percent of total assets between 1974 and 1981) not only from the government authorities but also from shareholders. This 'secret money' was mainly used to pay rates of interest above the legal limits (interest rates and dividends were severely controlled by the government at the time) and also to grant loans under very favorable terms to members of the inner circle of the bank. In fact, in many cases, these loans were never returned (Ríos, 2015, pp. 44-49). Second, the bank accumulated 'treasury stock,' i.e., it purchased its own shares. This operation is commonly forbidden; in Spain at the time it was not absolutely forbidden, but it required the approval of the Bank of Spain; Banca Catalan never requested this approval. In times of difficulties, as those years were, a common reason for accumulating 'treasury stock' is the wish to sustain the price of the stock and thereby to hide from the public the troubled situation of the bank, thus being able to sell stock at artificially high prices. According to the public attorneys, these fraudulent operations were repeatedly carried out by some Banca Catalana's directors.

The prosecutors also alleged that Jordi Pujol made an irregular donation of Banca Catalana's shares to a 'Catalan Foundation' in 1982. This donation was irregular because according to the bank's statutes, share donations should be officially notified to the rest of shareholders, so they could purchase them at the going price. This notification was not made, so the donation was invalid. Nevertheless, it was announced and registered at the Foundation, and the value estimated was of 187.7 million pesetas, a considerable figure at the time. However, after Banca Catalana was officially transferred to the FGD, the value of these shares plummeted and was reduced to one thousandth of that estimate. Thus, Pujol managed to appear as a great benefactor while he was donating something of little value. Furthermore, since the donation was not valid, Pujol in fact remained the owner of these shares, whose value recovered after Banca Catalana was acquired by the Bank of Biscay. According to Ríos (2015, pp 73-5 and 105), this may be one of the origins of Pujol's present colossal fortune.

The public prosecutors also found that the bank's directors took advantage of their privileged position to obtain special treatment. They illegally received high interest rates for their deposits, borrowed money at very favorable interest rates, money which often they never repaid, and, especially, they cashed in illicit dividends. These dividends were illicit because they were disbursed in years when the bank was suffering serious losses, although these losses were hidden by creative accounting. In this way, the prosecutors added, 'the accused reaped hefty profits in the knowledge that they thereby were driving the bank to its ruin.'

The accused defended themselves not by denying the facts, which were undeniable, but by alleging that their actions, though illegal, were standard practice in the profession. Cabana (1988, pp. 131, 224-32) and Pujol even affirmed that accusing them of illegal practices which were common in banking circles was blatant proof of anti-Catalanism. Of course, they omitted that the losses of Banca Catalana were the second largest experienced by a bank or banking group in the entire crisis and that they had to be supported by the national budget, i.e., by Spanish taxpayers. In general, according to Pujol and Cabana, everything the directors of Banca Catalana did was in the best of intentions and with the interests of the bank and of Catalonia at heart, while the intentions of the prosecutors, the Bank of Spain, and the Socialist government were invariably, sinister, perverse, and anti-Catalan.

In the middle of all this mess, Catalan local elections took place in April 1984. CiU, Pujol's coalition, which was governing jointly with ERC and UCD, obtained absolute majority and was getting ready to govern alone. A month later the indictment against 25 former directors of Banca Catalana, Pujol and Cabana among them, was submitted to a Barcelona court.

The newspaper *El País* had announced the indictment 4 days in advance. We know now that the source was one of the prosecutors, who talked to the newspaper because he feared that the government might quash the case for political reasons. Pujol and Cabana suspected exactly the opposite: that the indictment had been encouraged by the government. Pujol wrote in his memoirs that he believed as much (Ríos, 2014, pp. 112, 163-7). Cabana (1988, p. 192) wrote: 'I see the full participation of the government, with the help of Mariano Rubio, who wants to be governor of the Bank of Spain and is ready to do whatever necessary to support the Boyer-Guerra team.' Here Cabana showed considerable ignorance of the inner workings of the Socialist government. Alfonso Guerra, at that time vice president, and Boyer never formed a team, on the contrary, they were the visible heads of two rival teams; Guerra won and Boyer resigned in 1985. Both Pujol and Cabana believed they were being persecuted, but they do not show even the slightest evidence. Cabana's political conjectures are just plain wrong. Both Pujol and Cabana changed their opinions about who exactly was persecuting them. They blamed Guerra and Boyer, then they accused Felipe González (the then president) himself, later on they accused the minister of Justice (Fernando Ledesma) who would have forced the hand of the chief prosecutor; their last culprit was Narcís Serra, who was minister of Defense at the time but who, as the leading Catalan

Socialist, was viewed as an enemy by Pujol and Cabana. More recently, however, Cabana at least seems to have changed his mind again. When more recently asked by the journalist Pere Ríos (2015, p. 103) whether the prosecutors had been induced to act by the Socialist government, he answered: 'I don't think so.'

Pujol's certitude that there was a 'political hand' behind the indictment makes one suspect that he was attributing to the government what he himself would have done in their case: he would have pressured the public prosecutors to indict his political enemies. And in fact, he did similar things often when he could: he even accused one of his partners in Banca Catalana, J. Andreu Abelló, of having used the bank for his own enrichment after Andreu criticized Banca Catalana's policies (Ríos, 2015, p. 106).

The available evidence seems to contradict the statements by Pujol and Cabana after the indictment became public. In reality, it was the prosecutors themselves who were afraid that the government would pressure them to abort the indictment. This is why they publicized it as soon as it was ready. In turn, we know that their politics was to the left of the socialists: they were much closer to the Communists. Everything suggests that they acted according to their own convictions. Even today, they are convinced that they were right and Pujol and company were guilty as charged, and say so in their prologues to Rios's book.

What cannot be denied is that both the Spanish and the Catalan governments were aware of the political aspects of the affair. For Pujol, Banca Catalana was a Damocles's sword hanging over his head since he assumed power in 1980. He surely shared his partner and brother-in-law's opinion that the Socialist government were 'after Jordi, and to get him they must ruin and prosecute us' (Cabana, 1988, p. 181). Pujol was on the defensive because he knew that Banca Catalana was his weakest point; in September 1983 he was bitterly criticized in the Catalan parliament by Antoni Gutiérrez, the general secretary of the PSUC, who accused him not only of criminal responsibilities but also of having spoiled 'the possibility of having created a public sector bank and instead having made a gift to the Spanish big banks.' He was blaming Pujol for having let Banca Catalana fall in the hands of the Bank of Biscay. In fact, it is dubious that Pujol might have been able to determine the fate of

Banca Catalana after it was transferred to the FGD. Pujol answered evasively and profited from the occasion to blame the Bank of Spain. Gutiérrez's reply was hard and trenchant: 'Mr Pujol you not only commit errors. You yourself are an error, a historical error, I do not know of what dimension, but an error.'

Another deputy, the Socialist Lluís Armet, accused Pujol, in that same session, of being excessively linked to the Banca Catalana scandal, of lacking the independence and the 'political liberty' necessary to 'defend the national interests of Catalonia,' and this was shown, according to Armet, by 'the absolute and scandalous inhibition of the *generalitat* government in the final phase of the Banca Catalana crisis.' He therefore suggested that Pujol should resign. Harassed from the left, Pujol defended himself with his typically bungled and confusing oratory, but he had recourse to his ultimate rhetorical weapon: 'there has been a norm of my person which I have applied for better or worse, with more or less wisdom or success, but this has been serving Catalonia [. . .] my only motive is serving Catalonia' (Baiges, et al., 1985, pp. 205-9).

This was his last recourse, and to it he appealed when the great test arrived and he saw himself faced with the indictment in May 1984, just a few days after winning the local election with an absolute majority. The debates of the previous autumn had just been a sort of general rehearsal for the final act of May 1984. In autumn, he had accused the Catalan Socialists of disloyalty to Catalonia by being subordinated to the Madrid government. He used the same argument in the spring of 1984. He took advantage of the ceremony of his inauguration as president of the Catalan government to organize a mammoth street demonstration of support with personnel of his own party (CiU) in charge of keeping order. The slogans chanted in the demonstration expressed support for the leader and hatred for the national government, such as '*Felipe i Guerra ofesen nostra terra*' (Felipe [González] and [Alfonso] Guerra offend our land). In this hysterical atmosphere, Pujol appeared on the balcony of the *generalitat* and pronounced a short discourse full of demagoguery, whose best remembered phrase was the following: 'The central government has played an ignominious game [this was a veiled reference to the indictment] and, from now on, when the time comes to speak of ethics, morals and fair game it will our turn, not theirs.'

Typically, no hard details were given. There was no need, the masses knew perfectly well what Pujol meant and agreed with him that the indictment was not an attack against him as an individual, or against the former directors of Banca Catalana, but against Catalonia *in toto*. Once he had his followers in a frenzy, Pujol offered 'dialogue and cooperation.' It was a masterful performance in its own terms. Of course, we know now by his own confession that when Pujol proclaimed that it was his or 'their' turn to speak of ethics, morals, and fair play he had been defrauding and violating the tax code for at least 4 years.

In any case, both the speech and the demonstration were a resounding success which convinced friends and foes alike that Pujol and Catalan nationalism were better left alone. There were some exceptions, though. Jordi Solé Tura, wrote a newspaper article (*El País*, 27 May 1984) saying that he was in total disagreement with Pujol when he 'claims that submitting an indictment against the former directors of Banca Catalana is an attack against all Catalans. I consider myself as Catalan as he is and I do not feel I am being attacked.' This was considered by the Pujolistas as an unpardonable offense. From then onward, he was ignored by all CiU governments, even when he became minister of Culture. Cabana, nonetheless, thought everything in the demonstration had been 'impressive and correct.' Again, not everybody agreed about the correctness of the demonstrators; several top Socialist politicians were booed, insulted, threatened, and pushed around by militants of CiU (Ríos, 2015, pp. 143-5).

Pujol deftly took a leaf from his former enemy Francisco Franco and proclaimed a common political synecdoche: Franco identified his government with Spain and considered criticisms to his regime as attacks on Spain; Pujol decided that to indict him was to indict Catalonia in its entirety. It became obvious that a substantial part of the Catalan populace agreed with him. Although probably not the majority, it was a vocal minority and it had all the support of the *generalitat* and the party. Those who disagreed, like Solé Tura, became pariahs in their own region. The political attacks against Pujol in the campaign based on the Banca Catalana scandal misfired; instead of as a crook, electors saw Pujol as a victim. The Socialists, who thought that they could use the scandal as a political weapon and did nothing to stop the indictment, after they saw what happened in the elections and in Pujol's inauguration, changed tack and opted for achieving an entente with him and letting him do as he pleased in his Catalan fief.

The Spanish Socialists, who treat with contempt and animosity the parties to their right, show more respect for Catalan nationalism, no matter how dyed-in-the-wool conservative it may be, so they favor pacts of nonaggression and even mutual support with those groups. For similar reasons, Pujol and the nationalists have been ready to reciprocate. After all, their electoral support comes from different sectors, so there is no direct competition. The case is different with Catalan Socialists, whose electoral support overlaps considerably and therefore are seen as direct competitors by the nationalists.

After the victory in the battle of opinion, the judicial battle was relatively easy. Shortly after Pujol's inauguration, a decisive step was taken: the Supreme Court declined to take up the Banca Catalana case, which was returned to the Barcelona Audience, a collective body where the atmosphere was favorable for Pujol. In November 1986, the audience decided not to prosecute Pujol by 33 votes to 8. Then the cases of the rest of the indicted were moved to the ordinary jurisdiction. In January 1988, a Barcelona judge stayed the proceedings. The Banca Catalana affair ended without one single culprit.

After this episode and the triumph of Pujol before Catalan public opinion, his nationalist government had its hands free to carry out its linguistic, educational, and propaganda politics, which it had launched in 1980, but which now could be put into practice without any sort of hindrance. Some Catalan authors have described the ensuing situation. The essayist and journalist Arcadi Espada (2014) speaks of the 'ostracism to which dissidents were relegated in that asphyxiating and unanimous atmosphere.' According to Francesc de Carreras (2014), a law professor and political essayist, 'Catalan nationalism rapidly became the only legitimate and transversal ideology.' One could be conservative or leftist, this did not matter as long as one respected the limits of the 'nationally correct.' Any discrepancy was admissible but this one. Furthermore, if one was not a Catalan nationalist one automatically became a Spanish nationalist, there was no alternative. Pujol had succeeded in convincing a substantial section of Catalans that Catalonia constitutes a separate culture, very different from that of the rest of Spain, and that this separate culture only can survive if it is supported by an independent state.

Clemente Polo (2014), an economics professor, points to the success of Catalan nationalism in infiltrating left-wing parties, Socialists and Communists (now conjoined with ecologists), to the point that, when these parties displaced CiU and formed a coalition government with ERC, they surpassed their rivals in pushing an intensely nationalist program and in harassing non-nationalists. There was no political way out in the Catalan 'Animal Farm.'

Success and Failure of a Coercive Linguistic Policy

Linguistic policy is crucial to Catalan nationalism since the only clear element of the much touted *fet diferencial* is the Catalan language. An essential part of nationalistic policy is the attempt to turn Catalonia into a monolingual land, eradicating its long historical bilingual tradition. After the Banca Catalana affair, the nationalist *generalitat* had its hands freer to carry out its unconstitutional linguistic policies, because no matter what the Courts said on the matter (they repeatedly ordered the *generalitat* to go back to a policy of strict equality between the two languages), the nationalist governments carried on regardless and the central governments did nothing to force the *generalitat* to respect the law of the land.

As we saw earlier, the Constitutional Court struck down some minor sections but declared constitutional the 1983 Law of Linguistic Normalization, which was quite asymmetric in its preference of Catalan over Castilian in the educational area. Nevertheless, this seemed insufficient to the nationalists and in 1998 the Catalan Parliament approved a Law of Linguistic Policy which extended this asymmetry to practically all spheres. Before the passing of the law, the bill received numerous criticisms from leading Catalan intellectuals and linguists on the grounds that it ran counter the spirit and the letter not only of the Spanish Constitution but of the Catalan *Estatut*. To no avail: in Spain, not only in Catalonia, politicians rarely debate when they feel they can count on the necessary votes, as was the case at the time.

The linguistic policies of the *generalitat* not only are obnoxious and self-defeating, they are terribly expensive not only in strictly economic terms but also in that they create tensions and divisions in Catalan society. Catalan 'monolingualism' runs counter the history and tradition of Catalonia. The most distinguished Catalan writers write in Spanish, for at least a very simple reason: there are 500 million Spanish speakers in the world, while the equivalent number of Catalan speakers is at most some 8 million (and of those practically all can read in Spanish also).

It is a historical fact that during the Middle Ages the Castilian language expanded along the Iberian Peninsula with greater strength and extension than the other languages (Fig. 7.1). Catalan remained limited to the northeastern coast and Galaico-Portuguese was only spoken on the Atlantic facade. Basque was spoken by some groups in the Bay of Biscay and was divided into several dialects. Castilian not only was spoken by a vast majority in the Peninsula but was also used as

Fig. 7.1 The Iberian Peninsula in the Fifteenth Century

lingua franca among those who had other mother tongues. Basque and Catalan were also spoken in the adjacent areas north of the Pyrenees. I do not think that Castilian had any intrinsic superiority (although its spelling is simpler); its predominance seems to be due to historical factors. But the fact is that all other non-Castilian speaking areas were in fact bilingual, i.e., Castilian was spoken or at least understood everywhere in the Peninsula. This is a clear justification for the fact that Castilian should have become known as 'Spanish.' One significant consequence of this predominance of Castilian was that it was carried by the Spaniards to the newly conquered territories, so that it became the language of the Spanish Empire and the lingua franca in all of Spanish America. Simultaneously, Castilian literature produced numerous works of high quality and universal projection which contributed to the prestige of the language and to the spread of its knowledge. Although the later political and cultural decline of Spain affected the international status of the language, its historical and literary prestige and its presence in the Americas have preserved its importance, so that even today Spanish is one of the most widely spoken languages in the world; although clearly behind English in international diffusion, Spanish is ahead of other important European languages, such as French, German, Portuguese, or Italian.

Somewhat similar processes to that which took place in Spain occurred in other European countries since the Middle Ages, whereby one language has predominated and acquired national and official character. In the British Islands, English predominated and relegated other languages, of Gaelic and Germanic roots, mostly to the western Celtic fringes of Great Britain and Ireland. In Germany, France, and Italy, a single vernacular predominated over other languages and local dialects. In most countries where this has happened states have recently undertaken policies for the preservation of the secondary languages. Catalan may be the most important of those 'minor' languages and undoubtedly it deserves the respect and the consideration which Spanish legislation grants it. What is not comprehensible is that the Catalan autonomous governments should obstinately insist on imposing and artificial monolingualism by coercive and discriminatory means, such as eliminating Castilian from the official government communications and public signs, from public education (where Spanish is the facto considered as a foreign language), and from all means of communication subsidized by the *generalitat*. It is even less comprehensible if we take into account that this policy runs counter not only to linguistic logic, but also to Spanish legislation, and to the interests of the Catalan people. Not only does this policy border on totalitarianism (children in school are reprimanded if they speak Spanish even in their recreation time); the harm to the Catalan population is very serious. Could the reader imagine that in Scotland, for instance, the local government tried to stamp out English from public education and turn Scotland into a monolingual Scots-speaking community? One would expect that this should elicit an angry reaction from large sectors of the population, including nationalists, who would spurn such an attempt to deprive their children of one of the great assets which Scottish public education grants its students, i. e., a correct knowledge of the English language. This is what is being done to the Catalan population, depriving it of a correct knowledge of the Spanish language; there is a passive resistance on the part of large sectors, but the repression by the *generalitat* is considerable and many citizens quietly take their children to private schools if they can afford it.

To justify this imposition, it is said that Catalan has been an oppressed language and that under the Franco dictatorship it was not taught at school. This last statement is true. As to oppression, this is a debatable question. It is true that under Franco, especially in the early years, Catalan was relegated to private circles; but from 1950 onward, there was a growing tolerance toward the printing of books and newspapers in Catalan. It must be noted that those who speak of language oppression never mention that in northern Catalonia, which became French since the War of the Reapers, Catalan speakers are now a tiny minority and only French is taught at school; they never mention the oppression of Catalan in France. It is notable also that those brave defenders of the Catalan language, while denouncing Spanish 'oppression,' quote undoubtedly exaggerated figures of Catalan speakers (10 million) nearly all of whom are Spaniards; it thus turns out that Catalan is virtually spoken only in the country where it has suffered such terrible oppression. It simply does not seem credible. These glaring contradictions just show the lack of consistence of the nationalists' arguments. Catalan is certainly not an oppressed language today, rather the opposite. It is used to oppress Castilian speakers in Catalonia in an attempt to reel back history, in a sort of experiment of 'social engineering,' and impose a single language in a country that has always been bilingual.

Defending and promoting the use of the Catalan language is one thing; trying to erect a barrier between the Catalan and Castilian languages is something else again. This is something that has been tried repeatedly, especially since Pompeu Fabra, a philologist, rewrote the rules of Catalan grammar in the early twentieth century. Catalan is a romance language whose pronunciation is closer to French, but which has coexisted side by side with Castilian Spanish since the early Middle Ages and correspondingly, there have been intense mutual influences. Castilian Spanish has incorporated many Catalan words and expressions and the same has happened with Catalan, which has acquired many Castilian turns and voices. However, since Pompeu Fabra Catalan philologists, many of them under the influence of nationalism have tried to mark the differences and erase the parallels. This is well reflected in the book of one of those philologists, Xavier Pericay (2009), who after many years working on *Catalan Philology* (this is the title of his book in Catalan and in Castilian) at the service of the *generalitat*, reached the conclusion that 'philology is one thing and Catalan philology another [. . .] a Catalan philologist not only is an expert in linguistic variation [. . .] for the same salary he has a recognized authority in everything related to Catalonia and its problems.' And one of the favorite tasks of those 'Catalan philologists' is to weed out any trace of Castilian Spanish from the Catalan language. They are busily building up a new linguistic barrier between Catalonia and the rest of Spain.

Are they succeeding? In certain aspects, the response should be a rotund yes. In 1975, 74 percent of adults in Barcelona understood Catalan, but only 14.5 percent could write it. We have no data for other provinces. Today, in all of Catalonia, 90 percent understand it, between 70 and 90 percent can speak it, and 90 percent of the young can write it (while only 25 percent of those 65 years old or older can). This shows how compulsory education in Catalan has changed things.

The picture is different when the population of Catalonia are asked about what language they consider their own. Catalonia's own Statistical Institute (IDESCAT) carried out a two-stage survey in 2008 and 2013. The picture is quite similar in both years, but there are some minor differences. At any rate, the survey found that only 37 percent of those living in Catalonia consider Catalan their mother tongue, while 47 percent call Castilian their mother tongue; unlike what happened with the ability to write Catalan, in the matter of identification there are no generational differences. The inescapable conclusion is that, while coercive immersion in Catalan has improved the knowledge of the language among the population, it has not changed the population's allegiance toward their family's language. In spite of the 'normalizing' policies of the *generalitat,* Castilian Spanish still is the most widely used language in Catalonia, and it coexists normally with Catalan, as has been historically true. Thirty-seven years of Franquist imposition could not prevent Catalan being spoken in Catalonia and 36 years of nationalist totalitarianism have not been able to erase Castilian in Catalonia.

It may be due to the frustration caused by the stubbornness of facts that the *generalitat* and some related bodies keep proclaiming that Catalan is an oppressed language in need of ever more radical defense. Typical of this attitude is that they should consider that any attempt to apply the Spanish Constitution in Catalonia is an 'aggression against Catalonia.' For instance, the *Cercle Catalá de Negocis,* a nationalist business organization, published a pamphlet in 2012 entitled *Catalan: a language persecuted during four centuries,* which, of course, does not try to explain why this persecution has not prevented the survival and flourishing of this tongue in Spain while it virtually disappeared in France. What it does, though, is to define as an aggression against Catalan that 'the Superior Justice Court of Catalonia should have established the possibility that children be taught in Castilian if their parents so wish.' This freedom of choice, which Catalan speakers repeatedly demanded under Franco, is now denied to Castilian speakers under the nationalist governments, and labeled 'aggression against Catalan.' For the *Cercle Catalá de Negocis,* freedom of choice in education is oppression.

Pericay has denounced this self-defeating attitude of Catalan nationalism. Trying to put Catalan on a par with Castilian is like tilting at windmills: Castilian Spanish is in international language spoken by 500 million people, a figure Catalan will never approach, let alone reach. This condemns Catalonia, says Pericay (2009, 325), to 'linguistic normalization *ad aeternum*,' i.e., repressing Castilian speakers *ad aeternum*. Not only is Castilian one of the few international languages, it is also the lingua franca within the Iberian Peninsula, the language in which Catalans, Basques, Galicians, and Portuguese can understand each other.

Striving after Catalan monolingualism may have two outcomes, both of them terrible: it may fail or it may succeed. The most likely outcome is failure, and this will be bad if nationalist governments persist as they have done so far, to apply a policy which is expensive, which oppresses the majority of Catalans, and which borders on totalitarianism. But it would be worse if it succeeded, because this would create a linguistic barrier between Catalonia, the rest of Spain, and the rest of the world, a barrier which did not exist, say, in 1980.

Controlling the means of Communication

Even before he took over the government of Catalonia, since the time he was at the helm of Banca Catalana, Jordi Pujol made a point of controlling the means of communication, something he did through a policy of purchases, subsidies, and harassment. The final object was the creation of the '*Catalan space of communication* [whose mission is to oppose] the means from Madrid which operate and are distributed in Catalonia and which dare stick their noses where they are not welcome' (Pericay, 2009, pp. 327-8).

No sooner had Pujol been inaugurated, the *generalitat* set out to create its own television channel to propagate the Catalan language and culture. As Pujol said when the network was inaugurated in September 1983, 'a language cannot live without a means of communication like this one.' One wonders then how Catalan had survived for years and centuries before TV3 (the name of the new network) was founded. TV3 issues its programs in Catalan only, although it has to do a lot of translating from Spanish (it has created its own dubbing office). Pujol was in a hurry to have the program in place for the elections of the spring

1984 and he was successful. He was in such a hurry that the new network was created in violation of Spanish legislation, according to which regional channels were supposed to belong, at least formally, to the Spanish state. TV3 in fact belongs to a body dependent upon the *generalitat*, the so-called *Catalan Corporation of Audiovisual Means* (CCMA, in Catalan capitals). Pujol wanted this channel to be totally independent from the Spanish government, and the Spanish government let it pass. The year 1984 was a good year for Pujol's policies, who won other even more famous victories over the Spanish government at that time, such as the Banca Catalana affair with which we are already familiar.

Soon the CCMA had grown spectacularly. It now owns not only TV3 but six other different television stations, four radio stations, and also has participations in other news agencies; this has turned it into the most powerful communications agency in Catalonia. Its budget rivals that of the Spanish official television network (TVE) and is way ahead of those of other regional television networks. The Catalan governments have not spared means to bankroll this mammoth regional media network, especially its television branch because they know it to be a most powerful propaganda machine. In 2014, 82 percent of the CCMA budget was devoted to television and 13 percent to radio.

In spite of this pouring of millions, this oversize television network does not seem to have obtained spectacular results. For instance, in 2012, the Catalan television networks (the seven of CCMA plus the *La Vanguardia* network) jointly had a share of audience of 22.2 percent, while the national networks, in Spanish, had a share of 73.2 percent. And in fact the share of audience of the Catalan networks is mostly due to the transmission of football matches, especially those played by Barcelona F. C. Aside from this, Catalans seem interested in the same programs as the rest of Spaniards, not very high brow, certainly, and mostly in Spanish.

Regarding the paper press, the *generalitat* has also paid attention to this sector, although its diffusion is significantly less wide. The doyen of Catalan newspapers is *La Vanguardia*, established in 1881, since then controlled by the Godó family. It was founded as the Catalan organ of the Liberal Party, but it soon became independent. Presently it is the mouthpiece of relatively moderate Catalanism, although its financial dependence of the Catalan governments considerably shapes its outlook. The other provincial newspaper, *El Periódico*, founded in 1978, is slightly to the left of *La Vanguardia* and Catalanist but not nationalist. It is also partly financed by the *generalitat*, so its independence, like that of *La Vanguardia*, is in sufferance. Both *La Vanguardia* and *El Periódico* are printed in Spanish, but they have recently added smaller Catalan editions. Then there are some minor newspapers printed in Catalan, but their circulation is rather limited and they are heavily subsidized by the *generalitat*. In addition, there are a series of local newspapers with modest circulations, some in Catalan, some in Spanish, and there are several sports dailies, with much wider circulation. The most important one belongs to the *La Vanguardia* group and the second to *Grupo Zeta*, publisher of *El Periódico*.

More than 80 percent of the newspapers read in Catalonia are regional or local newspapers. *La Vanguardia* and *El Periódico* are by far those with the largest audiences in Catalonia (their respective circulations are 175,000 and 100,000). *El País*, the non-Catalan newspaper with the widest circulation there sells about 30,000 copies. One should add, however, that the circulations of *La Vanguardia* and *El Periódico* are boosted by the fact that the governmental subsidy takes the form of purchase of large numbers of copies, which the *generalitat* and its dependencies then distribute for free.

If we focus upon the language in which the newspapers are written, instead of upon their geographical origins, however, it turns out that about 75 percent of the newspapers sold in Catalonia are in Spanish. The *generalitat* subsidizes most heavily the Catalan editions of the papers whose main circulation is in Spanish and of course of those published wholly in Catalan. A case in point is that of the daily *Avui* ('Today' in Catalan). Founded in 1976 as the first newspaper published entirely in Catalan, it soon started to have economic problems so the *generalitat* subsidized it heavily. However, even with those subsidies, the newspaper suffered great losses and in 2004 it declared bankruptcy. It was saved by the *generalitat*, which acquired it through a *Catalan Communication Corporation* especially created for the purpose. The groups of *La Vanguardia* and *El Periódico* were compelled to buy 40 percent each of *Avui*. Even this was not enough and in 2009 *Avui* was merged with

Punt, another regional newspaper also heavily subsidized by the Catalan government. In conclusion, no matter how heavily subsidized, newspapers in Catalan have a rather restricted circulation. In 2013, Francesc Homs, at the time councilor of *Presidencia*, i. e., second in command to the Catalan president, announced that in those difficult times they were going to keep subsidizing those media using Catalan because this language 'in the field of means of communication, occupies a very secondary position.' In other words, the *generalitat* was, and is, throwing away large amounts of money in pursuit of a futile linguistic policy whose real justification is that it gives them the means and the pretext to keep alive the nationalist cause.

The Catalan Population

In all, 7.5 million people live in Catalonia, some 16 percent of the total Spanish population. Catalonia is the second community in terms of population, after Andalusia (8.4 million) and before Madrid (6.5 million). Historically, the population of Catalonia has grown much faster than that of Spain as a whole. It has doubled its proportion within Spain twice since the Middle Ages. Between 1600 and 1787, Catalonia's population went from 4 to 8 percent of Spain's total; by 1981, it had again doubled its weight to 16 percent, and there the proportion has hovered since then. Andalusia's population, although still the highest, has had a slightly declining share within the Spanish total, while Madrid has been the province (now community) with the fastest population growth in the last two centuries. The overall historical trend of Spanish population since the Middle Ages has been to move from north to south and from the interior to the coast, with the exception of Madrid.

An essential factor to explain the growth of Catalan population is migration. French immigration across the Pyrenees permitted Catalan population not to shrink between 1500 and 1700. The end of the War of Succession (1714) marked the beginning of a substantial population boom in Catalonia, which after many centuries went over the mark of half a million people. Immigration from other Spanish regions, attracted by the growing economic prosperity, had a role in this expansion. Local population also showed signs of renewed vitality, i.e., increasing birth and marriage rates. This demographic buoyancy leveled off in the second half of the nineteenth century, the unmistakable sign of having reached a certain demographic maturity. The leveling off became a topic of heated debate among Catalan demographers; the shrillest was Josep Vandellós whose book, *Catalunya, poble decadent* (Catalonia, a decadent people), expressed great alarm at the stagnation of Catalan birth rates, which he attributed to 'egoism.' Surprisingly, in a reputed demographer (he was hired by the Venezuelan government to organize its statistical office, and later worked for the United Nations), he does not seem to have remarked that Catalonia's population was just experiencing the well-known phenomenon called demographic transition to maturity, whereby birth and death rates decline in parallel to reach low or zero (or even negative) population growth levels. Furthermore, Catalan population did not remain static in the decades prior to the civil war, thanks largely to immigration from other regions of Spain, attracted by its wealth, higher standards of living, and demand for labor. As Nadal put it (1982, p. 119), 'around 1910 the self-sustained character of the demographic growth in the Principality [Catalonia] was at an end.' From 1911 to 1975, two thirds of the demographic growth in Catalonia was attributable to immigration. This permitted the region's population to reach 16 percent of the Spanish total in the early 1980s. Later on, around the turn of the century, a new type of immigration emerged: that coming from other continents, mostly Africa and Latin America (plus a respectable contingent from Eastern Europe), allured by the same stimuli which had earlier drawn in migrants from other Spanish regions: higher standards of living and good job opportunities. But this was now an all-Spanish phenomenon. Madrid and Catalonia were the main magnets, but many other regions, such as the Balearic Islands, Valencia, the Basque Country, even Andalucia, where unemployment has been chronically very high, attracted high numbers of immigrants.

The immigration boom stopped abruptly in 2007, and even a considerable reverse movement took place. In 2012, Catalonia lost some 10,000 inhabitants, 6,500 of which were Spaniards. Meanwhile, Madrid gained almost 3,000; although it lost 5,000 foreigners, it gained 8,000 Spaniards. This would suggest that Catalonia's linguistic policies repel

Spanish immigrants who instead feel attracted by the lack of linguistic imposition in Madrid.

During the twentieth century, an ambivalent attitude toward immigration has been perceptible in Catalonia: on the one hand, some influential Catalans have shown alarm that immigration would threaten their own identity (an obsessive preoccupation for nationalists); but on the other, they have been forced to recognize that they needed immigration as a source of manpower and to boost their numbers. In 1934, a manifesto entitled *For the preservation of the Catalan race* was published, signed by some influential Catalans, Pompeu Fabra and Josep Vandellós among them. The manifesto showed the aforementioned ambivalence; it conceded the need to accept immigration as a sort of necessary evil but proposed the creation of an Institute of Eugenics and to have recourse to all possible means to head off 'an essential transformation of our race.' Taking into account that at the time most immigrants in Catalonia were Spanish, this could be construed as meaning that for the writers of the manifesto Catalans were of a different race from the rest of their countrymen.

After the civil war, new writers participated in the discussion, among them Jordi Pujol, who showed his interest in the topic since very early, and published articles and books and made speeches since 1958. His ideas about immigration reflect the nature of his nationalism. He was concerned with 'what is a Catalan,' and offered the following definition: 'A Catalan is a man who lives and works in Catalonia, and who by his work, with his effort, helps to build Catalonia.' He added (2000, p. 18):

> The mission of Catalonia –a glorious mission, full of responsibility—is to welcome and to recast the immigrant mass into a new Catalan community [. . .] Catalonia has always been a melting pot, has always welcomed immigrants, who have made it richer and whom it [Catalonia] has given shape, created a community from dispersed people.

Not a word about Spain of course. At a time when most immigrants to Catalonia were Spaniards, Pujol considered them 'dispersed' and in need of being 'given shape.' Pujol's view of Catalonia is very close to that of Prat de la Riba (1906, p. 62) who considered it a sort of metaphysical entity, 'a community which is natural, necessary, previous and superior to men's will, who cannot unmake or change it.' Pujol seems to think that immigrants should be transmuted into parts of this 'community superior to men's will,' this immutable and eternal Catalonia. His thought is also close to that of Vandellós (1985, p. 26) who wrote: 'we must think in the future Catalonia, that of our children and grandchildren and we must try to make sure that it will have life and strength, that it will speak, think, and act in Catalan.'

Not everybody in Catalonia thought that way, fortunately. Jaume Vicens Vives, the greatest Catalan historian of the twentieth century, his legacy now relegated in nationalist Catalonia (even by some of his disciples), rejected nationalist interpretations of history, both the Spanish version propagated by Franco and the Catalan version spread by Prat de la Riba. In his celebrated *Notícia de Catalunya* (Report on Catalonia) originally published in 1953, he wrote: 'We Catalans are the product of many yeasts and therefore a sizable slice of our country belongs to a cross-bred culture and biology.' His theses seem to fit better the historical reality of the Catalan population, which Vicens's student Jordi Nadal studied so thoroughly, than those of the nationalists.

So far, however, it is the nationalist, essentialist version of Catalan demography that has prevailed there. In 1978, a book was published gathering the papers presented in a meeting in Barcelona about *Immigration and National Reconstruction in Catalonia* where one could read (p. 23) about achieving 'an irreversible Catalanization [which] requires a big double front of action: education and means of communication.' When Pujol and his party, CiU, took power in 1980, they put into practice the immigration policies which they had been dreaming up for years. In 1983, they drew up an Immigration Plan, one of whose objectives was 'to develop the participation of foreign immigrants in the national construction of Catalonia' through a 'Catalan path of integration.' The second version of the same plan (2001–2004) clearly states that this Catalan path of integration is aimed at making 'immigrants and their sons understand that it is necessary and just to preserve the elements pertaining to the Catalan culture, those which give it its own personality, starting with its own language' so as to prevent that Catalonia should become 'a dual or conflictive society [thereby obtaining . . .] the agreement of the large majority of the population involved, regardless of their original culture.' It is difficult to know whether Pujol himself wrote this paragraph, but even if he did not, the style is unmistakably his own: garbled, confusing, saying things by indirection and trusting that those who will have to carry out the policies know exactly what is meant even if it is not clearly spelled out. All this galimatias can be summarized in one single word: brainwashing, i.e., putting into the minds of the immigrants, who are normally in a weak and pliant position, that they learn Catalan and not Castilian or else. Bilingualism, according to this text is 'conflictive,' no matter that Catalonia, as we have already seen, has been a bilingual society from time immemorial. If all this were not clear enough, the Plan adds that 'public policies as well as the work of civil society must make foreign citizens understand and accept that although Catalonia is a part of the Spanish state, it is a nation with identity traits which are their own alone.' In other words, immigrants must become willy-nilly Catalan, not Spanish. Let us remark that, aside from language, those distinctive traits are never spelled out, for the simple reason that they are inexistent. Aside from the language, which after all is not that different either, Catalonia is just another region of Spain, with its cooking, regional dances and customs, just like any other Spanish region. Spain, for historical and geographical reasons, is quite a heterogeneous country, with marked regional differences. These special 'identity traits' of Catalonia are never spelled out because the enumeration would sound ridiculous: regional dishes, folklore, etc. In reality, the distinctive traits that are taught to immigrant and native alike are those of resentment and victimism. The official version is that Catalonia has been defeated, exploited, humiliated, and robbed by the Spanish state: this is the version of Catalan history that the generalitat circulates, and these are the supposed distinctive traits that the whole Catalan population must assimilate. We will see later how this is achieved through the school system.

In an effort to vie for the assimilation and support of Muslim immigrants, the administration of the then president, Artur Mas, created *Nova Catalunya* (New Catalonia) a foundation to welcome and assimilate mostly Muslim immigrants in 2012. The *generalitat* was worried that the new immigrants could vote against independence in an eventual referendum, as had happened in Quebec in the 1995 referendum. The nationalist governments have shown interest in attracting non-Spanish-speaking immigrants and have therefore drawn in a numerous contingent of Muslims, something which has created problems related to the spread of jihadism. Be is as it may, Nova Catalunya is closing after 4 years, due to all sorts of problems, from lack of funds to criminal charges against some of its personnel (*El Confidencial*, 26 September 2016).

Another undoubted distinctive trait of Catalonia is that its immigration policies are different from those of the rest of Spain. In Madrid, for instance, the Immigration Plan of 2001 emphasizes tolerance, pluralism, and respect for cultural differences, but says nothing about making the immigrants become *Madrileños*, or Spaniards, for that matter. The 2000 Spanish Law on Immigrant Integration, for instance, only says that the government shall promote 'the full integration of foreigners in the Spanish society in a framework of coexistence of diverse identities and cultures, with respect of the Constitution and the law as the only limit,' and that they will foster 'the knowledge and respect of the values of the Constitution and statutes of Spain, those of the European Union, human rights, public liberties, democracy, tolerance and equality between men and women [. . .] schooling at the ages when it is compulsory, learning of the official languages, and access to employment.' There is nothing about 'national traits,' 'preservation of Spanish culture,' 'divisive languages,' 'Spanish path of integration,' or any of the chauvinistic shibboleths that preoccupy Catalan legislators.

The Education Policy of the *Generalitat*

Monolingualism

A World Bank report of 1962 pointed out that the low level of human capital formation was one of the most serious obstacles to Spanish economic growth. A new General Education Law of 1970 tried to put a remedy to this situation by reorganizing the education system and making schooling compulsory until 14 years of age. The effects of the law were encouraging, but mixed. While the rates of school enrollment expanded notably, a new scarcity was felt: that of adequately trained teachers. While the problems posed by the implementation of the Education Law were still waiting to be resolved, the transition from dictatorship to democracy was taking place in Spain.

In 1980, both Catalonia and the Basque Country were granted competence in education in the middle of the decentralization wave which swept Spain during that transition. Their respective governments found a system in flux where the scarcity of teachers was acute. This was a windfall for them. They were thus able to devise the process of recruitment of new teachers, thus acquiring a powerful instrument to put in practice their plans to mold the minds of their respective populations. The Catalan government immediately developed its own methods of 'selecting and hiring teachers' of public secondary schools (De Riquer, 2004, pp. 390-1) precisely at the moment when the system was expanding. The debate in Catalonia was not, as in the rest of Spain, about public versus private education, but rather between bilingual (Spanish and Catalan) schools, as the Constitution establishes, and Tarradellas had introduced, and schools 'in Catalan,' as Pujol dictated against the constitutional mandate and against the advice of Rosa Sensat, a celebrated Catalan educational reformer who always recommended teaching in the mother language of students.

Now the shortage problem was double in Catalonia and the Basque country, because to the dearth of competent teachers was added the dearth of teachers in Basque or Catalan. No matter; one can be sure that proficiency in the language was considered more important than in the subject matter. In any case, many teachers were pressured to follow courses to learn or perfect the local vernacular; many others left Catalonia and the Basque Country if they could find an opening elsewhere. What followed was a process of 'nationalization' of the teaching bodies, so that mobility of personnel within Spain decreased. In the long term, the same phenomenon took place in other bodies of civil servants (judges, doctors, policemen, etc.), thus creating more barriers between Catalonia and the rest of Spain.

The instructions for the 'nationalization' of teaching circulated internally by the *generalitat* became generally known when *El*

Periódico published them on 28 October 2000 in an article under the title *The strategy of Catalanization.* One of those documents underlined the need for a 'plan of continuous re-education and recycling of teachers having in mind national interests [...] making sure that university-level schools for the education of secondary-level teachers promote the knowledge of the Catalan national reality [...] the body of inspectors must supervise the correct application of the norms about Catalanization of teaching. There should be a close watch over the selection of personnel [...] and the composition of selection committees.' All this is clear evidence that the *generalitat* not only wanted education carried out in Catalan and not in Spanish, it was also striving to transmit its nationalist principles to the students.

Thus, Catalan became the main language employed in teaching at Catalan schools, even for those students whose mother tongue was Spanish, who were (and are) the majority. A large-scale operation of 'social engineering' went under way. But the Catalanization of children which took place in the classroom did not seem sufficient to the CiU authorities; children were compelled to use Catalan also in their recreation time: 'students must use Catalan in their normal intercourse, not only as a learning language.' Later on, the imposition of Catalan was extended to the universities. Foreign students were encouraged to learn Catalan and were told this was the only way to be really integrated.

The imposition of Catalan found some resistance among Spanish speakers in Catalonia, but they were powerless in front of the determination of the Catalan government. The Spanish government did nothing to help them in their confrontation with the *generalitat*, who argued that teaching Spanish was not necessary, since everybody knew it already. Imagine that English were not taught in England because everybody there knows it already. The powerlessness of Spanish-speaking families in Catalonia was (is) pitiful. The Catalan authorities lent deaf ears to their requests for bilingual education. Only two ways of resistance were open to them. They could denounce an illegal policy at the justice Courts; but this was a very long process, which could not solve the problem of their children who would have to wait for years to get a favorable decision, which often arrived when they had already finished school. Furthermore, the Catalan government simply disregards Court decisions it does not like and the Spanish government does nothing to enforce them. So very few families would take the judicial route, which is expensive, long, and leads nowhere. Furthermore, many parents are afraid that by asking for bilingual education they and their children may be marked as anti-Catalans. The other solution was (is) to take their children to a private school. These, however, are expensive and not everybody can afford them. In addition, the *generalitat* does not view with sympathy the existence of these schools and certainly does not offer any information about them. According to an online newspaper (*El Confidencial Autonómico*, 16 September 2016), there are only 34 bilingual schools in Catalonia, 29 of them in Barcelona. The only help these parents receive from the Spanish government is the offer made in a recent education law to pay the registration fee in one of these schools to families who ask for it. Those who have asked for a reimbursement, however, complain about red tape. In any case, this pusillanimous solution reveals the fear Catalan nationalists inspire to Madrid governments and their unwillingness to confront them squarely.

The *generalitat*'s policy of Catalan monolingualism seriously harmed generations of students whose mother tongue was Spanish. In general, the Catalan education system has performed poorly since it started practicing coercive monolingualism. Its rates of school dropouts are among the highest in Spain, which are fairly high within the EU. In general, since the 1970 Law regional education indicators in Spain have shown a marked regional convergence; but the Catalan case, whose education indicators were well ahead of the national average in 1960, by 2011 were much closer to it, shows a very perceptible convergence downward; Madrid and the Basque country, for instance, which also show a relative decline, still remained well above the national average in 2011, unlike Catalonia.

The poor showing of Catalan nationalist education puts the *generalitat* on the defensive. They attribute it to 'alien' factors: immigration and the alleged 'stinginess' of the Spanish state. These explanations are not convincing. First, Catalonia is certainly not the only Spanish region which has experienced a flow of immigrants recently. Madrid, for instance, has been subjected to similar waves of immigration; after 1981, in particular, Madrid has received more immigrants than Catalonia and its educational index has not plummeted as that of Catalonia has done. Between 1930 and 1960, Catalonia had the second highest education index in Spain (average years of schooling) after Old Castile, which has been the historical leader in educational indicators until quite recently. This was also a period of intense immigrations for Catalonia (especially the 1950s) but at that time this did not seem to depress educational levels. Second, until 1980, Catalonia was subjected to the same educational policies as the rest of Spain and again this does not seem to have hurt Catalan educational indicators. Again, the comparison with Madrid is telling; Madrid has received less money earmarked for education than Catalonia has since they became autonomous communities, and Madrid has managed to maintain clearly better education indicators than Catalonia. Catalonia also has a relatively high rate of school dropouts, something which of course depresses those indicators. It seems reasonable to attribute these abnormally high rates of school dropouts to the imposition of Catalan on students whose mother tongue is Castilian Spanish.

Nationalism

For the *generalitat,* the question is not only in what language Catalan children are to be educated but also what they are taught. The contents of education are naturally very important, not only history, which we will study presently, but also geography, sociology, political science, the social sciences in general, which at the secondary level are offered in a sort of potpourri in Spain and in Catalonia. The documents reproduced by *El Periódico* which we cited before show how the *generalitat* considers these subjects as extremely important; so the instructions given by the authorities were to teach the 'values which are our people's own.' It seems obvious that 'our people' excludes the rest of Spain although, in a typical example of the Pujolesque style, it is left unsaid. 'Professors, teachers, and students must correctly know the language, history and geography of Catalonia and of the Catalan Countries.' Apparently, the rest of Spain is immaterial. 'Textbooks should be published and assigned on the history, geography, arts, literature, economy, etc. of Catalonia and the Catalan Countries. Agreements should be drawn up with publishers for the production and diffusion of those textbooks, subsidizing them if necessary. [...] Syllabuses should be "Catalanized" [sic]. People we can trust should previously analyze their contents and give their approval.'

It is obvious that the nationalist government has done a thorough job, leaving no loose ends: they have controlled and supervised the textbooks and they have also been careful to select the teachers who are in charge of teaching the subjects. Once again, the documents supplied by *El Periódico* show the basic ideas, or 'lines of sensibilization' (awareness guidelines) according to the *generalitat*'s terminology, that the students should absorb:

a) *Configuration of the Catalan personality.* Explanation and promotion of the basic, defining, and positive axes of our collective personality.
b) *Disclosure of the history and of the Catalan national fact* [sic]. Diffusion of the crucial events of our history and of our historical figures, as well as the contribution of the Catalan people to European science and culture. Promotion of popular holidays, traditions, customs, and their mythical background.
c) *New concept of the nation in the European framework*: Catalonia (Catalan countries), emerging European nation. Reaffirmation of the European spirit. A borderless Europe must be a Europe which recognizes nations [?].
d) *Discovering future possibilities*: Catalonia (Catalan countries) as center of gravity in the south of the EEC. Preferred area for economic-cultural action on the northwestern Mediterranean arc and the Occitan-Catalan space. Maximum attention to the nucleus within triangle Barcelona-Montpellier-Toulouse.
e) *The demographic factor*. Only young peoples move forward. We must make our people aware that it is necessary to have more children so as to guarantee our collective personality. We must take into account

the relationship of Catalonia with Aragon. And the area of mutual understanding from Alicante to the Alps.

f) *Memorial of grudges.* Catalonia is a discriminated nation which cannot freely develop its cultural and economic potentialities. We must discover, confirm, weigh and disclose the facts of discrimination, shortfalls, etc. in a clear, rotund and systematic way, underlining the negative incidence all this has for the whole of the Catalan people and each of its citizens.

g) *Collective awareness.* Catalonia is a people which walks in search of its sovereignty in a European framework. We must make citizens aware to reinforce the social *soul* [sic]. We must prop up our own center of gravity within Europe. Reform of the *Estatut.*

The reader can judge what these guidelines really are. We are not dealing with an educational, scientific program, we are offered an agit-prop blueprint for the indoctrination of the Catalan student body, with the purpose of 'making citizens aware to reinforce the social soul.' The indoctrination and social engineering plan of the *generalitat* obviously starts in the schools of Catalonia.

As Heras (2009, p. 173) pointed out, Catalan history and geography textbooks do not show the whole Iberian peninsula, but only the Mediterranean coast, including southern France. As the 'awareness guidelines' demanded, Catalan textbooks only pay attention to the 'northwestern Mediterranean arc' and totally disregard the rest of the Iberian Peninsula. Catalan children are educated in almost total ignorance of 83 percent of their country, Spain. In fact, a Catalan 'social science' textbook cited by Heras (2009, p. 179) defines Spain, or, rather, 'the Spanish state' as follows: 'it occupies the part of the Iberian Peninsula which does not belong to Portugal, Andorra, or the United Kingdom.' A geography textbook (cited by Heras, 2009, p. 175-6) says the following (italics added):

> In the Iberian Peninsula there are three states and a colonial dominion: the states are: Andorra, Portugal, and the Spanish state; the colonial dominion is Gibraltar. Catalonia is not a state, although it was so in the past, for many centuries, and now it is spread between Spain, France, and Andorra. Most

> Catalans are part of Spain [. . .] Since 1714 Catalonia was incorporated to Spain by the right of conquest, that is to say, because *they* won a war.

The readers of the present book can point out to the falsities contained in this short paragraph. Catalonia has never been a 'state' and it was never incorporated to Spain by the right of conquest. However, this is what children learn in Catalan schools and the 'Spanish state,' that monster of oppression according to the nationalists, allows these blatant lies to be taught there.

Nationalist History

Of course, history is the main battlefield where the nationalists fight (and almost invariably win) their ideological battles against 'the Spanish state.' For instance, we saw that during the discussion of the Constitution in 1978 the term 'nationality' was introduced as a euphemism for 'nation' when referring to regions with national aspirations. Some deputies warned that 'nationality' could become a Trojan horse through which national aspirations could be legitimized. They were not listened to, but they were prescient. The third Catalan Estatut (2006) says in its preamble: 'The Parliament of Catalonia, reflecting the sentiment and the will of Catalan citizens, has defined by an ample majority Catalonia as a nation.' Thus, the pessimistic prognoses made 28 years earlier were fulfilled: the term 'nationality' had served as a Trojan horse and Catalonia finally managed to be officially designated as a nation. Let me remark, by the way, that the wording of the third *Estatut* is misleading when it says it reflects 'the sentiment and the will of Catalan citizens' and that it is supported by an 'ample majority': it was supported by less than 37 percent of the electoral census. Anyway, the Catalan example was followed in Valencia, Majorca, Aragon, and Castile-León, which reformed or issued new statutes introducing terms such as 'national reality' and other strange expressions.

Alarmed by the pervasive influence of nationalism on history textbooks, the Spanish Academy of History published a report in 2000 where it said that it was its 'obligation to remark that, although in other countries history is as neglected as in Spain, in none of them is ignorance of the past utilized with the political intention of distorting and dissenting.' Only a few weeks later, a private Catalan institution, the Bofill Foundation, aired another, preliminary, report; a year later it produced the final version, which flatly contradicted the Academy report. A heated discussion ensued in the press and in the Spanish parliament. The immediate political effect of this controversy was the resignation of the education minister, Esperanza Aguirre, who had proposed to establish a nationwide agreement of minimum common contents for history textbooks.

The Academy report was a slender brochure (12 pages) offering a series of conclusions and examples, but whose method of work was not specified. The Bofill report was longer (125 pages) and explicitly based upon examination of a number of textbooks, something which lent it some more weight. It contained, however, some serious methodological flaws, even some errors and contradictions which seriously weakened its conclusions. In one of its strangest statements, it showed surprise that the Spanish history textbooks should devote more space to Spanish than to regional history; and it even erred in calculating the number of pages devoted to both subjects. So neither report is satisfactory, but prima facie one would think that the Academy was closer to reality when it said that history textbooks are biased by local nationalisms, especially in Catalonia. Here we are going to examine and compare two secondary school manuals by one of the main textbook publishers in Spain, Santillana. We will compare the History of Spain manual produced by this publisher for general use in Spain and the volume used specifically in Catalonia.

To start with, the aforementioned distinction is in itself quite marked. Santillana issues a textbook for general use in all communities but Catalonia. This general textbook is commonly sold in each community with a companion supplement on the history of that community. Of course, all the texts are presented in Spanish, although in the Basque Country, Galicia, and Valencia translations into the local language are also offered. But in Catalonia things are different. To start with, the text is in Catalan only; its content is supposed to be the History of Spain, but its title only says *History 2*. And, in fact, it is not a real history of Spain: its contents are different from the other Santillana textbooks and the bias is strongly Catalanist and nationalistic (Casassas, 2009).

In addition, the Catalan book totally omits prehistory, ancient and medieval history altogether: its opening chapter is on *Catalonia within the Hispanic Monarchy*. And this shows the focus of the book: it is not really a history of Spain: it is a history of Catalonia within Spain, where Catalonia is the hero and the victim, and Spain is the villain and the oppressor. About the **sixteenth century**, the golden age of Spanish power, the book has little to say. It resists calling the Spanish monarchy a state, so it speaks of the 'great Spanish empire,' but, surprisingly, says practically nothing about Spanish America, and shows Catalonia always resisting 'centralization.' Catalan nationalists do not like Fernando and Isabel, the Catholic Monarchs, because their marriage brought about the birth of Spain as a unified kingdom. The book therefore devotes little space to their reign; the two main topics it deals with are: the introduction of the Inquisition as a means to increase the monarchs' political power, a power based upon repression; and the authoritarian character of the new monarchy. There is absolutely nothing on the work and policies of Fernando, the greatest Catalan monarch ever and one of the most admired politicians of Renaissance Europe. Just as a token of the hostility of nationalists toward Fernando, suffice it to say that 2016 marks the fifth centennial of his death and that no commemoration has taken place in Catalonia; the only memorial Congress took place in Salamanca, sponsored by a private firm. Going back to the textbook, nothing is said in it about Fernando's policies in Catalonia (let alone its international policies), about which Vicens Vives wrote his important doctoral dissertation, where it showed how the king's measures contributed to the recovery of the region, devastated by epidemics and civil war. Naturally, the general manual presents a more balanced and complete picture of the reign of the Catholic Monarchs than the Catalan one.

The treatment of Charles V in the Catalan book is also biased: it seems to consider that the most important aspect of the Emperor policies is whether and to what extent it respected regional autonomy. And this is the prism under which all the problems of the Habsburg kings are analyzed. Curiously, not even the War of the Reapers appears to attract the interest of the book's authors, and is dispatched in just a few lines with glaring omissions and errors. The version offered of the War of Succession, a favorite topic of Catalan nationalists, is the standard. Not a word is said about the rest of Spain, let alone Spanish America, in the eighteenth century.

On **the nineteenth century**, the Catalan textbook still views Spanish history from the standpoint of centralization versus autonomy. This is no doubt an important topic, bet certainly should not be the only one. On the 1812 Constitution, a real watershed in the history of Spanish liberalism and of Spain in general, the manual's main statement is that 'it was the legal document essential for the centralizing and standardizing construction of the Spanish liberal state,' apparently forgetting that construction of this type of liberal state was one of the main political trends in all the nascent European nation-states (Herr, 2016, esp. Chs. 9-10). Similarly, the main educational law of the period, the Moyano Law of 1857, which had so many defects, is criticized only for following 'a centralizing and uniform model.' In general, among the many shortcomings of the Catalan manual stands its pervasive focus on the centralization versus autonomy question so that in the end it lumps together reactionaries and revolutionaries, Carlists and republicans, in so far as they represented a rebellion against the standard liberal centralization. As long as they wanted some sort of autonomy, no matter their political credos, Carlists, republicans, and anarchists are equally deserving of the sympathy of the manual's authors. This happens again when dealing with the 1868 Revolution and the ensuing Revolutionary Sexennium. The final failure of the successive regimes, monarchical and republican, elicits the following comment: 'with the failure of the monarchy of Amadeo and of the federal republic, the democratic and decentralizing political dreams which the Revolution of September 1868 had generated vanished.' In reality, democracy and decentralization were rather antagonistic dreams, especially in Catalonia, and this polarization strongly contributed to the failure of both regimes. This rather obvious analysis escapes the authors of the manual, almost exclusively focused as they are on the dichotomy centralization versus autonomy and on little else. Their evident purpose is to imprint on the students' minds that Catalonia had lost its (imaginary) autonomy in the fifteenth century (or in the eighteenth, what matters is the loss, not the actual facts) and that it fought to recover it but was thwarted by the repression of the Spanish authorities.

In the economic field, the Catalan manual states that 'the Spanish state as a whole, excepting the industrialized areas of Catalonia and the Basque Country, showed evidence of a serious economic backwardness with respect to the more developed European countries.' It seems that it was not the country, but 'the Spanish state' that was backward, so presumably the blame falls upon it, not upon the industrialized regions that are prosperous thanks to high tariff barriers which favor them but hurt the rest of the country. Thus, the Catalan manual cultivates the idea that Catalonia was prosperous and dynamic, an oasis in a country (Spain) whose name is seldom spelled out, but whose state was an obstacle that prevented the oasis from reaching the levels of development and welfare it was entitled to. It is true that the manual at some point admits that 'the Catalan industrialists arrived to control the Spanish market thanks to protectionist tariffs, to a significant reduction of smuggling, and to the competitiveness of their products, so that [by the late 1850s] they had a quota of more than 90% of the Spanish market,' which justified calling Catalonia 'the factory of Spain' (in praise of Catalonia, Spain can be named). Now the obvious question is: if Catalan products were competitive, what need was there for high tariff barriers? The manual offers no answer; it does not even pose the question.

The Catalan manual presents the history of **twentieth-century Spain** mainly as the history of Catalonia's struggle to become a nation and having a state. There are references to Ireland and to Woodrow Wilson's statement about the right of self-determination of oppressed peoples. The problem, however, is how to prove convincingly that the richest region of Spain is an 'oppressed people.' This is probably the reason why so many appeals are made to 'historical oppression.'

The manual accurately says that the first third of the century is 'a period of enormous tensions and spectacular changes in Spanish and Catalan history' something which is also true of the rest of Europe. But Catalonia 'showed a differential trait, its claim of a national character, something which gave a very particular character to its trajectory.' The manual presents Catalonia at this time as a monolithic block, whose all other problems pale before its main goal: to become a nation and have a state. So developments in Catalonia, 'the most important and old industrial area of Spain,' are studied in some detail at the expense of the rest of Spain, an unbalance which occurs all throughout the book but which is accentuated as we come nearer the present. Again, Spain is rarely mentioned, it is rather 'the Spanish state.' The same is true of the parliament (the *Cortes*): it is 'the Spanish Cortes;' the Army is 'the Spanish Army,' etc. Spain is systematically linked to military force and intransigence.

The book portrays the tensions and divisions of the 1920s and 1930s in considerable detail and presents them as a struggle between Catalonia and Spain, with very few nuances. The worst intentions toward Catalonia are always attributed to Spanish politicians and Catalonia, again, is presented as a unanimous body. A typical instance occurs when recounting the conflict created with the 1934 Catalan Agrarian Law about the right of vine cultivators (*rabassaires*) to acquire the land they farmed. This caused division in Catalonia between landowners and *rabassaires* as we saw in the preceding chapter, and the Supreme Court agreed with the landowners. In the Catalan textbook the division between landowners and farmers is not mentioned, and the conflict is presented, as usual, as an attack of the Spanish state against Catalonia. The same occurs when narrating the absurd proclamation of independence in October of that same year by president Companys. No mention is made of the lack of support the Companys rebellion found in Catalonia, but the harshness of the sentences received by the plotters is again treated as a sign of anti-Catalanism. Of course, military rebellion was punishable with death at the time and general Sanjurjo had been condemned to death 2 years before, commuted to life imprisonment. Companys was condemned to life imprisonment, not to death. Nothing is said about this in the Catalan textbook.

The treatment of the **civil war** is also full of inaccuracies and unfounded claims. For instance, the book says (attributed to other historians, but not refuted) that the Spanish Civil War had little to do with Catalonia: 'Catalonia was involved in a conflict that was imposed on it by outside forces.' The fact that many Catalans supported Franco (Cambó and some generals among them), for instance, is never mentioned in this context. The idea of Catalonia being a sort of oasis apart from the rest of Spain is repeated in several forms. In Catalonia, the manual says, there was a spirit of compromise, and 'the national political sense of collaboration among the right and the left never was totally lost.' Of course, it is difficult to see how this fits with the fact that 'the main victims of persecution [in Catalonia] were members of religious institutions and the more significant conservatives,' as the manual admits a few pages further. Even more difficult is to accord the vision of Catalonia as an Arcadian corner in an embattled Spain, which the manual offers, with the vicious battles that raged in Barcelona between communists and anarchists in May 1937, to which we referred before and which Orwell so vividly depicted in *Homage to Catalonia*. For the authors of the manual, however, the most negative consequence of this lamentable episode was not the loss of human life and the disorganization of the republican forces that this all entailed, but the fact that the republican government had to intervene to put a stop to this 'war within the war' and that it considerably reduced the wide autonomy (virtual independence) that the Catalan government had enjoyed so far.

As to the long years of **Franco's dictatorship**, the manual gives the reader the impression that Catalonia (together with the Basque Country and Galicia) was the main victim of the persecutions that ensued after the victory of the rebels, because the dictatorial governments repressed the use of regional languages. The authors betray their anti-Spanish prejudice when they decry that 'schools and universities [. . .] offered a discourse that was *pro-Spanish and reactionary*' (my italics). 'Spain' and 'reaction' seem to be closely related. Their bias shows again when writing about economics. According to them, Franco's economic policies greatly harmed Catalonia. In the early years, it was because his autarkic policies discouraged foreign investment and limited the supply of raw materials. They do not mention that autarky also had its advantages for Catalan industry because it put the Spanish market at its feet. As a matter of fact, this was a period when some Catalan industrialists and speculators made great fortunes, something not mentioned in the manual. When the Spanish economy opened up after 1959, and the Franco government took some decisions, such as making Barcelona a free port, locating the Seat automobile factory there, later locating one of the first nuclear generators near Tarragona, Catalonia undoubtedly benefited, but the manual does not recognize it. On the contrary, it offers a twisted vision of the wave of immigration that took place as a consequence of economic expansion in Catalonia. The impression conveyed is that the government fostered a flood of immigration so as to swamp the region with Spanish speakers and thus water down the strength of the Catalan language. The authors seem to lament 'the massive arrival of people coming from impoverished regions of the rest of Spain [. . . when . . .] Catalonia had not its own institutions to teach the Catalan language and culture among the newly arrived.' The conditions of accommodation of the newcomers do not appear to worry the authors of the manual: the important thing was that they should learn Catalan and forget Spanish.

When writing about the post-Franco period once more the writers of the manual translate the impression than Catalonia was unanimous in asking for democracy and claiming for autonomy. They never mention that even among those who demanded both things there was a clear rift between right and left and that both groups tried to bring the national government to their side.

Another unwarranted statement is to say, as the Catalan manual does, that the strong showing of the Basque Nationalist Party in the first democratic elections is a proof of 'a national community;' this probably would imply that the good results of CiU in the first regional elections in Catalonia would also prove that Catalonia was a 'national community.' Spain would not be such thing, since no Spanish nationalist party managed to get a single deputy elected. By the same token, however, Britain (before UKIP at least), Portugal, Germany (before AfG), or Italy (since the demise of the MSI) would not qualify as nations. This statement in the manual in fact makes little sense.

Further down the manual recognizes that 'Never, in the modern era, Catalonia had enjoyed such a long period of autonomy and political liberties.' However, 'fitting Catalonia within the Spanish context is still difficult.' What the manual does not recognize is that it is difficult to fit a piece in a puzzle when the piece does not want to fit: this is true of the nationalist *generalitat,* whose budget deficits are yearly financed by the 'Spanish context,' a *generalitat* which is in permanent violation of the Constitution and which claims that any attempt to apply the law in that region is an attack against Catalonia, a Catalonia which has already had three *Estatuts* (one under the Second Republic, two under the constitutional Monarchy) and is still unhappy with the 'Spanish context' and continuously complains that it is underfinanced or 'robbed' (we will shortly examine this claim.) In this last part of the book, its authors in fact become undisguised exponents and apologists of the nationalist policies of CiU. In general, following the rhetoric of Jordi Pujol and his party, the manual attributes every success or improvement in Catalonia to the work of the *generalitat* and blames every adversity on Spain or, better, 'the Spanish state;' for instance, the Great Recession of the twenty-first century seems to have been a Spanish problem: 'the Spanish economy entered into a phase of crisis and recession.' Not the world economy, not the Catalan economy: it was 'the Spanish economy' that entered into recession.

The manual depicts Spanish politics in black colors: corruption, intransigence, rigidity, etc. Catalan politics, which suffers from the same faults if not more, seems to be exempt from criticism. For instance, they state that the pacts between the Pujol governments and the central government under the socialists first and under the Popular Party later were severely criticized in the Spanish press. And the book adds: 'In reality, Spanish political culture could admit accords among parties of different ideologies, but did not admit a pact between a party of the Spanish ambit and parties of nationalities.' This statement is blatantly false; exactly the reverse is true. The manual itself just admitted that there were pacts between CiU and both socialists and '*populares*,' whereas never since the transition to democracy has there been a political pact (let alone coalition) between the Socialist Party and the Popular Party in the Spanish Cortes. Between the end of 2015 and the spring of 2016, two general elections took place in Spain in view of the inability or unwillingness of socialists and '*populares*' to reach an agreement. The situation was solved in extremis after a vicious fight within the socialist party in October, but there never was a pact.

The manual's version of the Banca Catalana affair is also full of falsehoods. It states, for instance, that the indictment against the 'ex-directors of Banca Catalana accused them of bad management.' This term (bad management) is generally interpreted, at least in Spain, as incompetence, rather than illegality. However, as we saw earlier, the indictment accused them of crimes such as double accounting, embezzlement, and illegal 'treasury stock' at the very least. The Catalan manual just covers this up. And then it makes an egregious mistake which as far as I know, has not been corrected in later editions: 'the indictment was submitted coinciding with the elections of 1984 [. . . and after the demonstration of support for Jordi Pujol on 29 May 1984 . . .] and the elections to the *Parlament* of November 1984 were considered as a sort of popular referendum' it says. Well, the elections to the *Parlament* took place in April and Pujol was inaugurated in late May, so these 'plebiscitary November elections' never took place. This is the type of history Catalan secondary school students are being taught and the kind of history of Spain they are exposed to. No wonder the separatist sentiment has grown in the last decades.

The last chapter of this manual of what is supposed to be (but is not) 'History of Spain' is entitled 'Catalonia in a globalized world.' In it we find that, among the difficulties to adapting to a fast-changing world, Catalonia has 'the added obstacle that it has no state of its own to support a protective unitary legislation [since] Catalan culture and language [are located] in a space scattered among four states: Spain, Andorra, France and Italy [. . .] and four autonomous communities within the Spanish state: Catalonia, the Valencia community, the Balearic Islands and Aragon . . . ' This, again, is too silly for words. Imagine then the plight for Spanish culture and language, without 'a protective unitary legislation' and scattered among Spain's 17 autonomous communities, 17 Latin American countries, plus vast Spanish-speaking communities in the USA and Brazil, plus Puerto Rico, Equatorial Guinea, etc. Terrible. But even worse is the situation of English culture and language without a 'protective unitary legislation' and the scattering of English speakers over England, Ireland, the United States, Canada, Australia New Zealand, plus being the lingua franca in many Asian and African countries and even around the world. Frightening. The authors of the manual must admit that the Catalan problem is dwarfed by those of English and Spanish. French is not in much better shape either. This is just another example of the nonsense Catalan students are taught in their classrooms and all of the above just a small sample of the kind of historical education Catalan students are subjected to.

The Social Support for Independence

We have seen that after Jordi Pujol's assumption of power, the *generalitat* undertook a thorough program of nationalist propaganda with the help of a host of very effective instruments: the schools, the media, immigration policies, plus the collaboration of cultural and educational organizations (*Assemblea de Catalunya, Omnium Cultural*), and even sports clubs, such as the Barcelona Football Club. Political parties have collaborated, some explicitly nationalist such as Unió and ERC, some not, such as the Socialist Party of Catalonia (PSC) or *Iniciativa per Catalunya-Verts* (ICV, an amalgam of postcommunists and ecologists). There is no doubt that the constant barrage of propaganda and indoctrination has had its effects and that the number of Catalans in favor of independence has increased. The problem is: by how much? As we will see, this is a much disputed question.

The *generalitat* makes frequent use of opinion polls and has them broadcast through the abundant media channels it has at its disposal, apparently showing that Catalan public opinion supports the separation ('disconnection' is the *generalitat*'s preferred term) of Catalonia from Spain. In order to better gather and handle its data, the *generalitat* created its own polling agency, the *Centre Catalá d'Estudis d'Opinió* (CCEO). A little comparison will give us an idea of the modus operandi of the Catalan agency. For instance, it carried out a poll in the fall of 2012, just ahead of the elections which took place in Catalonia on November 25 of that year. A comparison of its results with those of another poll taken by the *Real Instituto Elcano* (RIE), a Spanish government think tank, at around the same dates, is instructive. The poll by the RIE showed that 42.7 percent of Catalans favored independence and 43.4 were against. By contrast, the CCEO poll showed 57.5 of Catalans would vote for independence, while only 20.5 percent would vote against; abstention would be 14.3 percent, and 7.7 percent had no opinion or would not answer. The local elections which took place only a few days afterward belied the CCEO: abstention, including blank votes, was a hefty 34 percent. Of those who voted for an option 47 voted for nationalist parties and 53 percent for nonnationalists. This implies that of the total electoral census, only 30 percent voted for separatist options. The RIE poll was closer to the mark.

How could the CCEO be so wrong? The explanation may lay in the form questions are asked: people give different answers when asked 'what would you vote for?' or 'do you think Catalonia should be independent?' In any case, the CCEO work for the *generalitat*, whose interest now is to proclaim that their 'disconnection' plans are supported by a majority of Catalans. Their results were trumpeted through the media and by the 'organic intellectuals' of nationalism, so they were, and still are, believed by many people although election data contradicted them.

Electoral results show that today Catalonia is split in the middle between unionists and separatists, but while unionists remain silent and only make themselves felt at election time (and many, especially in villages, are afraid to vote) separatists express themselves openly and noisily. This asymmetry probably occurs also when answering opinion polls, something which could explain (partially at least) the bias of the CCEO poll.

If opinion polls and their interpretation are subject to debate, the results of actual elections are less problematic. This does not imply that they are straightforward in their meaning. If we are trying to determine whether voting for one given party means voting for or against independence, for instance, we find that parties have changed: the most characteristic case is that of CiU, which since its foundation was nationalist but, at least in appearance, not separatist. Here the appearance is important because, no matter what Pujol thought or was covertly planning, those who voted for his party were not voting for separation but for moderate nationalism. From 2011 onward, however, CiU has become overtly separatist, although a little bit more cautiously than are its present associates of ERC or *Candidaturas de Unidad Popular* (CUP), a lunatic fringe movement which is not only for Catalan independence outright but also against belonging to the EU and capitalism in general, in favor of collective marriage and, lately, has proposed to tear down the Columbus statue in Barcelona and replace it with a monument to

American natives who were the victims of imperialism. As we will see, incidentally, electoral support for CiU dwindled after its separatism became official.

The greatest electoral support for Catalan separatism was shown during the Second Republic, when the then recently founded ERC obtained 60 percent of the deputies in the *Parlament* in 1931. It is true, however, that at the time ERC was not strictly separatist, but rather 'confederalist.' When they twice declared independence (under Macià and Companys), they proclaimed that Catalonia would be part of an 'Iberian Federation' or a 'Spanish Federal Republic.' At that time, moderate autonomism was represented by the *Lliga*, Cambó's party. After democracy was restored under the 1978 Constitution, this political space was occupied by Pujol's CiU, which governed uninterruptedly from 1980 to 2003. If we consider CiU as a nonseparatist party, one can say that separatism, represented by ERC only, was a minority choice until quite recently. The main opposition parties during the 1980s and 1900s were the PP and the socialists. The PP posed quite a challenge to Pujol until 1996. It was led by Aleix Vidal-Quadras, a physicist turned politician and agile debater who made fun of Pujol's garbled dialectics. In 1996, the PP won the national elections but ran short of an outright majority. José-M. Aznar, its leader, requested the support of CiU in the Spanish Cortes. Pujol obliged, but demanded the removal of Vidal-Quadras as head of the Catalan PP. Aznar enjoyed 4 years of peaceful government and achieved many things which permitted him to win the 2000 elections with an absolute majority, but the Catalan PP, without Vidal-Quadras, went into decline. The socialists, meanwhile, fought tooth and nail to unseat Pujol, whose party suffered from so many years' attrition. Finally, in 2003, the socialists managed to wrest power from CiU by forming a tripartite government with ICV and ERC. Then it turned out that, once they reached power, they were more nationalistic than CiU, and even more inefficient. Seven years later, the tripartite government was totally discredited and CiU came back to power under Pujol's successor, Artur Mas. By that time the crisis had hit Catalonia hard, the Community's debt was increasing perilously and Mas started to use the menace of separatism to wring more money from the Madrid government, since the capital markets would not lend a cent to

Catalonia. It was a somewhat similar situation as in the nineteenth century, when Catalonia became increasingly hostile toward Madrid while at the same demanding help from it in the form of tariff protection.

The decline of the PP in Catalonia, plus the metamorphosis of the socialists into fervent nationalists prompted the foundation of a new party by a group of Catalan intellectuals who felt that a clear antiseparatist position was needed in Catalonia. The new party was called *Ciutadans* ('Citizens' in Catalan), the first word with which Tarradellas had addressed his audience upon arriving in Barcelona. *Ciutadans* gathered votes from disgruntled former voters of the PP and the Socialist Party. In the elections of 2006, it received almost 90.000 votes (3 percent of votes cast) and fielded 3 deputies in the Catalan parliament. From then onward, it has steadily enlarged its electoral base and number of deputies, probably at the expense of PP and socialists.

In fact, the electoral base of the separatists (the newly converted CiU plus ERC, plus the CUP) has remained rather stagnant since 2010: 48.72 percent of the vote in that year, 47.87 percent in 2012, and 47.80 in 2015. In fact, the trend has been of very slight decline, but remarkably stable all in all. The nonseparatists can be divided into two: those who want, or would accept, a referendum about the 'disconnection,' but say they would vote 'no;' and those who reject the idea of a referendum. Those who clearly reject a referendum are *Ciutadans* and PP. The socialists waver, while the postcommunists of IVC-V and the Catalan branch of Podemos support the idea of a referendum with varying degrees of firmness.

From the time CiU became openly separatist under Artur Mas, its electoral following has been declining: from 38.4 percent in 2010 to 30.7 in 2012. It also lost *Unió* as a partner; the party went back to calling itself CDC, for only a short time because, beset by scandals and desertions, it decided to change its name to Partit Democràtic of Catalunya (PDC), but internal dissension and legal problems keep even this name in doubt. Going back to electoral returns, those of 2015 are a little more difficult to interpret, but there is no doubt that support for CDC went down again. Mas was desperately seeking a massive show of support for his separatist policies, but he failed repeatedly. After his discomfiture in 2012, he organized, on 9

November 2014, an unofficial referendum where voters were asked a confusing double question. The Supreme Court ordered the referendum suspended, but Mas went on anyway. It was carried on without a reliable electoral census and with a rather objectionable system of participation. Most of those who voted did so in the affirmative, but they were, as usual, about one third of the electoral census. The organizers considered the 'referendum' a great success, but it really was not. Turnout was very low (less than 37 percent) and it embroiled Mas and some of his collaborators in a trial for disobeying the Supreme Court injunction. In March 2017 he was disqualified to stand for election for 2 years. After the 'referendum', Mas decided to call new elections for September 2015. He tried to whip up enthusiasm and said that these elections would be another 'referendum.' He reached an agreement with ERC to run a joint platform called *Junts pel sí* ('Together for a yes') and stated that if they reached 68 deputies (the majority threshold in the *Parlament*) or 51 percent of the vote (not of the electoral census) they would consider this a victory of separatism; they failed: they got 62 deputies and 39.59 of the vote. In the previous election, CiU and ERC separately had won a total of 71 deputies and 44.4 percent of the vote. Meanwhile, Ciutadans had become the second party in the Catalan Parliament with almost 18 percent of the vote and 25deputies, way ahead of the socialists and the PP.

However, there was the CUP. They ran separately (they consider all other parties 'bourgeois') and won 10 deputies and 8.21 percent of the vote. So even with them the separatists had less that 50 percent of the vote, but more than 68 deputies. The CUP at first showed honesty and good sense and said that the separatists had lost the 'referendum' and therefore had no mandate for independence. However, they had second thoughts afterward (they never explained why or how) and decided to enter negotiations with *Junts pel sí* to form a government. This would not be possible anywhere but in Catalonia, where the nationalist issue overrides any other political consideration. In a normal situation, it would seem impossible to have a government including almost all shades of the political spectrum, from 'bourgeois' conservatism to the lunatic fringe of the extreme left. In Catalonia, where the nationalists have made of separatism the only real political issue, such an impossible coalition can become a government. On one matter, however, the CUP imposed its will: Mas would have to go; and out he went. His replacement, nevertheless, was one of his faithful followers, the mayor of Girona, Carles Puigdemont. As can be imagined, in the months since this strange government was formed in January 2016, they have done little else than bicker about the new budget and about how to proceed toward independence: whether to do it unilaterally (as the CUP wishes) or try to reach an agreement with the Madrid government (as Puigdemont would prefer), something extremely improbable. And this is how Catalonia painted itself into a corner and got politically stuck in the mud.

Some Hotly Debated Issues

Fiscal Balances

This has been one of the main topics in the economic debate about the possible independence of Catalonia and has been used as a supposedly powerful argument in favor of independence. Let me warn the reader that fiscal balances are not often used or estimated, save in Spain, for two reasons mainly. First, their scientific value is limited; second, they are tricky to calculate, because they require unraveling a complex administrative tangle, an unraveling which often requires somewhat arbitrary decisions. Since they are of little value and so arduous to estimate, why, the reader may legitimately ask, are Spaniards devoting so much time and effort to try to measure fiscal balances? The simple answer is that Spain is a country where nationalist resentment has reached exceptional levels. Fiscal balances have been used by nationalists to support statements such as ‘Spain robs us,’ ‘we are fiscally mistreated,’ etc. For nationalists, their cause justifies the crudest and most vacuous of exercises.

As the saying goes, there are two inevitable facts in life: death and taxes. All citizens whose income is above a minimum must pay taxes; in exchange, all citizens are entitled to receiving some public goods. Traditionally, these goods were defense, public security, and justice.

Many modern states offer several other public goods, such as health care, education, and social security. There are some reasons for this, mainly that those public goods may be too expensive to be acquired individually (defense is a case in point). Equity and fairness are other reasons: basic vital public goods such as education or health care are often too expensive for families of modest means, but can be made available at acceptable levels of quality by the modern welfare state. The same is true of public transportation: most roads are built at public expense and are accessible for free, etc. These are the basic facts of a redistributive society.

As a consequence, income is redistributed to some extent. Very poor people do not pay taxes and have access to a series of free services. As one goes up the income scale, the balance tips in the other sense. People with high income normally pay more in taxes than the value of the services they receive from the state. Some among these well-to-do citizens may think this is unfair, or at least that they pay too much in taxes. Something similar may happen with collective bodies: people living in prosperous districts will pay higher taxes: their fiscal balances will be negative, while those of poor districts will be positive: they will receive more in services than they pay in taxes. And the same will happen with regions. London will pay much more in taxes per capita than, say Yorkshire, or, in the United States, Maryland or New Jersey than West Virginia or Mississippi. In Spain, Catalonia pays more than, say Extremadura or Andalucia. But, in per capita terms, Catalonia is not the wealthiest region: Madrid and the Basque Country are. Madrid pays more taxes than Catalonia in relative and absolute terms. The Basque Country, by contrast, pays much less than its fair share, thanks to its privileged 'foral' status (the same is true of Navarre, another wealthy region). Curiously enough, Catalan nationalists, who complain loudly about paying more in taxes than poorer regions, never complain about the privileged status of the Basque Country, for two reasons: first, they do not want to offend their Basque nationalist allies; and, second, they would like to share the Basque privileged status and, if not, secede. Mas became separatist when Rajoy refused to extend the privileged foral status to Catalonia in 2011.

Nationalist economists in Catalonia have made heroic efforts to convince their fellows that fiscal balances reveal tremendous injustices for Catalonia, which justify their claims that Catalonia is 'fiscally mistreated' and the 'Spain robs Catalonia.' They have certainly been successful in convincing many ordinary Catalans; but they have failed to convince their fellow economists who are not nationalist. Several of those economists, some of them Catalan (Josep Borrell, Toni Zabalza), have convincingly shown that the fiscal mistreatment of Catalonia is a myth. Ángel de la Fuente may be the one who has most thoroughly demonstrated that, although the Spanish fiscal redistributive system is seriously flawed, Catalonia is not the main victim of these flaws: Madrid is. In view of this overwhelming evidence, the nationalists have recently toned down their protests in this respect; the agit-prop work, however, has been done already, and it will be very difficult to make those who lent credence to the claims that Catalonia was 'fiscally mistreated' and 'robbed,' admit that they had been deluded and lied to.

Let me examine the problem in a little more detail. Two main methods have been used to calculate the fiscal balances. The simplest is that of the **monetary flows**. This method just finds out how much has Catalonia contributed to the Spanish Treasury and compares this with the total expenditure of the Spanish state in Catalonia. The difference between these two sums is the fiscal balance: if outlays are smaller than inflows, the balance will show a surplus; if they are larger, the balance will show a deficit. The case seems simple and easy, but it is not, because both taxes and state expenditures are very difficult to allocate territorially. Let us assume, for instance, a firm located in Catalonia but belonging to a Madrid family. The taxes it pays should be imputed to Catalonia or to Madrid? Or let us assume a reverse case: a Catalan family owns a firm in Madrid, and this firm receives a government subsidy. This government expenditure should be considered as made in Madrid or in Catalonia? Here is another often-cited example. The government wants to build a military airport offering protection to Catalonia. However, land is cheaper in neighboring Aragon, so the airport is built on adjacent land in Aragon. Now, the airport is to the benefit of Catalonia, but all the material investments are made in Aragon. Should this mean that in the fiscal balance no benefit should be imputed to Catalonia? Things are not as simple as those in favor of the 'monetary flows' system want us to believe.

The alternative method balances not monetary flows, but **cost and benefit**. It takes into account no only money flows, but real benefits, especially in the case of indivisible goods, such as military protection. In the military airport example, a part of the cost of building it would be imputed to Catalonia, as thanks to the construction of the airport this community would benefit from air protection. In general, military expenditure would be apportioned more carefully, taking into account land extension, population, and income. The final result of the cost–benefit analysis would be more nuanced than the mere study of monetary flows. Nationalist economists do not like this method because it reflects better the allocation of cost and benefit. Catalonia having a numerous and relatively dense population benefits more than the average from indivisible public goods and therefore its real fiscal balance calculated through the cost–benefit method shows a smaller deficit than the monetary flow analysis reports.

Another concept frequently mentioned in this context is **ordinality**. According to this principle, the fiscal impact of redistribution should not affect the original ranking of the different regions according to their income. In other words, Catalonia, ranked third in per capita income before taxes, should still rank third after taxes. Ángel de la Fuente (2014) has studied this matter and shown that this principle is not at all respected in Spain (data of 2011). The Spanish fiscal system distorts considerably the regional ranking by income. This is not too surprising if we take into account that the Basque Country and Navarre enjoy such fiscal advantage for being considered 'foral' territories. Catalonia is displaced from third to ninth rank, which certainly is a gross violation of the ordinality principle. But the Balearic Islands (displaced from second to eighth rank) and Madrid (from first to ninth, *ex aequo* with Catalonia) get equal or worse treatment, and hardly complain. As de la Fuente says, the system is terrible, but it certainly is not rigged against Catalonia exclusively.

An even more complex problem posed by nationalists is that of 'neutralization.' This is another accounting trick performed by nationalist economists in order to inflate the fiscal deficit of Catalonia. 'Neutralized' fiscal balances simply add to the 'real' deficit (normally calculated by them through the already biased method of 'monetary flows') a fraction of Spain's public debt, the fraction supposedly corresponding to Catalonia. The reason for this is that presumably the Spanish debt will be paid by future taxes and that a part of these taxes will be paid by Catalonia. This all the more surprising since many separatist politicians and economists claim that Catalonia should not pay its share of Spanish public debt if and when Catalonia became independent. At any rate, even if we accept that Catalonia will have to pay its share of Spain's public debt, adding this 'liability' to one single year's fiscal deficit is totally arbitrary, as some other Catalan economists (Borrell and Llorach, 2014 and 2015, Zabalza, 2013) have shown convincingly.

So, what is left of all these gigantic claims based on such flimsy exercises of creative accounting? Very little or, rather, nothing. Ángel de la Fuente (2014) has dismounted in just 18 pages the nationalist thesis of fiscal maltreatment, even including an international comparison with countries such as Germany, the USA, Italy, United Kingdom, Canada, and Australia, showing that the Spanish and Catalan case has nothing of extraordinary by comparison with those of these other countries. His concluding remarks are headed with the Shakespearean phrase: 'much ado about nothing.'

Commercial Balances

What would happen to commercial flows if Catalonia and Spain went their separate ways? This is another hotly debated topic. The Spanish economy (Catalonia, of course, included) during the last half century went from being almost autarkic to being very open. The main stages of this transition were closely linked to Spain's relations with the European community, from the old Common Market or EEC to today's European Union. The main milestones were the Stabilization Plan of 1959, which partially liberalized Spanish foreign trade, the Preferential Agreement with the European Community of 1970, which promoted reciprocal tariff rebates, and the accession of Spain to the EU in 1986, which stimulated a gradual integration of the Spanish economy with that of its European neighbors.

Catalan trade, as that of the rest of Spain, expanded rapidly, especially during the 20 years following accession to the EU. Today the main trading partners of Catalonia are the EU and the rest of Spain, which absorb about 45 and 35 of the exports form that community respectively. About 33 percent of Catalonia's GDP is exported to the EU (Spain excluded) and to the rest of Spain. Other estimates make this proportion a little higher, 35 percent. Catalonia's political separation from Spain is bound, therefore, to have serious commercial and economic repercussions. This problem is linked to that of the political and legal repercussion of separation. Separatists believe that these two sets of problems would be brief and small. The opposite is far more likely, as we will see. Fortunately, however, there are several estimates of the effects of separation upon trade based upon different assumptions. The one based upon the scenario most favorable to the separatist thesis is that of Comerford, Myers, and Rodríguez Mora (CMRM, 2014) which assumes that Catalonia would not be excluded from the EU after independence.

CMRM start by comparing the commercial relations which Portugal has with Spain and those Catalonia has with the rest of Spain. Portugal's relations are intense, but Catalonia's are even more intense, although Portugal's borders with Spain only while Catalonia borders not only with the rest of Spain but also with France and Andorra. The obvious reasons of Catalonia's greater commercial intensity are that it has much more in common with the rest of Spain: language (in spite of the Catalan nationalist's efforts to create a language divide), family relations, legislation, tastes, customs, and habits, all the product of centuries of coexistence as parts of the same nation. These intangible commercial barriers, which are higher between Portugal and Spain, are called commercial frictions and can be calculated numerically. Portuguese commercial friction with Spain is almost double that of Catalonia. The authors assume that after independence, the commercial friction of Catalonia would increase and in the end become similar to that of Portugal. The erection of such invisible barrier would cause impoverishment on both sides (Catalonia and the rest of Spain). It would involve a contraction of GNP to the tune of 3.3 percent for Spain as a whole, Catalonia included. This global figure, however, would be divided unequally: Spain's GNP would fall by 2 percent, Catalonia's by 10 percent. These losses would be due to the fall in efficiency and productivity which the shrinking of the size of markets entails, something economists know at least since Adam Smith published his *Wealth of Nations* in 1776. The greatest loss, naturally, would be supported by the smaller market.

Antràs and Ventura, two nationalist economists, criticized (2012) an earlier version of CMRM's paper and made their own calculations. Their results are, not surprisingly, much more optimistic than those of CMRM. They do not believe in 'frictions,' and think Catalan products would be sold in Spanish markets virtually at the same prices they now fetch and that exports to third countries would expand. Their rosy prognosis is completed with a total rejection of the possibility that Catalonia might have to abandon the EU if it abandoned Spain. On the basis of these favorable assumptions, they think that the GNP loss to Catalonia after leaving Spain would be 1 percent, 2 percent at most.

These two estimates assume (erroneously, as we shall presently see) that Catalonia would remain in the EU after exiting from Spain. Their results, different though they are, have therefore a downward bias. If we assume, more realistically, that if Catalonia left Spain it would automatically be leaving the EU, the estimated cost would of course be much greater. According to Polo (2013, 2014), an independent Catalonia would find itself separated from the EU by two barriers: the 'frictional' one estimated by CMRM and the tariff and bureaucracy barrier consequent to Catalonia's placing itself outside the Union. This, according to Polo, who has made his calculations using Spain's input–output tables, would cause a minimum reduction of Catalan exports to the rest of Spain of 50 percent, which would entail losses of 18 percent of GDP and 16.5 percent of total employment. To this the reduction of exports to the EU and to the rest of the world should be added. Spanish input–output tables do not permit a precise calculation of this fraction, but it is obvious that the effect of such reduction should be considerable, possibly equivalent to the losses in the Spanish market.

An earlier calculation by Buesa (2009) estimated Catalonia's loss as a consequence of separation at a little over 23 percent of GNP. There are other estimates, but all in all we can say the most likely estimates, and the most rigorous, are those by CMRM assuming that Catalonia would not have to leave the EU, and estimated around 10 percent of GNP, and that of Polo, assuming it would have to leave, and putting the loss at around 25 percent or more.

Political Consequences of Separation

The rosy economic prospects that nationalist economists promise for an independent Catalonia hinge largely upon the assumption that it would remain in the EU in the event of separation. As we just saw, the economic repercussions of independence would vary considerably if Catalonia found itself excluded from the EU, which would entail severe limitations to its possibilities of exporting to, and interacting with, the European market. Parenthetically, the economic repercussions of *Brexit* should serve as an experiment indicating how the economy of an independent Catalonia might fare, with the difference, of course, that the United Kingdom is a much larger country, and has a secular tradition of independence and nationhood totally lacking in the case of Catalonia.

Everybody in Catalonia admits that the possibility of losing the condition of member of the EU would constitute a great problem in the case of *Catalexit* from Spain. Massive demonstrations under the banner *Catalunya, nou estat d'Europa* (Catalonia, a new European state) have been organized by the *generalitat* to convince Catalans and to pressure the EU authorities that Catalonia wants, and should, remain in Europe even though it wants to leave Spain (as we saw earlier, Catalonia's real will to leave is a rather moot question). If Catalonia found itself excluded from the EU it would undo in a short time the way it traveled as part of Spain since 1986. More precisely, it would see itself separated from its Spanish and French neighbors by the border tariff of the EU. The Union's legislation would cease to be applicable in Catalonia, whose access to the EU's Structural Funds and Cohesion Fund as well as other lines of credit and support to countries and regions hurt by the crisis would be terminated. It would also be excluded from the Spanish Liquidity Fund for Autonomous Regions (FLA in Spanish) and other funds created by the Spanish state with the same purpose of helping in times of crisis. Due to its near bankrupt position, Catalonia has made, and is still making, frequent and substantial use of the Spanish lifelines. A measure of Catalonia's narrow dependence of these funds is offered by the fact that in 2014 it received more than 50 percent of the FLA funds destined to all communities (remember that Catalonia's population is around 17 percent of Spain's total). Even more eloquent and paradoxical, in October 2015, after the separatist parties which have a majority of votes in the Catalan *Parlament* (not of the popular vote) approved a declaration of intentions to work for independence, the *generalitat* asked the Spanish government for more funds to be able to pay its creditors, prominent among them its own employees. The Spanish government obliged.

In monetary matters, Catalonia could keep the euro even after quitting the Union, but the new Catalan state would have no say on the design of European monetary policy; it would not be subjected to the rules of the European Central Bank, but it would not be defended by these rules. This would mean that the Catalan monetary supply (total amount of money in circulation) would only depend on its balance of payments. If this were in deficit, as one would expect, the Catalan money supply would tend to decrease; this decrease would require either wage and price deflation or devaluation of the 'Catalan euro,' which would make this currency different from the 'Eurpean euro,' as the Canadian dollar is different from the US dollar. According to Feito (2014),

> The introduction of a new currency [. . .] would bring about a spiral of capital outflow-devaluation-inflation-devaluation-capital outflow which would lead to hyperinflation, thus annulling the positive effects that devaluation produces on competitiveness, and brutal falls of GNP [. . .] Catalonia on a new currency would suffer a very similar process to that of interwar Germany.

The Catalan balance of payments would in all likelihood be in deficit because the application of the European tariff would seriously affect its foreign trade. Its exports to the EU would fall and this would have to be compensated by finding new and distant markets; this rearrangement would cause great losses even in the best of cases. Furthermore, it would introduce a high degree of uncertainty (just remember that Ms. May's announcement early in October 2016 that conversations on Brexit would start in the spring of 2017 caused an immediate steep fall of the pound sterling) which would depress capital imports and stimulate capital outflows, something which is already occurring as a consequence of the *generalitat*'s secessionist pronouncements. All this would impinge negatively upon the level of employment and also on public finances, with a high probability that Catalonia would have serious problems to pay pensions, wages and salaries, and unemployment compensation.

It is obvious, therefore, that Catalonia is very much interested in remaining in the EU and keeping the euro as its currency. But, could it remain? The separatists refuse to admit that leaving Spain would entail leaving the EU. They try to convince themselves and their listeners that for the EU the loss of Catalonia would be terrible. They tend to adopt a denial position, as do the economists Antràs and Ventura (2012), who wrote: 'What would happen if Catalonia were left out of the European Union and were subject to its tariffs? Well, we already said that we think this cannot happen.' Or Francesc Homs, a leading member of CDC (now PDC?) and ex-spokesman of the *generalitat* (*El País*, 20 October 2013): 'Europe is finished if it expels seven million citizens.' Homs seems to forget that Catalonia's population is just 1.5 percent of EU population and produces just 1.55 percent of the EU's GNP, relatively modest figures. But, more importantly, he forgets that neither Spain nor the EU would 'expel' Catalonia. It would be Catalonia that would abandon the EU by seceding from Spain. Catalonia is a part of the EU because it is a part of Spain; if it would cease to be part of the one, it would cease to be part of the other. Jean-Claude Piris, a prominent French lawyer, former head of the juridical department of the European Council said (*El País*, 1 October 2013): 'There is no question of expulsion. The European Union would not expel anybody (never has done it). It all depends on the circumstances of birth of the new state.' Separatists become indignant and incredulous contemplating the consequences of their deliberate violation of clear and long established laws, and blame others for what is, or would be, their sole responsibility.

Those in favor of separation argue as follows to justify their incredulity that Catalonia's exit from Spain would inevitably entail exiting from the EU. First, they say that since Catalans are already European citizens, they could not be deprived of this condition (they omit to say that they are European citizens because they are Spanish citizens). Second, there is the curious statement by Oriol Junqueras, leader of ERC, who said (*El Mundo*, 22 September 2013) that after Catalonia's secession, Catalans would be able to adopt double nationality (Spanish and Catalan), so they could remain European citizens. The silliness of the idea is glaring: seceding from a country but keeping its nationality is equivalent to wanting to keep the cake after one has eaten it. Third, some claim that 'the treaties of the EU cannot be used against the democratic will of a people,' and introduce the novel concept of 'internal expansion,' by which they mean the increase in number of member states by division of former states, something like cellular multiplication by mitosis. Hoping to reinforce their argument, they cite German unification, which permitted East Germany to join West Germany, and thereby the EU.

Separatists distinguish between two possible scenarios for separation: cooperation or confrontation. According to Galí (2013), 'a friendly divorce with minimum costs for both sides is no chimera.' In a spirit of cooperation, the process of admission of Catalonia to the EU after separation would be 'simple and quick': Catalonia would remain out of the EU for a short time, while formalities of admission were fulfilled. This would require, of course, Spain's acquiescence of Catalonia being accepted as a new member. This *is* really a chimera: even in the extremely improbable case that Spain might agree, there are other states in the Union which might not, especially those that have problems of regional nationalism within their borders, such as France, Italy, or Belgium.

In the case that Spain proved uncooperative and vetoed the admission of Catalonia to the EU, 'this should not bring about adverse consequences for the Catalan economy,' says Galí, since nonmembers may still have rights of free circulation of people, commodities, and capital (he cites the case of Switzerland) and the EU would be 'the first interested in respecting those rights given the qualitative and quantitative importance of the Catalan market.' Catalonia would also be able to remain in the euro area by signing an agreement with the EU whereby it would be allowed to 'have access to the liquidity of the ECB.'

These pie-in-the-sky daydreams of professor Galí (a prestigious economist who ought to know better) are easily deflated just by referring to the Spanish Constitution, which does not contemplate separation of any region (very few democratic Constitutions do) and to the EU treaties. In the first place, those who say that Catalans are already European citizens who cannot be deprived of this condition ignore Art. 9 of the *Treaty on the European Union*, which says in part: 'Every national of a Member state shall be a citizen of the Union. Citizenship of the Union shall be additional to and not replace national citizenship.' Evidently, this means that if Catalonia separated from Spain its citizens would no longer be Spaniards (Mr. Junqueras notwithstanding) and they automatically would lose their EU citizenship. Furthermore, art. 4.2 of the same treaty says in part: 'The Union [. . .] shall respect [the] essential State functions [of Member States], including ensuring the territorial integrity of the State . . . ' This obviously means that the unconstitutional secession of part of a member state cannot be recognized by the Union.

In the second place, while it is true that the EU treaties contain no specific norms on secession, this does not mean that (against what the separatists say) in the case of secession, both the original state and the newly separated state would automatically become members of the Union, the supposed 'internal expansion' invented by the nationalists. Article 52 of the same Treaty enumerates all the member states belonging to the EU, the Kingdom of Spain among them. Any other state, new or old, is a 'third' state and must submit to a long procedure of admission to become a new member. Finally, regarding the German case, those who cite it as an example of 'internal expansion' forget three things: first, the union of both Germanys was by common agreement; second, it was unanimously supported by all Union members; and third, unite is just the opposite of separate, so that Germany's territorial integrity was not affected, rather the inverse.

In addition to the letter of the EU's basic treaty, there are the pronouncements of the top representatives of the Union. Romano

Prodi, the then president of the European Commission, said the following in response to a question by a British MEP (Eluned Morgan, 1 March 2004):

> When a part of the territory of a Member State ceases to be a part of that State, for instance if it becomes an independent State, the Treaties will no longer apply in that State. In other words, a newly independent region, by reason of its independence, will become a third State in its relation with the Union from the day of its independence, and the treaties will not be applicable in its territory.

This pronouncement was confirmed with almost exactly the same words by José Manuel Durao Barroso, Prodi's successor in response to a new question by a Dutch MEP (Auke Zijlstra, 13 November 2013). Similar opinions have been expressed at different times by the president of the European Council, Herman Van Rompuy, and by Joaquín Almunia, then commissar of Competitiveness of the EU.

In the third place, the possibilities of Catalonia being admitted to the so-called Economic European Area (EEA) to which Iceland, Norway, and Liechtenstein belong as do the rest of the EU states (Switzerland is linked to the EU through a series of separate treaties), the possibilities are far from simple. The EEA was conceived as a way to associate the old European Free Trade Area (EFTA) members to the EU (the EFTA was a looser association devised by the United Kingdom as an alternative to the then EEC—today's EU. When the UK became a member of the EEC, some members joined too, like Sweden and Denmark. The rest became associated through the EEA). Admitting a breakaway country, as Catalonia would be, could be a moot affair; it would be a special case, and Spain's position as a member of the EEA, would give considerable weight to its opinion.

In the fourth place, it is true that some countries, such as Montenegro, Andorra, Liechtenstein, San Marino, or the Vatican have adopted the euro as their own currency without formally joining the EU. Catalonia could do the same, but it is too big and its debt is too high. It is very unlikely that the ECB should take responsibility for Catalonia's problems or lend to its banks, since neither the ECB nor the Bank of Spain would have any control over the new country's monetary or financial matters.

It is highly unlikely, therefore that Catalonia could solve its already serious economic problems by separating from Spain: on the contrary, it would cut Catalonia's only lifeline, to Spain as lender of last resort and to the ECB.

Jaen-Claude Piris has clearly dispelled all illusions of separatists. There are three conditions, he says, for a state to be entitled to apply for accession to the EU. It must be recognized by the international community, it must be European, and it must comply with the rule of law. Its birth must be legal. A simple unilateral referendum violating a valid Constitution would not make Catalonia acceptable as a candidate to the EU. And he adds:

> Creating false illusions about unilateral independence is dangerous. Let us say the truth: if Catalonia undertook this way, this would involve a long path, which would require a modification of the [Spanish] Constitution, the EU treaties [. . .] A simple declaration of independence has no legal effects [. . .] A unilateral declaration does not mean they are really independent and may apply for accession.

Furthermore, even if Spain agreed to secession the new state could not be admitted immediately, since the inclusion of a new member would require changes in the treaties and in the laws, both of the new country and of the original country, in this case Spain. As Piris added later (*El País*, 25 August 2015) 'those who affirm that the EU would incorporate a hypothetical independent Catalonia demonstrate ignorance of the applicable legislation and of the political realities of the member states of the EU.' Or perhaps they demonstrate a will to deceive public opinion.

In spite of these evidence, Catalan nationalists still deny obvious facts and stick to their theory of 'internal expansion' in the infrequent cases when they are willing to frankly discuss these matters. They appear to be so accustomed to Spanish law being flouted in Catalonia that they think the same will happen with European law.

References

ANTRAS, Pau y Jaume VENTURA (2012) 'Dos más dos son mil. Los efectos comerciales de la independencia'. Col.lectiu Wilson. http://www.wilson.cat/es/

BAIGES, Francesc, Enric GONZÁLEZ y Jaume REIXACH (1985), *Banca Catalana. Más que un banco, más que una crisis*. Barcelona: Plaza y Janés.

BORRELL, Josep y Joan LLORACH (2014) '¿Dónde están los 16.000 millones?'. *El País*, 20 January 2014.

BORRELL, Josep y Joan LLORACH (2015), *Las cuentas y los cuentos de la independencia*. Madrid: Catarata.

BUESA, Mikel (2009), 'La independencia de Cataluña'. Published in his personal blog, 16 September 2009.

CABANA, Francesc (1988), *Banca Catalana, Diari Personal*. Barcelona: Editorial Tibidabo.

CARRERAS, FRANCESC (2014), 'La independencia que viene de lejos'. *El País*, 5 May.

CASASSAS, Jordi, *et al.* (2009), *Història 2. Batxillerat*. Barcelona: Grup Promotor/Santillana.

CHARRON, Nicholas, Victor LAPUENTE, and Lewis DIJKSTRA (2012), *Regional Governance Matters, A Study on Regional Variation in Quality of Government within the EU*. WP 012/2012. 2012. [Brussels], European Commission. Working Papers.

COMERFORD, David, Nicholas MYERS, and José V. RODRIGUEZ MORA, (2014), 'Aspectos comerciales y fiscales relevantes para evaluar las consecuencias económicas de una hipotética independencia de Cataluña', *Revista de Economía Aplicada*, 64, vol. 12, pp. 85–130.

ESPADA, Arcadi (2014), 'Fer país'. *El Mundo*, 27 July.

FEITO HIGUERUELA, José Luis (2014), *Razones y sinrazones económicas del independentismo catalán*. Paper, Panel Cívico.

FUENTE, Ángel de la (2014), '¿Maltrato fiscal?' in Fuente y Polo, pp. 11–29.

GALÍ, Jordi (2013), 'Cataluña, cooperación o confrontación. Un divorcio amistoso con costes mínimos para las partes no es una quimera'. *El País*, 12 October.

HERAS CABALLERO, Pedro A. (2009), *La España raptada. La formación del espíritu nacionalista*. Barcelona: Áltera.

HERR, Richard (2016), *Separate but Equal? Individual and Community Since the Enlightenment*. Berkeley, CA: Berkeley Public Policy Press.

MOLINERO, Carme and YSÀS, Pere (2014), *La cuestión catalana*. Barcelona: Planeta.

NADAL, Jordi (1982), 'La población catalana a lo largo del último milenio', reprinted in Nadal (1992), pp. 95–121.

Pericay, Xavier (2009), *Filología catalana. Memorias de un disidente*. Sevilla: Barataria.

Prat de la Riba, Enric (1998 [1906]), *La nacionalidad catalana/La nacionalitat catalana*. Madrid: Biblioteca Nueva.

POLO, Clemente (2013), 'El peso de las exportaciones en la economía catalana', in Amat, pp. 65–83.

POLO, Clemente (2014), 'Panorámica del argumentario economicista a favor de la independencia de Cataluña, mitos y realidad,' in Fuente and Polo, pp. 31–94.

POWELL, Charles (2001), *España en democracia, 1975–2000*. Barcelona: Plaza y Janés.

PUJOL, Jordi (2000), *Ante el gran reto de la inmigración, Casino de Madrid 4 de julio de 2000*. Barcelona: Departament de la Presidència, Generalitat de Catalunya.

REINHART, Carmen M. and Kenneth S. ROGOFF (2011), *This Time is Different. Eight Centuries of Financial Folly*. 13d. ed., Princeton: Princeton University Press.

Ríos, Pere (2014), *Banca Catalana, caso abierto. Lo que no se contó del escándalo que enriqueció a Jordi Pujol*. Barcelona: Península.

RÍOS, Pere (2015), *Banca Catalana, caso abierto. Lo que no se contó del escándalo que enriqueció a Jordi Pujol*. Barcelona: Península.

RIQUER, Borja de (2004), *Història de Catalunya*, Volume 9 ("La Catalunya autonómica, 1975–2003, primera parte"). Barcelona: Edicions 62.

RIQUER, Borja de and Jordi MALUQUER (2004), *Història de Catalunya*. Volume 10 ("La Catalunya autonómica, 1975–2003, segunda parte"). Barcelona: Edicions 62.

SOLÉ-TURA, Jordi (1984), 'El respeto a Pujol y la querella contra Banca Catalana,' *El País*, 27 May.

VANDELLÓS, Josep A. (1985), *Catalunya, poble decadent*. Barcelona: Edicions 62.

ZABALZA, Antoni (2013), 'La imaginación al poder,' *El País*, 4 June.

8

Conclusions

> *...sono tanto semplici gli uomini, e tanto obediscano alle necessità presenti, cho colui che inganna troverrà sempre chi si lascerà ingannare*
>
> *...men are so simple and obey so much to momentary needs that whoever wants to deceive them will always find an easy victim*
>
> (Macchiavelli, 1994, p. 156)

The Weight of History

The first document where the words 'Catalonia' and 'Catalans' appear belongs to an Italian poet from Pisa in the early years of the twelfth century. A few decades later, in 1137, Catalonia (the county of Barcelona) was united to the kingdom of Aragon through the betrothal of count Ramon Berenguer IV and Petronila, heiress to the throne of Aragon. In 1479, upon the death of King Juan II, the father of Fernando the Catholic, Aragon and Castile were united by the marriage of Fernando with Isabel of Castile.

G. Tortella, *Catalonia in Spain*, Palgrave Studies in Economic History, DOI 10.1007/978-3-319-54951-4_8

This means, therefore, that Catalonia has been a part of Spain for some 536 years and a part of Aragon for nearly nine centuries. The relations between Catalonia, Aragon, and Castile (in turn a composite of pre-existing kingdoms) have experienced long periods of harmony and shorter lapses of conflict. Although the consequences of conflict have almost invariably been lamentable, conflicts themselves have not been historically exceptional. European history teems with conflict; the Catalan case is not extraordinary. The history of medieval Spain is quite complex, and Spain was formed through the successive accretion of kingdoms and suzerainties with very distinctive traits; Catalonia was one of them. The slow formation of the Spanish nationality has quite original traits due to the frontier character of its medieval components, which had an influence in molding them and its sui generis feudalism, but it also has much in common with the formation of other large European kingdoms, such as France or Great Britain, which were equally the result of protracted processes of amalgamation of preexisting kingdoms and territories, through long and tortuous episodes along the Middle Ages.

Catalanist historians have repeatedly affirmed that the union of Castile and Aragon through the marriage of Fernando and Isabel did not create a new, superior unit, the kingdom of Spain, but just the juxtaposition of two kingdoms. This is not wholly true: Isabel considered herself queen of Castile and queen consort of Aragon, but her husband, her second degree cousin, thought of himself as king of both kingdoms and therefore as king of Spain. He was called 'king of Spain' (*Hispaniae rex*) in the inscription of a monument built in 1502 in what today is the Spanish Academy in Rome. He was the first statesman to put into effect policies which affected equally Castile and Aragon (i.e., he viewed both units together as a single kingdom). And he was considered as such by the greatest social scientist of the Renaissance, Niccolò Machiavelli, who, in *Il Principe* repeatedly calls him *re di Spagna* (king of Spain) and speaks of him with undisguised admiration.

Even though Renaissance Spain was not properly a nation, it was the embryo of a nation, and the same applies to Great Britain, France, or Portugal. The consolidation of those kingdoms for several centuries produced long periods of coexistence between their various territories, a process which would crystallize in the formation of nations in the modern sense.

History shows that Catalonia has hardly ever been independent. Perhaps it was semi-independent during the eleventh century, but then it was a group of counties under the suzerainty of the 'principal' county of Barcelona. We do not know exactly when it started being called Catalonia, but what is certain is that it was first called Spanish March or Spanish frontier, as Denmark was the Danish frontier, and both were part of the Carolingian Empire. Catalonia's medieval greatness (approximately from the mid-thirteenth century to near the end of the fourteenth), when it conquered Valencia and Mallorca and created a Mediterranean empire reaching all the way to Greece and Byzantium, arrived when it was part of the kingdom of Aragon.

The demographic crisis of the fourteenth century affected Catalonia more severely than the other Hispanic lands; the Aragonese-Catalan dynasty died out in 1410 and a scion of the Castilian Trastámara lineage was crowned king of Aragon as Fernando I. This was an important step toward the union of Castile and Aragon. When Fernando and Isabel married, Aragon was weaker than Castile; and Catalonia, decimated and divided by internecine wars, was even weaker. Socially static and rent by dissension, it almost vanished from history in the early modern period. Its rebellion against Felipe IV and the Count-Duke in 1640 (War of the reapers) lasted 12 years because the monarchy also was exhausted. Elliott's book on the war is subtitled 'A Study in the Decline of Spain.' France took advantage of this long combat between two groggy fighters and in the Peace of the Pyrenees (1659) the defeat of Spain in the Thirty Years' War and the loss of northern Catalonia were ratified.

But Catalonia recovered from this war and from the ensuing War of Spanish Succession and, starting in the third decade of the eighteenth century it followed the path of economic growth which, with inevitable ups and downs, has continued to this day. The profound renovation which followed the War of Succession was vital for Catalonia. The *Nueva Planta* decrees abolished medieval *fueros* and privileges and established a modern and equitable tax system; the administrative union of Castile and Aragon gave Catalan industry access to the peninsular and

American markets, while strong protection benefited the Catalan textile industry. Catalonia became 'the factory of Spain,' the economic leader of the country, a situation which convergence in the last 50 years or so has attenuated. There are other 'factories of Spain' now, although Catalonia still is the more powerful. There can be no doubt, therefore, that Catalonia has benefited 'unsuspectedly' (as Vicens Vives wrote) of its centuries of integration within Spain.

Nation and Nationalism

The word 'nation' has become an emotionally charged term which politicians, Catalan in particular, bandy about with the purpose of rousing their followers, talking of a medieval Catalan nation and apparently forgetting that the modern concept of nation is rather recent. A nation is just a convention: it has no real existence, as all collectives, such as committees, political parties, corporations, or football teams; these are just sets of individuals, grouped together for some reason. Nations are political entities, aggregations of people under a single government, occupying a given territory, sharing a common history and a common legislation, and enjoying the recognition of the world community. This applies clearly to Spain, which is one of the oldest European nations, although, as Fusi (2000) shows and as is the case of other old European nations, it is a conglomerate of preexisting communities, and its population has gradually acquired the conscience of being a nation and adopted the unitary administrative structure in a gradual, secular process.

Catalonia, in contrast, has never been a nation (neither has Castile nor the other regions which are parts of Spain), and there has never been talk of a 'Catalan nation' until the end of the nineteenth century or the beginning of the twentieth, when Enric Prat de la Riba published a book called *La nacionalitat catalana* (The Catalan nationality, 1906), where, in what seemed to be a fit of inspiration, he decided to erase four centuries of history and proclaim that Spain was not a nation but a 'state' (in his own words 'an artificial entity'). The bases of this assertion were a foggy historical introduction and an essentialist definition of 'nation,' which he characterized as 'a unity of culture o of civilization' (p. 74), 'a fundamental unity of the spirits' (p. 99), 'a collective spirit, a Catalan social soul' (p. 109), 'a natural community, necessary, previous, and superior to the will of men, who cannot undo it or change it' (p. 62). This is pure metaphysics. Brubaker (1996, p. 15, n. 4) notes that 'No serious scholar today holds the view [. . .] that that nations or ethnic groups are primordial, unchanging entities. Everyone agrees that nations are historically formed constructs.' Prat de la Riba, meanwhile, never makes explicit his criteria to determine that Spain is 'an artificial entity' whereas Catalonia is 'a natural community.' But a nation is not a 'social soul,' or a 'unit of the spirits,' as he says, but just a juridical, conventional body, as we just said.

Essentialist definitions of nation remind us of Lüthy's (1962, p. 85) statement that

> All discussions on nationalism in general are marked by the proliferous and glittering sterility characteristic of discussions of undefined and indefinable subjects [. . .] dealing with the shadowy realm of collective psychology, which eludes rational consciousness. Every attempted definition of 'the nation', 'the nationalist idea' or 'national feeling' ends in mysticism or mystification.

This of course applies to the essentialist definition of 'nation' so well reflected in the book by Prat de la Riba. The term 'nation,' however, in a nonessentialist sense has a precise meaning, the one we gave it at the beginning of this section, and a chronological origin quite clear also, the final decades of the eighteenth century, when the American and French revolutions took place. Among other traits, both revolutions were antimonarchical, rebelling against the *Ancien Régime*, striving to substitute the term 'citizen' for that of 'subject' and that of 'nation' for that of 'kingdom.' The revolutionaries fought for a new type of society whose members would be free and equal, and where sovereignty would reside in the people. When in France the States General, divided into estates of the realm, decided to constitute themselves into an assembly representative of all the French people without distinctions, they gave themselves the name of *National Assembly*. And the American Constituent

Congress, in the preamble of the 1787 Constitution, in representation of all the inhabitants of the new country, defined themselves as *We, the people of the United States*. In this country, the term 'nation' took longer to become generally used, probably due to the sovereign velleities of several states of the Union. Be it as it may, instead of the traditional monarchical legitimacy, a new national or popular legitimacy was born, and both terms, 'nation' and 'people,' became virtually synonymous.

Of course, although the irruption of the term 'nation' in modern history is revolutionary, it had been evolving gradually, especially during the period separating the English and the American revolutions. Thinkers and political philosophers had been questioning the legitimacy of absolute monarchy, and the idea that the power and privilege possessed by kings was justified by the effectiveness of the monarchy in promoting the happiness of its subjects rather by divine will or hereditary rights, spread gradually. Thus developed the idea of the monarchy as an *enlightened despotism*; this was the product of a paternalistic social philosophy which linked the legitimacy of the monarchy to its administrative and political ability. In England (soon Great Britain), since the Glorious Revolution of 1688, the principle of shared sovereignty between king and parliament brought about a feeling of national consciousness. Nevertheless, the American revolutionaries tried to carry further the democratic principle and this was the main motive of their rebellion against Britain in 1776. In France, Louis XVI was much closer to the figure of a benevolent ruler, an enlightened despot, than any of his predecessors; however, this did not satisfy French revolutionaries, who wanted liberty, equality, and popular representation. The American and French revolutions thus put an end to the ideal of enlightened despotism. In this sense, therefore, the national principle is democratic, even though the new American and French nations were not wholly democratic, since universal suffrage of both sexes took almost one and a half century to become established in both countries.

The word 'nation,' however, is much older than its modern meaning; its origin is Latin, the verb *nascere*, to be born. From Antiquity 'nation' designed a collective of people from the same region, and also of followers of some religion, speakers of a language, or even members of an extended family. In convents, universities, and armies, people were often lodged according to their 'nations,' a division which was more ethnic, linguistic or geographic than political. Mostly during the eighteenth century, the word 'nation' gradually acquired a political connotation. We then find more commonly the term 'Spanish nation' to mean the collective of subjects of the Kingdom of Spain, an expression more frequent after Felipe V became king. The first Spanish official bank was founded 1782 with the name *National Bank of Saint Charles*, surely to underline that it was not a Royal Bank, although promoted by Carlos III. At the time, the word 'national' referred to the realm. The Spanish flag which was established also under Carlos III was equally called 'national flag.' The word nation became more politicized with the French Revolution; it is well known that during the Peninsular War in Spain and the conflicts that followed, the absolutists cried: 'Long live the king, death to the nation!' And when the official bank was founded anew under Fernando VII in 1829, it was called *Spanish Bank of Saint Ferdinand*, because the word 'national' had acquired subversive overtones.

In Spain, the word 'nation' acquired its revolutionary and democratic meaning during the Peninsular War. The two Constitutions of those years (the Napoleonic Statute of 1808 and the liberal Constitution of 1812) speak of the Spanish 'nation,' although the Constitution does so more frequently and emphatically (see Chapter 4). From then onward, although there were several Constitutions, the national principle was never abandoned in Spain.

During the nineteenth century, however, the political meaning of the word 'nation' changed again. In the early decades of that century, in contrast to the idea of a democratic or revolutionary nation, the ethnic or spiritual concept of 'nation' took form. This new sense was also linked to that of 'people,' but it transcended the merely factual meaning of a collectivity of individuals submitted to a representative government and a system of laws equal for all. This new meaning of 'nation,' not necessarily democratic, rather mystical (recall Lüthy's words), implied that there was something more to the nation than a mere group of individuals organized according to some political principles, was born in Germany and Italy, and had Greece as its origin; it could be characterized as 'romantic' or 'essentialist.' At the time this idea originated, none of these three countries was properly a nation; their names were simple geographical expressions, although in all three cases there existed historical precedents of unitary states: Classical Greece or the Macedonian Empire, the Roman Empire, and the Holy Roman (German) Empire. The idea was thus born of a *Volksgeist*, the soul of the people, an idea which posited the existence of a collective being over and above the individuals who were part of it and who were united by cultural, ethnic, religious, and linguistic links; the image of these 'stateless nations' was that of a sort of collective disembodied souls wandering around in history, in the hope of becoming embodied in a state which would put an end to their painful roaming around. These three stateless nations became real nations during the century and thereby became an example for other groups in similar situations: typical cases were Poland, partitioned and dismembered by three adjoining empires (Russian, Austrian, and German) and the Balkan peoples subjected under the Russian, Austrian, and Ottoman empires. The end of these empires after the First World War gave birth to a host of new nations; this, however, became the source of new problems.

The world suffered greatly during the twentieth century as a consequence of the essentialist definition of nation. The greatest damage originated in the triumph of the Fascist and Nazi parties in Italy and Germany, and the growth of extreme nationalism in Japan, and the waves of totalitarianism, violence, and war those parties and movements brought about. Essentialist nationalism took root in countries which, for one reason or another, thought themselves wronged by the distribution of power in the international settlement after World War I. Victimism played a key role in the growth of essentialist nationalism. Germany felt hurt by the Versailles Treaty, Italy considered itself relegated by her allies, and Japan felt threatened by China's resurgence and the hegemony of the USA in the Pacific. These were not the only factors, but they played a paramount role in the takeover of extreme nationalism in those countries.

Spain was by no means free of the essentialist scourge. As a relatively backward European nation and with serious problems of internal order, it was prey to a lot of victimism and, consequently, of extreme nationalism of the national and regional varieties. The clearest manifestation of this was, of course, the civil war, and the victory of the Franco side, who called themselves 'the nationals.' The Franco regime made extensive use of the nationalist rhetoric and of the nationalist fascist party *Falange*

Española (Spanish Phalanx; see Payne 1961). Extreme nationalism usually has a period of exaltation and then one of decline. This happened in Spain and, during the second stage of the Franco dictatorship Falangist nationalism faded gradually, and in fact disappeared with the demise of the Franco regime. But if essentialism went out through the door, it rebounded and came back through the window in the shape of provincial nationalisms whose potential danger was overlooked by the protagonists of the transition to democracy. Spain is still paying for that oversight; Spanish nationalism is under the stigma of being linked to Francoism while regional nationalisms enjoy surprising support and are hard at work trying to demolish the democratic edifice built with a substantial share of goodwill (and of naïveté) by the so-called fathers of the Constitution.

The Causes of Catalan Nationalism

We have seen that Catalan nationalism appeared at the end of the nineteenth century and at the beginning of the twentieth century acquired its founding manifesto from Prat de la Riba. Several factors contributed to its birth and growth. Perhaps the most important and decisive was the gap between Catalan and Spanish per capita income, a gap that grew during the nineteenth century and reached its maximum around 1930. Catalan economic development, in good measure led by the textile industry, brought about the growth of an industrial proletariat who became quite militant and of a large and cultivated bourgeoisie whose attention was more focused upon France and Europe than upon the rest of Spain, valued only as a market and as a source of political power, buy not as a cultural focus or as a social model. As a consequence of this economic and cultural mismatch, there was a sort of irritation and sneer toward the rest of Spain, whence Catalonia depended politically and economically, but with growing impatience and dissatisfaction (let me point out, however, that cultural contempt was unjustified, as letters and sciences in Madrid reached remarkable levels in the first decades of the twentieth century).

These feelings reached a maximum with the 'Disaster' of 1988, which is a second explanatory factor. The Catalan bourgeoisie thought that the rest of Spain had failed in being defeated in the war with the United States and in being forced to abandon Cuba and the Philippines, which had been such good markets for Catalan exports. The opinion became widespread in Catalonia that the defeat was entirely the fault of the rest of Spain, conveniently forgetting to what extent Catalonia had been a leading partner in the conception and the development of that policy and that defeat.

A consequence of the development of Catalan industry was not only the income gap (undeniable *fet diferencial*) but also the arrival of a steady wave of immigrants from the rest of Spain (the third factor). This is a common phenomenon in developing countries: a transfer of manpower takes place from backward, agrarian regions, toward industrialized areas, which offer higher wages and better opportunities; this is the well-known model of a 'dual economy.' In Catalonia, this inflow of manpower was received with decidedly mixed feelings. There was a xenophobic, even racist strain in the attitude toward the newcomers, a malaise enhanced by the fear that the Catalan 'culture' or language may be swamped by the arrival of so many Castilian speakers. Something similar took place in the Basque country at around the same time (late nineteenth, early twentieth centuries). It seems alarming that these sentiments should appear at all, but that the hostility should be directed to other Spaniards is even more lamentable.

The fourth factor is the weakness of Spanish nationalism, whose main cause was the failure of the educational system since the nineteenth century and which is still with us (Álvarez Junco, 2001, pp. 545-65; Boyd, 1997; Núñez, 1992). Political dissension and the weakness of the state in the nineteenth century were obstacles to the creation of an effective educational network able to train the population and combat illiteracy, to popularize the speaking and writing of standard Spanish, and to offer a coherent and accurate version of Spanish history. The inefficiency of the Spanish state, furthermore, left a considerable part of education in the hands of the church, a largely ultramontane institution whose version of Spanish history was unfavorable to liberalism and in general to the small but undeniable progress achieved in the nineteenth century. As a consequence, unlike in France, where the school system turned French peasants in citizens (Weber, 1976), in Spain a large section of the population remained illiterate and an even larger share acquired a very nebulous notion of what it meant being a Spanish citizen. The Spanish Army did not play a very useful role in this respect until well into the twentieth century, at least as regards literacy (Álvarez Junco, 2001, pp. 550-2; Quiroga, 1999). It is understandable that local nationalisms should fill the void left by the national educational system. And the persistency of the failure of the Spanish educational system (Chapter 7 provided a glimpse of this) remains alarming even today.

Why Now?

After years of Francoist repression, Catalan and Basque nationalisms awoke with renewed energy and found sympathy and comprehension in all of Spain. In the long term, Franco got exactly the opposite of what he strived for: he totally discredited Spanish nationalism and reinforced the prestige of regional nationalisms. This explains the sympathy with which these were generally viewed, and the irresponsible passivity which democratic governments have shown toward the continuous violations of the law by Catalan nationalists, which nonnationalist Catalans have repeatedly decried, and which the courts have often but ineffectually condemned. This attitude of sympathy for regional nationalisms was reflected in the new Constitution and in other laws of the new democracy. It also contributed to the victory of Jordi Pujol's party (CDC in coalition with Unió, forming CiU) in the 1980 elections. This triumph surprised everybody and turned out to be one of the direst misfortunes which could hit Catalonia and Spain as a whole. As Antoni Gutiérrez, leader of the PSUC, would say a few years later in the Catalan parliament, Pujol not only committed errors, he was a living error himself.

In effect, Pujol embodied a grave historical error of Catalan electors, some for voting for him, others for abstaining. Since his inauguration, Pujol undertook a thorough program of popular indoctrination and of repression and harassment of the nonnationalists which could only affect the behavior of considerable numbers of citizens. The instruments employed in this program have been all available state resources, especially the school system and the media. The Catalan population has been subjected at school and from the newspapers, the radio, and especially the TV networks, to a deformed and victimist version of history, teeming with outright lies, such as, for example, that the Catalan nation was crushed in 1714, that this 'nation' was fighting for independence, that the conquering army imposed an unfair exploitation, that Catalonia endured long-term spoliation and oppression, etc. That there was alleged spoliation and oppression is contradicted by the remarkable spurt of economic growth which a supposedly 'oppressed' Catalonia enjoyed in the eighteenth century after 300 years of stagnation. Catalonia became the economic leader of Spain and kept this role until Pujol assumed the presidency. The transcendental significance of the 1714 defeat seems rather dubious if we keep in mind that all those gestures of heroism remained almost forgotten for almost two centuries, until they were unearthed and dressed up by nationalists very late in the nineteenth century. Among other widely diffused myths, there is, for instance, that Catalan has been a systematically persecuted language in Spain (its renaissance in the mid-nineteenth century and its virtual disappearance in France belie it), that Catalonia was excluded from the levers of power in Spain, that the poverty of Spanish peasants was an obstacle to the development of the Catalan textile industry, that Franco persecuted Catalonia and Catalanism with special animosity, that he encouraged emigration to Catalonia to dilute Catalan 'culture,' etc. In this book, we have tried to examine and dispel these myths and others, whose list would be too long to enumerate here.

The reason for this steady barrage of fabrications is simple: nationalism needs it to maintain the fervor of the faithful and thus remain in power and go on stirring up anti-Spanish feelings. In other words, it needs to create domestic and exterior enemies and to stimulate xenophobia. The *Brexit* movement in Britain and the victory of Donald Trump in the USA are good illustrations of this kind of nationalism. All nationalisms need myths (i.e., more or less invented histories that justify their militant theses and slogans). Francoism, that extreme version of Spanish nationalism, also expounded a Manichean and xenophobic version of Spanish history, whereby democrats were the bad guys and authoritarians the nice characters. According to this version, Spain had not one, but many enemies, domestic and foreign which came in handy as scapegoats to blame for all problems and shortcomings: freemasonry, communism, socialism, 'demo-liberalism,' and so on. For Catalan nationalism, one enemy seems to be enough: Spain, the 'Spanish state,' the cause of all the ills of Catalonia—and of which Catalonia is a part since 1479 no less.

There is also the often repeated *fet diferencial*, the Catalan language. But there is no reason for this to pose a problem: there are many multilingual countries; Catalan nationalists prefer to exaggerate and agitate around this topic, alluding to an imaginary persecution of the language precisely in the only country where it is spoken, written, and read by several million people; anything goes to rouse the masses. There is also a vague frustration felt by many Catalans that the Principality is not the political center of Spain and that Catalan is a respectable but minor language. But history is not fair or just; all in all, however, it has treated Catalans rather fairly and there is no way to reel it back. Another complaint is more justified: very few non-Catalans in Spain speak Catalan or are knowledgeable with Catalan history and institutions. As we just saw, the nationalist authorities are doing their best to make this ignorance reciprocal, so where there was one wrong now we have two.

On the other hand, rivalries between cities and regions are common in all countries. Rome, Milano, and Napoli are bitter rivals, and the mutual hate between northerners and southerners in Italy is proverbial; in Belgium, Walloons and Flemings are always on the verge of tearing the country apart; the same could be said about Scots and English in Great Britain; regional and racial divisions in the USA are universally known; etc. Coming back to Spain, there is a famous dictum by José Ortega y Gasset in the Spanish parliament in 1932:

> The Catalan problem, as all those similar ones which have existed and endure in other nations, is a problem which cannot be solved, it may only be put up with, and when I say this I mean not only that the other Spaniards must put up with Catalans, but that the Catalans must put up with the other Spaniards.

The real problem crops up when a substantial minority of Catalans, stirred up by the Catalan government, do not want to put up with (*conllevar* in Spanish) the other Spaniards, and make impassable mountains of very surmountable problems. Disagreement is not oppression; higher taxes for the rich is not spoliation, it is justice; differential facts turn up everywhere. In Spain, almost all regions have differential traits which distinguish them from the others. Putting up with your neighbors has been a constant in Spanish history (in all national histories), and Spaniards never had it so good as in the recent decades, even taking account of the Great Seven Years Recession of 2007–2015. Why then this recent surge of separatism?

It undoubtedly seems paradoxical that in 2016, when Catalonia has attained all its self-government objectives and enjoys the longest period of autonomy in all its history—as De Riquer wrote (2004, p. 401), the 25-year period after the approval of the Constitution was, for Catalonia 'a historical epoch [. . .] exceptional [. . .] because it is the longer stage of Catalan self-government of all the modern era'—when Catalan governments violate systematically and with impunity the Constitution and other legislation, when those governments have accumulated enormous public debt nobody wants to finance but the Spanish state, we find that those same governments are the prey of righteous indignation against that same state and complain of 'grievances,' about a 'putting a Court sentence before the ballot box,' about 'the dignity of our institutions' having been offended, and that 'one after another, doors were slammed,' as Artur Mas, the then president of the Catalan government wrote recently (2015).

The article by Mas in *El País* takes the form of a complaint for a series of offenses the Spanish government is supposed to have inflicted upon Catalonia; it is written in a garbled style no doubt learned from his mentor Jordi Pujol. Those offenses boil down to two: that the Constitutional Court struck down some blatantly unconstitutional clauses in the 2006 *Estatut* after it had been approved by referendum ('Court sentence before the ballot box') and that the Spanish Constitution does not allow the secession of a region ('slammed doors'). Let us examine those in turn: the 2006 *Estatut* has always been controversial. Many of its clauses were clearly unconstitutional; it was a pet project of the then Spanish President J. L. R. Zapatero, who needed the Catalan vote to be reelected. It should not have been submitted to referendum until after being revised by the Constitutional Court, but Zapatero permitted it for his own reasons. Its popular support, in any case, was scant: less than 37 percent of the electoral census (more than 50 percent abstained).

With such weak popular support and such high rate of abstention, it should not have been considered valid. When the sentence of the Court struck down or modified only a few articles, many people criticized the Court's excessive tolerance. But, of course, nationalists made a big scandal about the will of the Catalan people having been suppressed. The truth is that even the nationalists strongly disagreed about the *Estatut*, but now they all agree in calling the affair a terrible offense against Catalonia. They seem to have forgotten that the *Cortes* of the Republic in 1932 carried out a much more radical paring down of the draft *Estatut*, approved in referendum with much larger support than that of 2006.

The second offense is that the Constitution does not allow secession, or local referendums on secession. First, if this offends Catalonia, it should offend the other Spanish autonomous communities and it does not seem to. But second, and more important, no written Constitution of a democratic country allows secession (not even the Canadian one), so that all federal states, provinces, *länder*, cantons, *départements*, regions, etc. of all the world should be offended for not being constitutionally allowed to secede. But only Catalonia seems to be. Catalan nationalists appeal to the right of self-determination proclaimed by President Woodrow Wilson after World War I, but we saw in Chapter 6 that Catalonia does not at all fit in the Wilsonian—and later UN—definition of 'subjected peoples.' Doors to unilateral secession, therefore, are closed in all democratic nations—save Great Britain, but this is a very special case.

The paroxysm of secessionism, however, is being reached in the current years. We saw how after the failed 'referendum elections' of September 2015 a strange Catalan government running from the moderate right to the extreme left was formed in January 2016. This government has done practically nothing but bicker among themselves on how to achieve independence or 'disconnection.' The linchpin here is the maverick CUP, whose ten deputies dictate on the other members of the coalition because without them the government would fall to pieces. They have forced President Puigdemont to proclaim that a unilateral referendum (i.e., even if the Spanish government does not agree—which is a foregone conclusion) will take place in Catalonia in September 2017 at the latest, to decide about a unilateral declaration of independence. All this is in violation not only of the Spanish Constitution but also of the Catalan *Estatut*, which says that it can be modified only by two thirds of the votes of the Catalan *Parlament*, approval of the Spanish *Cortes*, and a referendum in Catalonia. Since a declaration of independence would be a modification of the *Estatut*, they would need 90 parliamentary votes to start with, which they do not have (they have 72). But these legal niceties are not paid attention to in nationalist Catalonia.

Let us go back to our question, why are the separatists in such a hurry to declare independence, ready to violate every law in the books, if necessary, and not even counting with a majority of the popular vote? The reasons seem clear: for a generation and a half, the Catalan population has been indoctrinated in the gospel of nationalism and secessionism; the children of the 1980s are today adults who feel angry for the alleged 'oppression,' 'spoliation,' 'offense,' 'incomprehension,' etc., they have supposedly been submitted to by the rest of Spain. As a consequence, the share of the population who support independence has grown considerably. They are not the majority of the population, but they are near. As happened under Franco, corruption and incompetence have become evident and they have to be covered by something: in both cases, nationalism is the curtain that deflects criticism. According to a recent EU survey (Charron, et al., 2012), Catalonia is the worse governed region in Spain. Nationalists have put Catalonia just at the border of bankruptcy; in Catalonia, corruption is even more scandalous than in the rest of Spain. Pujol himself confessed in 2015 that he had been defrauding the state for decades and that he had fraudulently exported millions of euros to Andorra and other tax heavens. Everybody knows that his enormous fortune has dubious origins. The rest of his party has had problems with the police since the Banca Catalana affair if not earlier.

Then came the Seven-Year Recession and things became even more complicated (see Fig. 8.1). A large part of the protest vote in Catalonia shifted to extreme nationalism; expenditure cuts were extremely unpopular. Seeing his vote base shrink, Mas, the successor of Pujol, was loath to cut expenditures: this is how Catalonia's debt ballooned. It soon found himself unable to finance his deficits, because his government's credit plummeted. In desperation, he went to Madrid to ask Mariano

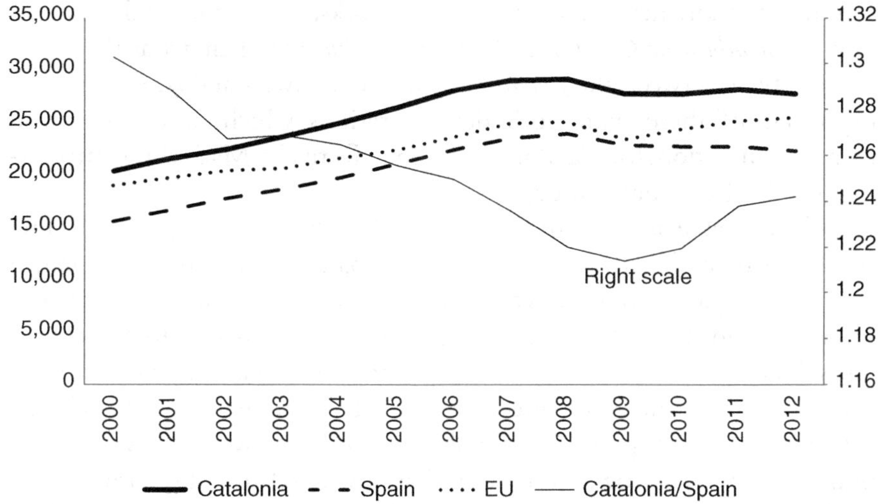

Fig. 8.1 Income (GDP) per capita: Catalonia, Spain and European Union, 2000-2012 (euros)

Rajoy for a privileged tax treatment, such as the Basque Country and Navarre have. But Catalonia is too big for this privilege. The Spanish budget is in dire straits already; privileging Catalonia would put Spain on receivership. Mas threatened with independence, but Rajoy did not budge. Mas returned empty-handed and facing the need to economize. His only solution was to agitate, point the finger to Madrid as the cause of Catalonia's problems, and call for independence.

Threatening and posturing is a good tactic with Spanish governments, who are always afraid that if they are perceived as dealing harshly with Catalonia, the people there will become even angrier and more pro-independent. So even if not willing to give Mas his *foral* tax system, Rajoy was willing to lend generously. We already saw how Catalonia got a disproportionate share of the loans of the Fund for Autonomous Regions (FLA). In fact, for Catalonia's nationalists, all this confrontation and bluster is a win-win game. All the concessions gained are steps of no return toward independence. The hush money dished out by Madrid goes in large part to pay the faithful, to create miniembassies to spread the independence gospel abroad while offering plump salaries to members of the party, to subsidize friendly newspapers and TV networks, and to the 'civil organizations' (*Assemblea de Catalunya, Omnium Cultural*) which act as the transmission belts between the *generalitat* and the followers and supporters, the organizers of these mammoth demonstrations which have become so common in nationalist Catalonia, etc. So, effectively, Madrid is contributing to subsidize Catalan independence.

Independence is the Promised Land for the Catalan political elite. Although treated with kid gloves by all Spanish governments, Spanish courts and Spanish police, even Spanish newspapers, can be a nuisance. Pujol has had his bad moments and embarrassments due to these nosy 'outsiders,' and a fair number of his friends and collaborators have been processed and a few even ended up in jail. In an independent Catalonia, this would not happen. The Catalan government would have its own public finances, its own judges, and its own police. They are already there today, but there is too much interference from 'Spain.' The nationalist vote in Catalonia is located in the rural districts, which are overrepresented, and then in the wealthy districts of Barcelona, and other large cities; in other words, the old Carlist districts in the countryside and the urban prosperous upper middle class. These people would be the absolute masters of an independent Catalonia. The rest would pay a high price for independence in terms of economic difficulties (inflation, unemployment) and for being at the mercy of those in power.

References

ÁLVAREZ JUNCO, José (2001), *Mater Dolorosa. La idea de España en el siglo XIX*. Madrid: Taurus.

BOYD, Carolyn P. (1997), *Historia Patria. Politics, History, and National Identity in Spain, 1875-1975*. Princeton: New Jersey, Princeton University Press.

BRUBAKER, Rogers (1996), *Nationalism reframed. Nationhood and the national question in the New Europe*. Cambridge, UK: Cambridge University Press.

Quiroga, Gloria. (1999), *El papel alfabetizador del Ejército de Tierra español*. Madrid: Ministerio de Defensa.

CHARRON, Nicholas, Victor LAPUENTE, and Lewis DIJKSTRA (2012), *Regional Governance Matters, A Study on Regional Variation in Quality of Government within the EU.* WP 012/2012. 2012. [Brussels], European Commission. Working Papers.

FUSI, Juan Pablo (2000), *España. La evolución de la identidad nacional.* Madrid: Ediciones Temas de Hoy.

LÜTHY, Herbert (1962), 'A Rehabilitation of Nationalism?', in Jelensky, pp. 85–99.

MAS, Artur (2015), 'A los españoles'. *El País*, 6 September 2015.

NÚÑEZ, Clara E. (1992), *La fuente de la riqueza. Educación y desarrollo económico en la España contemporánea*. Madrid: Alianza Editorial.

PAYNE, S.G. (1961), *Falange. A History of Spanish Fascism.* Stanford, CA: Stanford University Press.

RIQUER, Borja de (2004), *Història de Catalunya,* 9 vols. ("La Catalunya autonómica, 1975–2003, primera parte"). Barcelona: Edicions 62.

WEBER, Eugene (1976), *Peasants into Frenchmen. The Modernization of Rural France, 1870–1914.* Stanford, California: Stanford University Press.

Bibliography

ABELLÓ, Teresa *et al.* (1998), *La resposta catalana a la crisi i la pèrdua colonial de 1898*. Barcelona: Generalitat de Catalunya y Editorial 92.

ÁLVAREZ DE CIENFUEGOS, Isabel *et al.* (1963), *Homenaje a Don Ramón Carande*. Madrid: Sociedad de Estudios y Publicaciones.

AMAT, Oriol *et al.* (Ed.) (2013), *La cuestión catalana, hoy*. Madrid: Instituto de Estudios Económicos.

ANES, Gonzalo (Ed.) (1999), *Historia económica de España, siglos XIX y XX*. Barcelona: Galaxia Gutenberg-Círculo de Lectores.

ARTOLA, Miguel (1959), *Los Orígenes de la España Contemporánea*. 2 vols. Madrid: Instituto de Estudios Políticos.

CALATAYUD, S., J. MILLÁN and M. CRUZ ROMERO (Eds.) (2009), *Estado y periferias en la España del siglo XIX. Nuevos enfoques*. Valencia: Universidad de Valencia.

CAPMANY, Antoni de (1808), *Centinela contra franceses*. Madrid: Gómez Fuentenebro y Cía.

CARRERA PUJAL, Jaime (1961), *La economía de Cataluña en el siglo XIX*. 4 vols. Barcelona: Bosch.

CARRERAS, Albert (1990), 'Cataluña, primera región industrial de España', in Nadal and Carreras, pp. 259–295.

G. Tortella, *Catalonia in Spain*, Palgrave Studies in Economic History, DOI 10.1007/978-3-319-54951-4

CIPOLLA, C.M. (1973), *The Fontana Economic History of Europe, IV. The Emergence of Industrial Societies. Part Two*. London: Collins.

FERNÁNDEZ, Roberto (Ed.) (1985), *España en el siglo XVIII. Homenaje a Pierre Vilar*. Prólogo de J. Fontana. Barcelona: Crítica.

FONTANA, Josep (2003), *La revolució liberal a Catalunya*. Lleida/Vic: Pagés/ Eumo.

FUENTE, Ángel de la and Clemente POLO (2014), *La cuestión catalana. II. Balanzas fiscales y tratamiento fiscal de Cataluña*. Madrid: Instituto de Estudios Económicos.

GERMÁN, Luis, Enrique LLOPIS, Jordi MALUQUER and Santiago ZAPATA (Eds.) (2001), *Historia económica regional de España, siglos XIX y XX*. Barcelona: Crítica.

HERNÁNDEZ ANDREU, Juan (1981), 'La polémica Cambó-Calvo Sotelo sobre la valoración de la peseta', *Hacienda Pública Española*, 69, pp. 291–302.

JELENSKY, Konstanti A. (Ed.) (1962), *History and Hope. Progress in Freedom. The Berlin Conference of 1960*. London: Routledge & Kegan Paul.

LYNCH, John (1969), *Spain under the Habsburgs. Volume Two. Spain and America, 1598–1700*. New York: Oxford University Press.

MALUQUER DE MOTES, Jordi (1974), 'El mercado colonial antillano en el siglo XIX' in Nadal and Tortella, pp. 322–357.

MALUQUER DE MOTES, Jordi (2011), 'El turismo, motor fundamental de la economía de Cataluña, 1951–2010', *Historia Contemporánea*, 42, pp. 347–399.

MORALES, Antonio (Ed.) (2014), *1714. Cataluña en la España del siglo XVIII*. Madrid: Ediciones Cátedra.

MORILLA, José, Juan HERNÁNDEZ ANDREU, José Luis GARCÍA RUIZ, and José María ORTIZ-VILLAJOS (Eds.) (2010), *Las claves del desarrollo económico y social. Homenaje a Gabriel Tortella*. Madrid: LID/Universidad de Alcalá.

NADAL FARRERAS, Joaquim and Philippe WOLFF (Eds.) (1992), *Historia de Cataluña*. Barcelona: Oikos-Tau.

NADAL, Jordi (1984), *La población española (siglos XVI a XX)*. Ed. corregida y aumentada, Barcelona: Ariel.

Nadal, Jordi. (1992), *Bautismos, desposorios y entierros. Estudios de historia demográfica*. Barcelona: Ariel.

NADAL, Jordi, Albert CARRERAS and Carles SUDRIÀ (Eds.) (1994), *La economía española en el siglo XX. Una perspectiva histórica*. Barcelona: Ariel.

NADAL, Jordi and Gabriel TORTELLA (Eds.) (1974), *Agricultura, comercio colonial y crecimiento económico en la España Contemporánea*. Barcelona: Ariel.

NADAL, Jordi *et al.* (1988–1994), *Història econòmica de la Catalunya contemporània*. 6 vols. Barcelona: Enciclopèdia Catalana.

ORWELL, G. (1952), *Homage to Catalonia*. New York: Harcourt, Brace, Jovanovich Inc.

PÉREZ MOREDA, V. and D. S. REHER (Eds.) (1988), *Demografía Histórica en España*. Madrid: Ediciones El Arquero.

PRAT DE LA RIBA, Enric (1998), *La nacionalidad catalana/La nacionalitat catalana*. Madrid: Biblioteca Nueva.

PUJOL, Jordi (1976), *La immigració, problema i esperança de Catalunya*. Barcelona: Nova Terra.

PUJOL, Jordi (2002), 'Cataluña, tierra de acogida', in *Cataluña hoy. Ciclo de Conferencias de la Universidad Menéndez Pelayo*, 23–29 July, Barcelona: Generalitat de Cataluña, pp.13–28.

SÁNCHEZ-ALBORNOZ, N. (1987), *The Economic Modernization of Spain, 1830–1930*. New York: New York University Press.

VICENS VIVES, Jaime y Montserrat LLORENS (1958), *Industrials i polítics (segle XIX)*. Barcelona: Teide.

VICENS VIVES, Jaume (1936–1937), *Ferran II i la ciutat de Barcelona, 1479–1516*. 2 vols. Barcelona: Universitat de Catalunya.

VICENS VIVES, Jaume (2013), *Notícia de Catalunya*. Barcelona: Editorial Vicens Vives.

VILARASAU, Josep (2012), *Memorias. El extraño camino a "la Caixa"*. Barcelona: RBA.

Index

G. Tortella, *Catalonia in Spain*, Palgrave Studies in Economic History, DOI 10.1007/978-3-319-54951-4

C

9783319855295